THE TRAVELER'S KEY TO
ANCIENT GREECE

THE TRAVELER'S KEY TO

ANCIENT GREECE

A GUIDE TO THE SACRED PLACES OF ANCIENT GREECE

RICHARD G. GELDARD

With photographs and illustrations
by Astrid Fitzgerald

Alfred A. Knopf   New York   1989

THIS IS A BORZOI BOOK
PUBLISHED BY ALFRED A. KNOPF, INC.

Grateful acknowledgment is made to the following for
permission to reprint previously published material:

Penguin Books Ltd.: Excerpt from *The Greeks* by
H. D. F. Kitto. Copyright 1951, © 1957 by The Estate of
H. D. F. Kitto. Reprinted by permission of
Penguin Books Ltd.
Shrine of Wisdom: Excerpt from *The Golden Verses of the
Pythagoreans,* published by *The Shrine of Wisdom.*
Reprinted by permission of the editors of *The Shrine
of Wisdom.*

Grateful acknowledgment is made to the following for permission
to use photographs:
Deutsches Archäologisches Institut, Athens: pages 4, 16, 21, 76,
202, 203, 204, 205, 214, 229, 260, 300, 301, and 303. Alison
Frantz: pages 10, 117, 128, 138, and 142. National Archeological
Museum, Athens: page 118.

Library of Congress Cataloging-in-Publication Data
Geldard, Richard G. [date]
The traveler's key to ancient Greece.

Bibliography: p.
Includes index.
1. Greece—Antiquities—Guide-books. 2. Greece—
Description and travel—1981–   —Guide-books.
3. Greece—Religion. I. Title.
DF127.G45   1989   914.5′04928   88-45268
ISBN 0-394-55631-3

Manufactured in the United States of America
First Edition

CONTENTS

Acknowledgments   vii

Introduction   ix

1   The Background   1
      Historical Overview   3
      Greek Religion   35
      Sacred Number and Geometry   69
      Sacred Architecture   80

2   **The Palace Cultures**   91
    Crete and the Minoans   93
      Knossos   95
      Phaestos   122
      Mallia, Gournia, and Zakros   133
      Iraklion: The Museum   137
    The Mainland and the Mycenaeans   146
      Mycenae   148

3   **The Temple Cultures**   173
    Athens   177
      The Acropolis   184
      The Theatre of Dionysos   205
      The Asklepieion   211
      Other Minor Sites   212
      The Agora   216
      The National Archaeological Museum   226
    Eleusis   230
    Epidauros   252
    Delphi   269
      Athena Pronaia   277
      The Kastalian Spring   280
      The Sanctuary of Apollo   283
      The Museum   299

4   The Lesser Palace and Temple Sites   305
      Bassae   307
      Brauron   308
      Corinth   308
      Delos   309
      Dodona   310
      Olympia   310
      Pylos   311
      Sunium   313
      Tiryns   313

Glossary   315

Further Reading   317

Index   318

ACKNOWLEDGMENTS

A great many people make a book such as this possible. There are teachers, those who helped to shape an appreciation for the Greek experience. Among the most important were T. B. L. Webster, William Arrowsmith, and William Sharp. Many people also helped to guide me through the labyrinths of history, religion, and archaeology, especially the staff of the American School of Classical Studies in Athens. I am grateful to the librarians of the Bodleian in Oxford, to Phyllis Brugnolotti at the Collegiate School in New York City, to Elias Kulukundis of the Collegiate Hellenic Studies Program, to Vincent Scully at Yale for his vision of the landscape, and to John Anthony West, whose insights into sacred science inform much of this entire series on the sacred sites of the world.

Special thanks also go to Olympic Airways whose support made travel to Greece possible; to my friend and former colleague Vassili Attaliades, whose invaluable help in Greece made our work so enjoyable; to Andy Vassiliades, whose travel arrangements supported the research; to Alison Frantz for her photographs of Minoan artifacts; and to Olivia Bauer for the special care she took printing the photographs.

Particular thanks and deep affection go to Toinette Lippe, my editor at Knopf, whose dedication to detail and consistent support through two difficult years made publication in this decade a reality. Together with my wife, Astrid Fitzgerald Geldard, whose love, encouragement, and talent brought the text to life, I wish to offer whatever value this book may have to those pilgrims who share our love of Greece and its living heritage of sacred places and abiding spirit.

Finally, this book is dedicated to the memory of my daughter Cynthia. . . .

> *and from her head*
> *and her dark eyes there was*
> *a blowing grace, as if it were*
> *from Aphrodite, the golden*
> —HESIOD

INTRODUCTION

The Traveler's Key to Ancient Greece is divided into four sections: The Background, The Palace Cultures, The Temple Cultures, and The Lesser Palace and Temple Sites.

In the first section the reader will find a general history, a description of ancient Greek religion, and introductions to the sciences of sacred number, geometry, and architecture. The second section is devoted to the palace cultures, those sites in Greece where the ancient Minoans and Mycenaeans established themselves and left for modern pilgrims and inquisitive archaeologists a record of their distinctive cultures. The third section covers the major sacred sites from the Archaic, Classical, and Hellenistic periods of ancient Greek history, and the fourth the lesser of the palace and temple sites.

Each site has its "myth," a term which means a story of the life of a place, human being, or god. All myths have meaning, and the task has been to translate the myth into the myth-language of our own era. For the most part, the language of our mythology is the language of psychology. And of course there are several styles of psychological language: Jungian, Freudian, Adlerian, and so on. In this case, the language goes back to Plato and has been brought to the present idiom through the work of Paul Diel, the late Austrian psychologist.

Plato, the great voice of the journey of the human soul, was the first Western writer to speak of the idea of spiritual development, the idea that a human being might lead his life in such a way as to awaken within himself the divine life. The possibility of such a discovery makes Plato's works a psychology, or a study of human behavior in the physical, intellectual, and spiritual sense. Plato was indebted to the voices of his own culture and his predecessors in philosophy, both Eastern and Western. These fragments from the past form a living mythology which still has power to transform lives.

The sections on each site have information on history, mythology, and the site itself. The ancient pilgrim would have known some of the history of the site and would have been familiar with its mythology—or living narrative. The purpose of a visit or pilgrimage to the site was to perform an act of worship there, to purify the body and the mind, to make a sacrifice to the god or gods of the place, and to seek spiritual knowledge in the experience.

This book, then, is designed to emulate the journey of the pilgrim to a sacred site. The reader is presented with the context and some historical knowledge and is then guided onto the site "in a sacred manner." The gods have not vacated the holy places of Greece. If there has been any vacating, it is our own "vacation" from the myths of sacredness within ourselves. A sacred place is, after all, a place on the earth which men have set aside as a symbol of their own spiritual being. It is as much inside as it is out there. What the ancient Greeks understood was that the aim of spiritual work was to make their gods manifest through acts of creativity, devotion, and sacrifice. What we are able to see in Greece today of these attempts at manifestation are the stones, columns, walls, statues, paths, and artifacts of evolving spirit.

The requirements of length have not permitted a full treatment of a few of the more important sacred sites in Greece, namely the island of Delos, the oracle at Dodona, and the great sanctuary at Olympia. The final selection of sites to receive full attention was made on the basis of accessibility and historical continuity, that is, the pattern of development from Minoan and Mycenaean to Classical and Hellenistic times as revealed by clear and existing evidence from all of the major periods.

The oldest road in Europe—the Sacred Way, Knossos, Crete.

Finally, a note about spelling. For many years all things Greek were sifted through the Roman experience via Latin. Heroes of Greek myth acquired Latin names, such as Hercules rather than Heracles or Herakles. Since the Greek language has no *c* in its alphabet, the letter *k* is used for the hard sound, which in English is used with both *c* and *k*.

For this text, as in many others of recent vintage, a compromise position has been selected. Wherever possible the Greek language has been translated directly into English, without a Latin influence. The exceptions to this general rule will include those names which have become established in English with the Latin influence, such as Sophocles, Socrates, Pericles and Aeschylus. Other names and places, such as Asklepios and Epidauros, being less familiar, retain their Greek influence. The author makes no claim of immunity from inconsistency. Decisions have been made based on familiarity so as not to startle the eye too much in the reading process. In general, the decisions involve the use of "*u*" vs. "*o*" or "*c*" vs. "*k*." In the text alternative spellings of words first encountered appear in parentheses.

1
THE
BACKGROUND

HISTORICAL OVERVIEW

PREHISTORY

When the interested traveler comes into physical contact with the remnants of ancient Greek civilization, he is exposed to an unaccustomed breadth of human history. The results can often dazzle the senses and dull the mind, both reactions not helpful to the understanding. Historians and archaeologists have marked out distinct periods, beginning for Greece at about 3000 B.C., the start of the so-called Bronze Age, when evidence of human activity first reveals organized settlements and social groupings larger than the clan or tribe.

But for our purposes, the human history prior to that significant change in culture is still very important. In terms of the sacred life of human beings, the written record has yet to establish a beginning. We do know, for example, that human beings buried their dead in a sacred manner 60,000 years ago. And if we know little or nothing about human life then, it is because people lived a nomadic existence, constantly moving and following the horned and cloven-footed herds in their seasonal wanderings in search of grazing pastures.

Much still needs to be learned about this long period of nomadic life, when we lived with few possessions in minimal shelters, hunting, telling stories, fighting to protect our own, praying to the spirits who dwelled in the caves, gorges, springs, and mountains—the landscape which formed the only home we knew. To these nomadic peoples, the landscape was full of powers, which gradually acquired names and qualities. Spirits had wings, teeth, horns, claws, and more human qualities like mind and emotion. To placate these spirits and to bring human life into the protective shelter of their power, we developed a ceremonial recognition of divinity.

Nomadic peoples began to follow sacred paths through places of danger to where game was available. These routes are still followed and still have the touch of spiritual power in them. In addition, the landscape itself was recognized as having divine qualities. The most important belonged to the Earth Mother Goddess around and within whom the people lived and died. The earliest evidence we have of sculpted figures reveals an overwhelming interest in and devotion to the earth as mother. Artists molded the earth itself into images their minds perceived as the likeness of life-giving power. The life-bearing hips and the life-sustaining breasts dominate these early figures. These features corresponded to the hills, clefts, and springs of actual landscape.

Gradually, there came to be specific places set aside as more sacred than other places. It is as if recorded history began with the separation of existence into spiritual and material elements. As long as the nomadic peoples regarded the whole of their world as sacred, we can view them as being integrated with the world of spirit. As soon as special sanctuaries were marked out, the boundary marked separation as well as devotion and, in a sense, modern man was born. We cannot know at what point in time human beings conceived the sanctuary, but it must have been before the time of settlement since the archaeological evidence suggests that dwellings gradually grew up around established

Earth Mother or Goddess figurine, Neolithic Period, from Sparta.

places of worship and that the sense of the landscape itself as sacred was a factor in the choice of settlement.

The sanctuary began either as an area of landscape set aside for the gods or as an altar around which a sacred precinct gradually developed. The altar was probably a flat rock in a position facing features of the sacred landscape. On the rock, sacrificial offerings were made. Thanksgiving and appeasement were typical of the offerings made after the hunt. In ritual it was recognized that spirit had left the animal and that its life-giving meat, bone, sinew, and skin were now available to the group. Such a gift required thanks and the hope that the Earth Mother or the sky gods were not offended by the killing.

The Earth Mother was relatively fixed in her places in the landscape, and specific locations were set aside for her worship. Lesser gods and *daemons* (or spirits) were less permanent, appearing here or there like the wind or the weather. Places and rituals were also established to honor and, to some extent, to attempt to control these powers, to make access to this power more common. These places and rituals, too, became the foundations of the Greek religion, which in history actually developed with greater consistency than did the political and social history of the region.

One brief comment also needs to be made about climate in Greek prehistory. Geological evidence, Plato's own account in the *Critias,* and centuries of deforestation and overgrazing show us that prior to 3000 B.C.—the date generally taken as the start of the Bronze Age—Greece had a more fertile and wooded landscape. The hills and mountains were covered with mature forests, and streams and rivers flowed abundantly. The present harshness is a late development. The gradual drying must have driven the herds north or killed them off, and the end of abundant water ended the nomadic life. The Indo-European migrations into the relative void brought the beginnings of agriculture and the domestication of cattle. The Neolithic Period began, but with it remained the reality of the Earth Mother, giving form to the civilization despite the changes in the landscape that remained as an image of her protection and power.

We began with a description of the earth and the landscape as sacred. Certainly occurring at the same time was a human awareness of and interest in celestial bodies—sun, moon, planets, and stars, including comets, eclipses, shooting stars, and the like. But the overriding interest was in the sun, giver of life and power supreme, and the moon, giver of time and dreams. We know from the evidence of Stonehenge and other prehistoric astronomical sites, that man calculated the rising and setting of the sun and established the moon-year based on the cycle of twenty-eight days, further broken down to patterns of seven days or weeks. One of the earliest references to the week occurs in Genesis in the account of the creation of the world. As we will see later, these early calculations were sacred expressions of the divinity residing in the sun, moon, and stars. The calculations themselves were given expression not in numbers—a relatively late invention—but rather in geometry. The circle expressed both sun and moon; it came to be the perfect expression of divinity. Within that circle, contained by it and held in its embrace, emerged the cross, emblematic of man and nature. From the cross came the square, the expression of the manifest creation. This geometric language spoke of the divine, just as light expresses the Light of Truth in man's quest for knowledge and meaning.

That these developments are connected to prehistory has been revealed by archaeological discovery and analysis in any number of sites throughout Asia and Europe. It is the combination of the sacred landscape and the rudimentary development of geometry that provides the frame for our picture of the sacred places of ancient Greece.

The Lion Gate, Mycenae, as it looked in the nineteenth century.

THE BRONZE AGE

Before setting out to describe the essential features of the rich and varied period known as the Bronze Age, let us look at a table which sets out the flow of years and shows relationships from culture to culture throughout the Mediterranean.

Key to Bronze Age Periods

BRONZE AGE		HELLADIC	MINOAN	EGYPTIAN
Early	3000 B.C.	Early Helladic I	Early Minoan I	1st Dynasty
	2800 B.C.	"	E.M. II	4th D.
	2400 B.C.	E.H. II	E.M. III	7th–10th D.
	2200 B.C.	E.H. III	Middle Minoan I	11th D.
Middle	2000 B.C.	Middle Helladic	M.M. II	12th D.
	1800 B.C.	"	M.M. III	13th–17th D.
	1600 B.C.	Late Helladic I	Late Minoan I	18th D.
Late	1500 B.C.	L.H. II	L.M. II	—
	1400 B.C.	L.H. III	L.M. III	—
	1100 B.C.	(End of Mycenaean Rule—Dorian invasions)		

The term Helladic refers to the civilizations of the Greek mainland, which in this period means primarily what has come to be called the Mycenaean civilization. The Mycenaean priest-kings flourished throughout what is now modern Greece from 1600 B.C. to 1100 B.C., or the Late Helladic Period. The Minoan civilization takes its name from the legendary King Minos of Crete. This distinctive civilization, characterized by the unprotected palaces of Crete and the Cyclades, came into existence soon after 2200 B.C. and came to a disastrous end in 1450 B.C. in what many observers believe to be the great earthquake and tidal waves of the Thera eruption. Thera, now the modern Greek island of Santorini, remains an active volcanic island in the middle of the Mediterranean Sea. Visitors can see the great crater and smoking dome that remind us of the end of a great civilization. There are even Minoan remains on the island still under investigation.

Other significant dates in the Bronze Age include the Homeric story of the sacking of Troy, which archaeological investigation of the Troy site places near 1200 B.C., at the close of the Mycenaean era. We will often need to refer to these periods, which correspond to the archaeological record of levels in the various digs as carefully determined by the dating of pottery. Thus, a Late Minoan I piece of pottery is dated at 1600 B.C. and corresponds to the Late Helladic I period on the mainland and so on.

SETTLEMENT

At the start of the Bronze Age, there was no line which marked off east from west in the Mediterranean. Trade on the sea spread its influence from Egypt in the south across the islands to the mainland and to the western boundaries of the known world. The dominant culture was Minoan, a people whose background was either Egyptian or Near Eastern in origin. Between 2000 B.C. and 1900 B.C. a herding people from Indo-European stock came from the north and settled in Thessaly and the lands spreading out from Mount Olympus. These Indo-Europeans brought with them a strong tradition of worship centered on the sky gods, chief of whom was Zeus, the great spirit. They brought with them a spoken language that was a form of archaic Greek. In what is now northern Greece they encountered the indigenous culture, the eastern peoples whose religious belief and tradition centered on the Earth Mother Goddess. The Middle Bronze Age, then, begins the marriage of gods. It was not always a smooth relationship or a peaceful union, but there were principles of spiritual law related to nature and human life that made this marriage a logical and important development in human history.

The major influence in Greece at the time of the Indo-European migration was clearly Minoan civilization, which evolved on the island of Crete. The Minoans were a peace-loving, creative people whose culture centered on elaborate, beautiful palaces, most of which can be dated from 2000 B.C. The Minoans sailed the Mediterranean freely and established trade routes and colonies throughout the Aegean. Their major conflicts seemed to be with pirates, who raided the trading routes and disrupted the flow of goods. But they apparently had no difficulty protecting their own palaces since evidence shows them to be unfortified during the height of the Minoan civilization.

However, by 1500 B.C. a new dynasty established itself on the mainland of Greece, no doubt supplanting the Minoan colonies in the process. This new civilization was known as Mycenaean and was characterized by massive hilltop fortresses and aggressive control of subjugated peoples. The evidence suggests that the Mycenaean culture was formed from the model of the Minoan.

MINOAN CIVILIZATION

The great artistic and religious culture called Minoan thrived on the island of Crete between 2200 B.C. and 1450 B.C. Archaeological remains at Knossos reveal evidence of habitation at the site for at least four thousand years before the construction of the first Minoan palace. Thus, the Minoans supplanted an indigenous population who well may have developed a religion similar to the Minoan, based in great measure on the worship of the Earth Mother and closely associated with the landscape surrounding the palace and the sea over which they traveled and which they painted so lovingly in their frescoes.

Where the Minoans came from we can only speculate. Most likely they landed on Crete from the south or east. The history of Egypt indicates that upheavals in the Fourth Dynasty may have stimulated emigration. In any case, these remarkable people settled in Crete, built astounding palaces, developed a sophisticated religion, made pottery and paintings second to none in the world, and died out in violence.

Their contributions to art in particular have, however, survived them. In 1967 on the island of Santorini, the Minoan town at Akrotiri was uncovered and revealed a treasure of wall frescoes now on display in the Archaeological

The Dolphin Room in the Queen's Megaron, Knossos; a reproduction based on fragments.

Museum in Athens. The fresco of the fisherman holding his blue and golden catch, the antelope fresco showing a power and line unexcelled in later art, these reflect a harmony and a vision missing from much of Greek art, and yet the debt is clear.

It is, indeed, the art of the wall frescoes that reveals something of the later history of the Minoan culture. After 1700 B.C. and before the final destruction of the great palaces, the frescoes begin to show scenes of war and portraits of warriors. The Minoans began to reflect the general level of violence and upheaval typical of the Aegean in those years. Other scenes of daily life and the evidence of Linear B script give us a picture of Minoan religious and economic practice.

The king ruled in the palace, with a hierarchy of officials taking responsibility for the economy, which included grain production and extensive herds of sheep, goats, and pigs. The king seems to have been responsible for the religious life of the settlement, a ritual existence about which we shall have much more to say later. There was also a full range of craftsmen and professionals in fields related to building, farming, and sailing. Women were very much part of the life of the palace and participated in most aspects of life, even sport and religious ritual. The wall frescoes picturing women reveal a sense of style and grace unsurpassed in later Greek art.

The key to the Bronze Age periods shows Minoan civilization divided into nine parts. For the most part, the divisions are based on the changes in pottery design, but they also reflect specific events, often cataclysmic ones. In general we can point to new migrations to Crete in 3000 B.C., opening up contact with Egypt (Early Minoan I); to a great earthquake which marked Middle Minoan III; to political change shifting control to the mainland in Late Minoan I,

*Detail of female bull leaper
from the famous bull-leaping
fresco at Knossos (see p. 138).*

and so on. In the development of pottery, fabrics, and fresco painting, the highlights are the development from polychrome black-glaze ware in Middle Minoan II, to glazed black on buff in Late Minoan I and finally to the so-called palace style of Late Minoan II. The general reader need only realize that a history this long and rich will reveal many changes of style and quality. What is remarkable, however, is that there remains a Minoan style which, once studied, will be recognizable through a period of nearly two thousand years.

There is a common element in the frescoes which suggests an overwhelming interest in idealized ritual movement and harmony. The priest-king fresco from Knossos shows a young man moving in what we might call a sacred manner (the content is uncertain). His hair flows in harmonies of three, his step is sure and measured, his pose serene. Surrounding nature blends in with his purpose, whatever it is. The rope in his left hand suggests that he may be leading a bull or a griffin. (See illustration, p. 117).

MYCENAEAN CIVILIZATION

Mycenaean culture begins on the Greek mainland in 1600 B.C. or the Late Helladic I Period. The first appearance of the culture in the archaeological record is the great circle shaft grave at Mycenae. What this site reveals, first, is the existence of a burial cult. The elaborate grave sites, with their rich tomb offerings, gold masks, and ornaments, suggest a reverence for the divinely ordained kings who ruled these outposts, which spread quickly throughout the Mediterranean.

The characteristics of Mycenaean culture—the citadels with their massive walls, the beautifully wrought shaft graves, and the beehive tombs of Mycenae—are still visible throughout the Aegean, to the western island of Kephallenia, to the north in Thessaly, to the east at Troy and Kolophon, and to the south in Rhodes and Crete. Over two hundred sites have been identified and there are undoubtedly many more to be discovered.

The heritage of the Mycenaeans is not only reflected in the grandeur of their monumental citadels and their obvious wealth but also in their legends of heroes, the flavor of which was captured years later by Homer and passed along as the foundation of Greek culture. These bearded warriors were not merely barbarians, as we might think of the hordes invading Rome from the steppes of Asia. Rather, the Mycenaeans farmed the land, established trade, and developed beautiful pottery and bronzeware of delicate design.

The reasons for the decline of Mycenaean culture are not clear. However, it seems logical that with the development of trade and modern weapons, the citadel was no longer a viable form of military organization. A social revolution may have occurred, one based on democratic instincts, which certainly emerged later after the Dark Age. The invasion from the north of the Dorian peoples clearly played a part as well. The development of iron supplanted bronze in weapons

Early engraving of so-called Tomb of Atreus at Mycenae.

and tools, perhaps hastening a decline in the fortress citadels. No longer were the dead buried with the same reverence. Cremation became commonplace, signaling a decline
in the cult of the dead. The heroic values immortalized by
Homer were set aside in the general atmosphere of disorder
and political chaos.

The end of the Bronze Age marked the end of the reign of
the priest-kings. During the Bronze Age, in both the Minoan
and Mycenaean cultures, the apex of the social, economic,
and religious pyramid was the *wanax* or priest-king. The
resulting integration of all aspects of life produced a harmony
and unity within the culture which was the source of its
great strength. The inevitable challenges to that leadership
and the corruption which is bound to befall such a mortal
structure produced schism and eventually revolution. Combined with the arrival of a new race of people with new
values and a spirit of competition, the internal rivalries were
too much, even for a system which had survived so much
warfare and possessed such a unified worldview.

Key to Periods of Greek History

1100 B.C.–800 B.C.	The Dark Age
776 B.C.–480 B.C.	The Archaic Period
480 B.C.–338 B.C.	The Classical Period
338 B.C.–146 B.C.	The Hellenistic Period

THE DARK AGE

It is a concession to the archaeologists and historians that we
refer to the three hundred years (from 1100 to 800 B.C.) as
the Dark Age. The term has survived the advances of new
discoveries in art and architecture because this period was
one of chaos and transition on the mainland of Greece. The
Mycenaean age was over, by virtue of internal revolution and
invasion, and a new order was yet to establish itself. From
the north, brown-haired Dorians, speaking a dialect of
Greek, swept into the territory once dotted by fortified
citadels. Or, as recent historians argue, unknown tribes from
the north invaded the south in vast numbers, destroying and
wasting the land, only to die out or be absorbed. It may be
that in the wake of this chaos the Dorians moved south and
restored order with a new vision of political and social
organization.

In any case, one race did not obliterate another. There was
a process of assimilation. This time the former occupants
held onto a few centers of culture, such as in Athens, where
the Mycenaean citadel on the Acropolis remained fairly
undisturbed and where the memories of the *wanax* as
priest-king lived on, although in changed political form. But
for the most part, we suspect that the Dorian migrations
produced a period of disruption and change from which the
Greek civilization as we know it finally emerged in about
800 B.C.

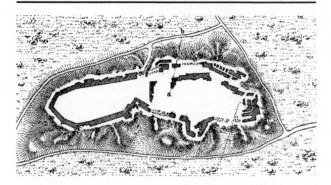

Engraving of the fortress at Tiryns, a port city in the Mycenaean Period.

In religion, the Dorians continued the shift of emphasis from the Earth Goddess as dominant deity to Zeus the sky god and ruler of the universe. As symbols of the human relationship to the divine, these gods demonstrated man's new distance from the powers of nature and the earth spirits who dominated the prehistoric era. With the Dorians came a fresh intellectual power and a new understanding of human potential. They were a people more at ease with language and expression. Their sense of relationship to the land and to the universe in general expressed itself in new and powerful myths, later written down by Homer, Herodotos (Herodotus), and Hesiod, to name a few of the later figures whose work established the Greek culture we have come to know and admire.

Herodotos, for example, called all the indigenous peoples living on the mainland prior to the Dorian invasion, Pelasgians, a name referring to the remnants of the Minoan culture, the Mycenaean, and even the lately arrived Ionians. This assertion from Herodotos, the first great historian, makes the Dorians the true Greeks, or Hellenes as he called them. The search for racial purity is perhaps understandable, but it is hardly realistic given the mixing of racial types living together and the freedom of travel permitted by the sea and island stepping-stones to the east and south.

By the time the Dorian invasion was complete, the entire eastern coastline of Asia was Greek. And by Classical times the survival of Greek dialects shows that the Doric remained in the southern Peloponnese and Crete, the Ionic dialect in Asia and the Cyclades, the Aeolic near Troy, the Arcadian in the central mountains of the Peloponnese, the Attic in the vicinity of Athens, the Thessalian to the north, and Northwest Greek in Epirus. So many dialects must reveal not only isolation but also a variety of racial influences over thousands of years.

It is in art and religion that we are able to follow a connecting thread in this labyrinth of history. The two come together when we realize that scenes on pottery and religious rituals both contain elements of design which reflect a worldview, a sense of man's place in the universe. Despite the darkness of this period, we are able to see two major developments. First, rational thought emerges as religion becomes public and secrets are shared by a wider spectrum of the population. No longer does the *wanax* serve as intermediary between the gods and men. Second, the new political and religious life of the community is organized around what will come to be known as the *polis*, or city-state, the most important political and social development in human history. Thus, as the Dark Age comes to an end, the Archaic Period emerges and with it a new idea in government and relationship of men to their gods or to the presence of the divine within man.

THE ARCHAIC PERIOD

The story of what we call Greek history usually begins in 776 B.C. with the first recorded victors in the Olympic Games. The alphabet used to chronicle this event was Phoenician, an alphabet borrowed through trade from across the Mediterranean. The rapid spread of this alphabet began the process of written records and thus the true historical record of the Greek civilization.

The Archaic Period begins in 776 B.C. and lasts until the Persian Wars in 480 B.C., which is the date normally marking the start of the Classical Period. Historically, the importance of the Archaic Period is the emergence out of the Dark Age of a new form of social and political organization, the *polis*. With the demise of the priest-king the battle of authority among warring factions and competing groups went through a period of chaos and experimentation. What generally emerged from the struggle was rule by successful aristocratic warriors who brought communities together by a combination of leadership, consensus, reason, and force to form a loosely bundled confederacy of families and their retainers in a given geographic area, usually centered on an acropolis, the "high place" of the city. The resulting city-state, both small and sovereign, arrived at a middle ground of authority by the few (*aristoi*) for the benefit of the whole (*demos*), with the many (*hoi polloi*) sharing in the resulting security and wealth.

In place of the Mycenaean palace on the acropolis, there were now temples to the gods of the *polis*. The rest of the community, including the *basileus*, or king, lived nearby but not within the sanctuary set aside for the worship and veneration of the gods. The life of the *polis* centered on the *agora* or marketplace, where business was carried out, but, most important, where the affairs of the *polis* were publicly debated. This new emphasis upon debate and public life was the heart and blood of the *polis* and marked a new thing in the civilization of the world. It is in this Archaic Period that political power and religious ritual come out of the darkness of the palace into the light of the marketplace.

THE LAWS

Late in the Archaic Period, inscribed codes of laws began to appear in the *agora* of many a *polis*. Rather than arbitrary or sacred law imposed from above, these new codes reflected the efforts of an intellectual elite to establish order and justice through consensus, at least to a limited degree. Far from being democratic in ideal or practice, these codes set forth for the first time the *nomoi,* or customs and laws, of the state. An example of such a code was discovered on Crete in 1884 in a streambed at Hagios Deka. These Archaic inscriptions covered walls 30 feet (9.1 m) in length and 6 feet (1.8 m) in height in a circular building. The 600 lines in the code address nearly all phases of life in the *polis* of Gortyn. The rights and duties of citizens and slaves were set forth, as were laws governing inheritance, marriage, and divorce. A good deal of attention was paid to matters of landownership, which is an indication of the development in the Archaic Period of the relationship between land and power. Indeed, much time seems to have been spent establishing family ties to the heroic past as a basis for authority in the new structures of power in the *polis*.

EXPANSION

So successful were these new entities that wealth and power increased at a rapid rate, as did the desire for expansion. The

Remains of the Archaic Temple of Apollo in the Agora in Athens.

Greek city-states, particularly Athens, Corinth, Sparta, and Argos, expanded their influence and successfully colonized throughout the Mediterranean. Colonies ranged as far as southern Spain and east into the Black Sea. While the Persians under Cyrus and Darius were busy conquering Egypt and expanding to the east, the Greeks were establishing profitable trade routes and colonies wherever boats could sail. Even Tyre and Sidon on what is now the coast of Israel were under Greek influence early in the eighth century B.C.

The most important development during the Archaic Period in the life of the *polis* and its influence was the birth of alliances and political control, a moving out from the isolated city-state to a more regional base of power. Sparta, for example, expanded within the Peloponnese to control other city-states as far north as Elis and east to Megara and Epidauros. Such imperialism would have devastating effects in the Classical Age when rivalry between Sparta and Athens broke out into war.

ARTS AND LITERATURE

The extraordinary energy of this period is also reflected in the arts and literature. New ideas and forms typify the sculpture and pottery of each *polis*. Particularly in pottery and sculpture the development is extraordinary. Examples of Archaic amphorae and marble and bronze statues have been found throughout northern Europe and Asia Minor. This work shows a vision and a skill unmatched anywhere in the world at this time. Also, architecture saw the development of the temple, as new forms found monumental expression for the first time since the height of Mycenaean brilliance. Although architecture did not see its best work during this period, the principles were being discovered that would transform the landscape of the Classical era.

Late in the Archaic Period a new phenomenon in the world began to emerge in the Ionian islands of the eastern Aegean Sea. In the realm of thought, partic-

Marble statue called the Almond-Eyed Kore, *500 B.C., Acropolis Museum, Athens.*

ularly expressed by the early philosophers but also by the epic and tragic poets, the Archaic age reaches a climax in the sixth and early fifth centuries B.C., actually ending with the death of Sophocles at the close of the fifth century B.C.

Before that, however, in the works of Homer and Hesiod, the mythology of the earlier Greek heritage, both Mycenaean and Minoan, takes on a new form and expression. The new mythology assumes a psychological style as the narratives of the gods and their relationship to men begin to express an evolving awareness of the relationship in man of body, mind, and spirit.

HOMER

To say that Homer is important to the culture of the Greeks is an absurd understatement. Homer *is* Greek culture after the Archaic Age. The heroic ideal, the standards of conduct, the concepts of excellence, honor, justice, harmony, and moderation, indeed the whole *ethos* of a race is written out in the *Iliad* and the *Odyssey*. During the late Archaic and early Classical periods schoolchildren memorized long passages of these works as the basis for their education.

It is probably true that the long epic poems we now have in our possession were not written by a single poet named Homer. None of the history is trustworthy, but it is generally accepted that the poems emerged from bardic tradition and most likely from the island of Chios in the eastern Aegean. The dialect of the poems is Ionian, which places them in the east, and for years Chios boasted a family called the Homeridae who claimed descent from the poet. As to the dates of his life or lives and the composition of the poems, we can only guess. Some suggest 950 to 900 B.C. as the time when epic poetry reached perfection. Others place Homer in the eighth century. We do know, however, that by 753 B.C. both the *Iliad* and the *Odyssey* were firmly a part of the Greek culture. We also have, in addition to these two epics, five hymns credited to Homer and twenty-nine shorter poems, all dedicated to various gods. Taken together, these works form the largest and most important source of knowledge about pre-Classical Greece.

HESIOD

The other important epic poet, Hesiod, lived in the eighth century (probably) and came from Boeotia. His life is presented to us as full of turmoil and tragedy, ending in his murder. But tradition places him in a position of honor next to Homer for the strength and importance of his work. *Works and Days* is a collection of myths and fables which give us a good picture of the life and values of the period. It was much cherished for its moral teaching. The *Theogony* (see the text on Religion) is an account of the beginning of the universe and of the gods. This poem can be read as a view of the human condition and of man's divine origins and destiny. Although it is not designed as a spiritual guide—like the Vedic Upanishads—the *Theogony* is nonetheless a mirror of human spiritual awareness and conflict.

THE BIRTH OF PHILOSOPHY

Philosophy takes its life from Eastern influences of religious thought (the concepts of unity and being) and the development of natural science in the sixth century B.C. Also, thinkers wanted to reflect upon the new political organization of the *polis* and its effect on a new entity called the individual.

This mode of thought centered in the eastern colony of Miletos. The so-called Milesian thinkers rejected the simplistic mythologies of polytheism and began a search for first causes and a more philosophic cosmology, no doubt influenced by Egyptian and Far Eastern theology and philosophy.

The Milesian Thinkers

The ideas of unity and being found their Western source in Xenophanes, who lived some time between 570 and 480 B.C. He was also the first Westerner to conceive of mind as an entity larger than personal thought and to see mind as the source of being in the universe. Known as the Eleatics, Xenophanes and his fellow philosophers Parmenides and Zeno thought of the visible world as an illusion and of eternity as the basis of reality.

Heraclitus (Herakleitos) of Ephesus, who lived at the close of the Archaic Period, was in many ways the most modern of the "new" thinkers. He said that "this world, which is the same for all, none of the gods or men has made, but it was ever, is now, and ever shall be an ever-living fire, with measures of it kindling and measures going out." He asserted that divine law governs the universe and that the law is rational. He conceived of deity as the underlying harmony of the universe and that unity was the supreme lord of all.

In many respects this flowering of thought bears fruit with Pythagoras, who lived from 570 to 500 B.C. and who was the most influential among these early thinkers. He founded a school which outlived him and which influenced the monumental work of Plato and Aristotle during the next era. Pythagoras traveled widely in Egypt and the East before settling down to teach in Italy.

The foundations of the Pythagorean school are belief in God as the principle of order in personal life and in society. The way to achieve this order is through discipline in all aspects of personal life: habits, diet, study, and religious practice. His great discovery was the relationship between number and divine laws of the universe. Central to these laws was the discovery of basic harmonic laws as demonstrated by the ratios and progression of tones produced by lengthening and shortening of a vibrating string. The development of the monochord is credited to the Pythagorean school. His greatest contribution, which we shall see in much greater detail in the section on sacred number and geometry, was the application of number to the universe.

THE CLASSICAL PERIOD

Because our sense of time reduces history to qualities instead of chronology, we often affix labels to a span of years and forever regard the era as a name. Throughout guidebooks as well as histories of the world "Classical" has come to mean what is properly "ancient." Classical Greece is a period in ancient history usually beginning in 480 B.C. with the brave defense of the Greek mainland at Thermopylae and ending with the commencement of Alexander the Great's campaign against Persia. Thus, the Classical Period begins with the arrest of Persian ambitions in Greece and ends with invasion of its own lands by Alexander. The significance of the latter's campaign in terms of Greek culture is that with Alexander's successful invasion of Asia Minor, the Greek culture once again became orientalized, that is, influenced by the grandeur and artistic styles of the East for the first time since Archaic times.

THE PERSIAN WARS

A run of twenty-six miles up the coast from Athens is Marathon, the town where in 490 B.C. a defensive force of 10,000 Greeks, mostly Athenians, overwhelmed a superior Persian force and lost only 192 men. The grave mound erected in their memory still attracts thousands of visitors each year. These "Men of Marathon" represent all that is

Northwest corner of the Parthenon, Athens.

heroically Greek in the Homeric tradition, and the memory sustains to this day the distinctive sense in the Greek mind of independence and freedom.

The victory at Marathon merely delayed further Persian attempts to conquer Greece, and ten years later, a force under the fated leadership of Xerxes made another attempt on Athens. This time huge land and sea forces attacked at Thermopylae and in the Bay of Eleusis, near Salamis. The Persian land force was enormous, some say over a million but probably more like 200,000, and it streamed through a pass, the Hot Gates, toward Athens. The Persians were delayed by a heroic force led by Leonidas, the Spartan king. The defenders all perished, but their defense stood throughout ancient times as the ideal of pride and courage.

At sea, within sight of Xerxes, who sat on a throne carved out of the hillside above the scene, the great Persian fleet sailed out to meet the meager Athenian fleet of 280 ships which had been sent north to delay the superior Persians. The day was the twenty-seventh of September, 480 B.C., at a time when the Athenians would have been celebrating the Eleusinian Mysteries. The site of sacred Eleusis was within a few miles of the Persian invasion force. Athens had been evacuated. No citizens remained and only a small defensive force remained on the Acropolis. Normally, on this day, a huge crowd would have been making its way up the coast to begin the rituals connected with Eleusis. But now the roads were silent. We have the story from Herodotos, who reported the following scene from the account of two renegade Greeks in the Persian camp that day.

The account says that the two Greeks, the Athenian Dikaios and Demaratos, banished king of Sparta, watched from the plain of Thira through which ran the Sacred Way to Eleusis; suddenly a great cloud of dust arose in the distance from the direction of Eleusis. The two heard voices shouting "Iakchos! Iakchos!" which was the usual cry of the celebrants in honor of Dionysos (Dionysus). The Spartan asked the Athenian what the dust and the shouting could be. As Herodotos tells it, Dikaios replied, "Demaratos, it can only be that the king's army will suffer a great defeat. For this is clear: since all Attica has been abandoned by its inhabitants, those sounds must be a divine host that has come from Eleusis to help the Athenians and their allies. If it makes for the Peloponnese, it will endanger the king and his army on the mainland; if it turns toward the fleet at Salamis, the king is in danger of losing his fleet. For this is the feast that the Athenians celebrate each year in honor of the Mother and the Daughter (Demeter and Kore). At this festival all the Athenians, as well as those other Greeks who so desire, are initiated. The voices you hear are the cries of 'Iakchos!' that resound at the feast." The cloud of dust did indeed drift toward Salamis and the two men watching knew that the Persian fleet was doomed.

The victory of the Greek fleet at Salamis will always have that religious connection and the belief that the Mysteries were intimately involved with Greek life and destiny. In this way the history of the ancient Greeks is intertwined with images of spiritual presence.

Despite the great victory of the Greek fleet, the Persian army was successful in overrunning Athens and burning the Acropolis. The sanctuaries were torn apart, the temples gutted, and the treasures of Archaic Athens stolen. So devastating was this destruction that the citizens of Athens chose to allow the devastation to remain as a testimony to the bravery of those who died defending Athens and to the constant danger of attack from abroad. It was not until the time of Pericles, thirty years later, that the Acropolis was rebuilt.

The Calf-Bearer, 570 B.C., Acropolis Museum, Athens.

A year after the fall of Athens, in 479 B.C., the most important victory over the Persians took place, this time at Plataea on the Theban plain. There, an army made up of Spartans, Athenians, and other allied city-states met the Persian force and destroyed it completely. The Greeks captured Persian treasure far more impressive than anything they had ever seen. Years later, next to the Theatre of Dionysos in Athens, Pericles built the famous Odeion using for his design the royal tent of Xerxes captured at the battle.

ATHENIAN DEMOCRACY

In the midst of the concerns over foreign invasion and the expansion of cultural and economic influence, city-states such as Athens were experimenting with a new form of government: democracy. The groundwork for this important experiment in social organization had been laid by Solon, who at the beginning of the century had established the rule of written law in Athens. The combination of a code of law and the decline of the four leading Ionian tribes or clans as a ruling oligarchy, eventually produced a new vision of government.

The leader of this change was Cleisthenes. His contribution was to formalize what had already taken place in the social structure of the *polis*. Under his leadership the ten families whose ownership of the land in and around the growing city constituted districts or *demes* became the basis of political structure. In this arrangement there emerged an organization from which representatives might be selected to exercise power and to conduct the business of the *polis*.

The next important development, again from the leadership of Cleisthenes, was the Council of 500, a ruling body made up of fifty men from each tribe, chosen by lot from lists drawn up by each *deme*. In addition, there developed in this period a system by which the citizens might control the excesses of a particular individual who was deemed to be a detriment to the *polis*. Every year, on a certain day, citizens could scratch the name of an offending person on a piece of broken pottery (an *ostrakon*) and submit it to an official especially appointed to receive it. The names were counted, and if 6,000 citizens (out of 30,000, say, in the fifth century) voted ostracism, that individual was banished from Athens for ten years.

PERICLEAN ATHENS

After the establishment of democratic principles under the leadership of Cleisthenes, Athens reached a level of development we have come to call Periclean Athens, that period between 460 B.C. and 430 B.C. when this one city achieved a level of timeless success. In the arts of vase painting, sculpture, architecture, drama, and politics, Athens, as Pericles (Perikles) himself claimed, "was the school of Hellas." Actually he need not have limited himself to Greece, since the influence of Athens went beyond the bounds of the Hellenic world to the known world in the fifth century.

Much of this success came about because of two seemingly opposite forces: one, the impulse to promote and achieve democratic ideals of equality and justice in the *polis*, and two, the willingness of the aristocracy of Athens to take an active part in the government. Pericles was such an

Engraving of the Acropolis in Athens, showing templelike propylon and statue of Athena.

aristocrat, a member of the ancient family known as Alc-
maeonidae, from which Cleisthenes had also come.

Pericles served as general, an appointed position of leadership corresponding to executive responsibilities in a representative government. Pericles maintained power for
nearly thirty years through eloquence and political skill, and
firm grasp of principle. Forty times a year, on a regular basis,
the Assembly met on the Pnyx, a hillside overlooking the
Acropolis, where five thousand persons could gather to hear
and take part in debate. All major questions of foreign and
domestic policy were decided by the Assembly of 500. On
one such occasion, Pericles spoke in praise of those young
men who had died in the conflict with Sparta. It is a political
speech, but it also reflects in its finer moments some of the
principles which supported the best of the age. Here is an
excerpt from that oration:

> Our love of what is beautiful does not lead to extravagance; our love of
> things of the mind does not make us soft. We regard wealth as
> something to be properly used, rather than something to boast about.
> As for poverty, no one need to be ashamed to admit it: the real shame
> is in not taking practical measures to escape from it. Here [in Athens]
> each individual is interested not only in his own affairs but in the
> affairs of the *polis* as well: even those who are mostly occupied with
> their own business are extremely well-informed on general politics—
> this is a peculiarity of ours: we do not say that a man who takes no
> interest in politics is a man who minds his own business; we say that
> he has no business here at all. We Athenians, in our own persons, take
> our decisions on policy or submit them to proper discussion: for we do
> not think there is an incompatibility between words and deeds; the
> worst thing is to rush into action before the consequences have been
> properly debated. And this is another point where we differ from other
> people. We are capable at the same time of taking risks and of
> estimating them beforehand. Others are brave out of ignorance; and,
> when they stop to think, they begin to fear. But the man who can most
> truly be accounted brave is he who best knows the meaning of what is
> sweet in life and what is terrible, and then goes out undeterred to meet
> what is to come.

The first remarkable thing about this address is that it was
delivered in public to the assembled citizens of Athens. It is
not a private treatise on society. The second important idea
in it is the recognition of the role of debate and conscious
understanding as a prelude to action. Knowing "the meaning
of what is sweet in life and what is terrible" is an expression
of principle that understanding is the foundation of human
action, a characteristic of Athenian society which gives to its
history a special significance. This self-awareness expresses
the unique quality of the Classical Age in Greece. It also
begins to help us define the idea of tragedy as it was used in
drama and as it reflected the decline of the Athenian culture
soon afterward.

CLASSICAL DRAMA AND PHILOSOPHY

The origins of drama are much debated among historians
and literary critics. The archaeologists and anthropologists

have also made their contribution to the discussions, leaving us all with heads spinning with theories. The traditional view is that a singer of choral odes named Thespis, who, in 540 B.C., engaged in a dialogue with the lyric chorus, became the first actor. The combination of choral ode and dialogue was developed in Athens and the form known as tragedy gradually evolved. In addition to this tradition, however, there are also theories based on Dionysiac religious ritual and the festivals of the cult of Dionysos. More of this religious background will be examined in the sections on religion and the site description of the Theatre of Dionysos. It does need to be said here, though, that in the fifth century B.C. dramatic festivals were state occasions and were competitive. This mixture of contest, holiday, and religious ritual was surely unique and contributed to the high level achieved by this art form and religious expression.

The Theatre of Dionysos beneath the Acropolis in Athens.

Aeschylus

The first great tragic poet was Aeschylus (525–456 B.C.), who was a native Athenian and had fought in the battle of Marathon. He took for the subject matter of his plays the myths of Homer, the myths of the Olympian gods, and current history. Developing the form inherited from Thespis and adding his own elements, including masks and costumes, Aeschylus was responsible for the birth of the tragic form and its growth to maturity.

In the years between 484 and 468 B.C., the height of his career, Aeschylus was awarded the first prize thirteen times by the judges of tragedy. In the competition, the poets wrote three plays, usually but not always connected in theme and content. Of the eighty titles left to us of his work, we have only seven plays, the most important of which is the trilogy of the House of Atreus. *The Oresteia* details the story of Agamemnon's return from the Trojan War, his death at the hands of his wife Clytemnestra, the revenge of that murder by their son Orestes, and the subsequent trial and release from guilt granted to Orestes by Athena and the tribunal at Athens.

When Aeschylus was living and writing in Athens, the *nomoi* were being established. Not merely an artist on the fringes of society, Aeschylus took an active part in politics. Part of his sacred vision of man's relationship to the gods and to justice and fate is articulated in his description of the trial of Orestes. This close relationship between the drama and civic affairs as well as foreign policy was unique in Athens during the Classical Period.

Sophocles

The second great tragic poet of the age was Sophocles (496–406 B.C.), also a native Athenian. As the dates of his life show, he lived a long life, and it was a productive and prominent one. Gifted from birth, Sophocles won his first prize in 468 B.C. with his first entry. He was also a priest, a general, an ambassador, and once a treasurer in Athens. His good friend Pericles said that as a general Sophocles was a good poet, no doubt true enough, but it is still a mark of the age that citizens were able to undertake such contrasting responsibilities at all.

Sophocles wrote well over one hundred plays, of which seven remain. His major trilogy, written over a long span of his later life, included *Antigone, Oedipus Tyrannus,* and *Oedipus at Colonus,* written in that order. Sophocles did not live to see the final defeat of Athens in the Peloponnesian War but must have understood the drift of the times. His loyalty to Athens and devotion to truth emerge in all his plays. The Sophoclean vision sees man aspiring to overcome limitation and to understand his place in the universe. His great hero Oedipus blinds himself from the horror of his fate, wanders in suffering, but then finds the grace through his suffering to understand and accept his life. The acceptance of fate through suffering was a message that Sophocles meant to leave Athens when he died.

Sophocles was a conservative, that is, one who wished to conserve the values of an earlier time. Some say he was the last of the Archaic thinkers, an assessment too radical but one which reflects the times in which he lived. He always affirmed that the gods in their own time worked out reality, and men struggled and suffered to understand that reality. The works of Sophocles may be read as a history of the human spirit during the fifth century.

Euripides

It is perhaps significant that Euripides, the third of the great tragic poets, was not an Athenian, but was born on the island

The fourth century B.C. theatre at Epidauros, where the classical dramas are played each summer.

of Salamis in 480 B.C., the day of the great battle, when the Persian fleet met defeat. Not being born to the Athenian inner circle, he looked on from the outside and wrote as an outsider. His revolutionary plays stirred strong feelings— both admiration and animosity. His was a tragic vision of human nature as a destructive force working out its destiny in the face of divine *ananke*, or necessity.

Euripides won the prize only four times and yet was prolific, credited with over one hundred plays, nineteen of which are extant. His best and most famous plays include *The Bacchae, Medea, Electra,* and *The Trojan Women.* Close friend of Socrates (Sokrates), he took issue with the common thought of the day and was a strong critic of the war. In 409 B.C., just before the death of Sophocles and the downfall of Athens, Euripides left Athens and went north, first to Thessaly and then to Macedonia, where he died in 405 B.C. at the age of seventy-five.

The plays of Euripides which remain to us show a variety of subject matter and artistic powers. In his plays, man fights necessity and is overcome with his own passions to the point of self-destruction. The gods are indifferent to this suffering, remaining aloof. But man is still able to rage against this indifference and to create new values which transform society even though he may be destroyed in the process.

Aristophanes

At the same festival where the tragedies were played, comedies were presented on the final day. During the fifth century, the comic form evolved as a celebration of man's release from necessity, his freedom to live like a god or to escape the realities of existence. Aristophanes (444–380 B.C.), the master comic poet, was known to have written forty-five plays, eleven of which have come down to us. These are the only comedies to have survived, which may be a reflection of the superior quality of Aristophanes' works.

The comic poets were free to mock both men and gods and to name names in the process. There was little censorship of either language or content, and the plays are graphic in portraying sexual and bodily functions. *Lysistrata*, performed in 411 B.C., was written to protest the conduct of the Peloponnesian War and was, at the same time, a marvelous parody of human nature.

Both Euripides and Socrates were targets of this biting satire and it was said that the former might well have left Athens to avoid further jabs from the comic sword of Aristophanes. Careful study of these plays reveals a genuine concern for the decline of values in Athens toward the end of the fifth century. In that sense Aristophanes was a conservative, even though his inventive genius produced revolutionary plays.

Socrates

It is difficult to measure the influence and effect of the presence in Athens of Socrates, born in 469 B.C. and condemned to death by the Assembly in 399. Trained as a sculptor by his father, Socrates gave up this art in favor of conversation. He was to be seen almost daily in earnest discussion with the citizens of Athens in the *agora,* adjacent to the Acropolis. His topic was always the truth: What was it? Could one know it? His method was the dialectic, or what Plato later called the science of philosophy.

Remains of the state prison where Socrates died—the Agora, Athens.

As we shall see later on in our glimpse of Greek religious thought, Socrates engaged his students, friends, and opponents in dialogue, the purpose of which was to uncover the truth. He believed in the soul, or *psyche,* which lived within man and was accessible to the power of reason. He referred to this soul on occasion as a *daemon,* a power within like a voice which if obeyed gave warnings and led in the direction of the Good, or the Supreme Being.

Tireless and always poor, Socrates spent little of his time maintaining himself or his family. He went barefoot through the Athenian marketplace engaging citizens in endless conversation. He described himself as a gadfly, biting the reluctant Athenian horse, stinging it to action and reflection. He taught purity of thought and action, honesty in all things, respect for the Good and the Beautiful. Plato was his student, as were many of the young aristocrats of Athens, but his thought confused and deceived most people. What many thought was a disregard for the gods was in Socrates a firm belief in divinity within himself and any other who cared to seek it out.

By the end of the century Athens had lost the tolerance that had always marked it as a great city. Reasons were sought for the defeat by Sparta. Many accused Socrates of corrupting the youth of Athens and teaching them to be critical of their elders and to be skeptical of the gods. At his trial Socrates spoke of his beliefs and his life. Again, little of what he said was understood. He said, "The simple truth is, O Athenians, that I have nothing to do with physical speculations." And, "Is there anyone who understands human and political virtue?" He told the Assembly what it did not want to hear, namely that "I found that the men most in repute were all but the most foolish." He knew that "not by wisdom do poets write poetry, but by a kind of genius and inspiration; they are like diviners or soothsayers who also say many fine things, but do not understand the meaning of them."

These words are, of course, Plato's, who reported what Socrates said at the time. We do not know how accurate these statements are of Socrates' intent, but the evidence is clear that he was badly misunderstood and that his values were not commonplace in the culture. When he died an important spirit died out in Athens.

THE PELOPONNESIAN WAR

After the defeat of Persia, finally achieved in 449 B.C., Athens and Sparta fell into a period of imperial competition. Both cities expanded their influence throughout the Aegean and the mainland of Greece. The Athenians established the Delian League, with its center on the sacred island of Delos, where the treasury of the league was guarded. The Spartans established the Peloponnesian League, which also included the mainland cities of Thebes and Delphi. Although sporadic

fighting broke out from 457 B.C. onward, a full-scale war did
not begin until 430 B.C.

The Peloponnesian War lasted for twenty-five years off
and on and was finally won by Sparta in 404 B.C. What is
important about this war is that it could have been resolved
peacefully many times. But as Thucydides tells us, vanity
and arrogance combined with fear and ignorance eventually
brought Athens to its knees. His account of the war is a
powerful description of the changes that had taken place in
society from the period of the Persian Wars to the close of the
fifth century, in 404 B.C. It is important to note that our view
of Classical Greece should not be clouded by fantasies of
purity and heroic idealism. Rather, Greek culture at this time
was convulsed with revolution, not only of cities and classes
but also of values and ideas. Indeed, we can see, looking
clearly, that Classical Greece of the fifth century B.C. resembles our own time more than we might wish to admit. What
we can see is who we are and what we struggle to overcome
in ourselves and in our culture. Listen to Thucydides
describe the effects of the collapse of the culture as Athens
and Sparta lost their control over events:

> Words had to change their ordinary meaning and to take that which
> was now given them. Reckless audacity came to be considered the
> courage of a loyal ally; prudent hesitation became specious cowardice
> and moderation was held to be a cloak of unmanliness; the ability to see
> all sides of a question became inaptness to act on any. Frantic violence
> then became the attribute of manliness and cautious plotting a
> justifiable means of self-defense. The advocate of extreme measures
> was always trustworthy and his opponent a man to be suspected.
>
> The cause of all these evils was the hunger for power arising from
> greed and ambition . . . The leaders in the cities, each provided with
> the fairest professions, on the one side with the cry of political equality
> for the people, on the other of a moderate aristocracy, sought prizes for
> themselves in those public interests which they only pretended to
> cherish, and recoiling from no means in their struggles for ascendancy,
> engaged in the direct excesses.
>
> Thus, religion was in honor with neither party, but the use of fair
> phrases to arrive at guilty ends was in high reputation. Meanwhile the
> moderate part of the citizenry perished between the two, either for not
> joining in the quarrel or because envy would not suffer them to escape.
> Every form of evil took root in the Hellenic countries by reason of the
> troubles. The ancient simplicity into which honor so largely entered
> was laughed down and disappeared, and society became divided into
> camps in which no man trusted his fellow.

It is difficult to realize that this description is a so-called
Classical commentary. So contemporary is it in fact that we
realize how much our own struggles are reflected in the
history of peoples and events covered in the dust of neglect
and ignorance. We should remember, as we move among
the weathered stones, that those who planned, carved, and
raised them were not so very different from us, except in the
effect of culture on our personal lives. Their spiritual struggles are our own and we can learn from their words and
sanctuaries how to remember what we have forgotten and

how to learn from the stones what powers they were meant to evoke.

The Peloponnesian War ended in defeat for Athens, but the terms were good and Athens soon recovered some of its influence, although not in terms of imperial power. A period of despotism set in during which much of the glory that we think of as the height of the Classical Period diminished as those in power sought to assign blame and to gain control. When, for example, Socrates received the death penalty, he became the scapegoat for the failures of Athenian foreign policy and for the moral decline described above by Thucydides.

THE FOURTH CENTURY B.C.

The second half of the Classical Period is characterized by a movement away from the independence of the democratic *polis* in Greece to a unification of the states under the power and leadership of King Philip II of Macedon and then his son Alexander the Great, who in a brief explosion of a lifetime created a Greek empire. It was also a time of intellectual growth, as Plato and then Aristotle changed the culture by virtue of the power of their thought.

The years following the Peloponnesian War were, for Sparta in particular, years of frustration and disappointment. First Sparta, then Thebes, then Athens once again, and so on, the city-states of Greece tried to gain supremacy over one another and to turn their attention once again to the east and Persia. The history of the first two decades after the defeat of Athens contains accounts of deceit, bribery, treachery, and intrigue, as leaders scurried around seeking allegiance and developing plans for new conquest.

In 377 B.C. the Spartans attempted once again to assert their control and to impose their rigid value system on the Greek world. The Battle of Leuctra ended that dream and Athens, once again, rose in influence, but only temporarily. The defeat of Sparta meant that the way of life so jealously guarded for a thousand years had finally ended. The closed society of physical and mental discipline, of unquestioned obedience and high ideals, had finally broken down under its own weight and internal decay.

Philip of Macedon

For a time Thebes gained in prominence only to decline in turn when Philip of Macedon gradually gathered the cities of Greece under his control. In 355 B.C. a struggle began over the control of Delphi. To the north, in Macedonia, a race of peoples whose manner of life and temperament brought back memories of the Mycenaean kingdoms, began to gain ascendance in power and wealth. Their king, Philip II, began to look to the south as the first step in gathering the necessary force to attack Persia.

Philip seized an opportunity in a conflict over the administration of Delphi to play one city off against another and to impose his might on the weaker states. Finally, in 338 B.C., a battle took place between Philip and the federated Greek states. The decisive event in this battle, in which 75,000 men took part, was a successful cavalry charge led against the Greek forces by Alexander, the eighteen-year-old son of Philip. This battle, in which the forces of Macedon prevailed over the remnants of the once mighty Greek armies, marked the end of the age of the *polis,* and hence, the end of the Classical Age.

Philosophy in the Fourth Century

Before we leave the historical background of the fourth century B.C. we must recognize the impact of the work of Plato and Aristotle on the period. Plato was born in Athens in 428 B.C., early enough to be exposed to high points of the fifth century but too late to have seen its glory. He was an aristocrat by birth and an intellectual by gift and inclination. Soon after joining the group around Socrates he began to observe with care and devotion the words of the master. Most of his written work in later years would recapture the dialogues of Socrates in the *agora.*

From the historical point of view, Plato's Academy in Athens was really the world's first university, a place to withdraw temporarily from society to study. As such it was a new idea. Outside the walls of the city, near the *deme* of Colonus, Plato lived apart, not participating in the life of the *polis,* and there in his garden he taught and wrote. It was there that he died in 348 B.C. at the age of eighty-one.

Romantic engraving of philosopher's garden, with a view of the Acropolis.

The political impact of Plato's work is difficult to measure in the short term. He lived and wrote at a time when the democratic impulse was waning and Greece was about to unite under the leadership of Philip of Macedon and his son Alexander. But while he lived, Athens remained independent and essentially democratic. Plato was convinced that the ideal state should be ruled by a philosopher-king, a man who was wise and who understood the relationship between justice and the good. He had seen a democratic state condemn his teacher Socrates and had witnessed the greed and vanity of tyrants. His most important work is the *Republic,* which sets forth his concept of the just society.

Aristotle was born in Macedonia in 384 B.C., the son of a court physician. He came to Athens at the age of eighteen and entered Plato's Academy. He remained in residence for twenty years and left upon the death of Plato to return to Macedonia, where in 342 B.C. he became the young Alexander's tutor. From what we know about Alexander's later philosophy, Aristotle's major impact was to instill a deep respect for the heroic values of Homer. Beyond that, Aristotle and Alexander appear to have had little in common.

In 335 B.C. Aristotle returned to Athens and established the Lyceum, a rival school to the Academy. Much closer to Plato's philosophy than most observers believe, Aristotle took the concept of the ideal forms of Plato and applied them to the natural world. He also divided knowledge into its natural divisions and examined the nature and functioning of the human mind. It is his study of the relation of the world to the human mind that signals a beginning of the science of knowledge.

When Alexander died in 323 B.C., Aristotle lost favor in Athens and went into voluntary exile, where he died the following year.

THE HELLENISTIC PERIOD

The Hellenistic Period begins, traditionally, in 338 B.C., at the time when Alexander the Great undertook the campaign against Persia. The first aim of the young Macedonian king was to recapture for Greece the cities along the coast of Asia Minor. The king was only eighteen, but he possessed the scars of earlier battles and had qualities of leadership that men willingly follow throughout the world. Little did his armies know just how far Alexander would ask them to go.

Legend has it that Alexander began the Persian campaign by hurling his spear ashore at Troy in honor of the heroes he so admired. In 334 B.C. he refounded Troy and captured the Ionian cities formally belonging to Greece. His style won him quick, thorough victories. He was a brilliant and ruthless general and an enlightened ruler. Rather than sacking cities and enslaving populations, he made it clear that he wished to institute democratic principles in the conquered territories.

As he moved south along the coast, Darius III, the Persian king, pursued him. In a masterful attack, Alexander surprised the Persian army near Issos. It was reported that 110,000 Persians died in this one battle, yet only 302 of Alexander's men were lost. Darius fled, leaving behind his queen and all the treasure of his kingdom.

ALEXANDER'S KINGDOM

Within the brief period of Alexander's life, the kingdom established by his military might and genius stretched south to include Egypt, east beyond the Indian Ocean to India itself, and north beyond the Caspian Sea to Armenia. By the end of 330 B.C. he was well north in Afghanistan and planning a westward campaign to Italy when he became ill. Returning south to Babylon, he died in 323 B.C. at the age of thirty-two. Within his lifetime he had succeeded in creating a Greek empire which lasted, even in fragmented form, for several hundred years.

The chief influence throughout the Alexandrian empire was all things Greek: art, literature, philosophy, and scholarship. In Egypt, where he was proclaimed a god, he founded his own city, Alexandria, which eventually replaced Athens as the center of Greek culture. Here it was that the famous library was established which began to collect the world's literature. Here scholars from around the empire gathered to study.

HELLENISTIC CULTURE

After Alexander's death, the kingdom was divided into territories ruled by his former generals. The system was too loose and chaotic to last more than a generation, and soon local peoples began to revolt. Thus, the political structure dissolved quickly. The culture which Alexander spread, on the other hand, lasted until the Roman invasions and even then was to influence the next five hundred years, or until the Dark Ages of the Christian era.

What seems most striking about these rapid developments is the sudden change in values brought about by imperial expansion. The splendors of the East, the sudden availability of large amounts of currency, and the appearance for the first time of large mercenary armies all contributed to the dramatic change of values in Greece. Private houses became opulent, art was created for homes rather than for temples, and expensive buildings were constructed for secular purposes.

As well, the *polis* disappeared as an independent political entity. The decisions affecting daily life and public policy were made somewhere else, by strangers. It was said that at this time the oracle at Delphi was asked who was the happiest man in the world. The answer forthcoming was that it was a farmer tucked away in the hills of the Pelopon-

nese, isolated from the world. There is in this story something of the loss of an earlier innocence, already long gone,
of course, but only now understood. There is also an
anticipation of the loss to come, when Roman armies would
sweep into Greece to end this brief dynasty.

ROMAN CONQUEST

While Greek imperialism to the east held the spotlight of
history, the Romans were gradually increasing their control
of the Western Mediterranean. By 200 B.C. Rome was in
control of the city-states of the Italian peninsula, had defeated the powerful Carthaginians and their commander
Hannibal's attempts to invade from the north. To the east,
Rome concentrated its attention in the Adriatic and on the
ambitions of local Achaean rulers. New federations of Greek
states formed to counteract the influence of Macedonia, now
led by Philip V. His feeble attempts at leadership were kept
in check by Roman power.

During the next fifty years Rome increased its influence in
Greece. Roman commissioners settled conflicts among states
and slowly but firmly established Roman-style rule. The
instinctive desire for freedom, so typical of the Greeks,
exerted itself finally in Corinth, where in 146 B.C. Roman
envoys were attacked. A Roman army descended upon
Corinth, completely destroying the city. Hereafter Roman
law and military control were imposed throughout the
former Greek empire. Democracy was abolished, taxes imposed, land ownership controlled, and for a thousand years
events in Greece became a part of someone else's history.

*Corinthian column from the Roman period with the Temple of
Hephaistos in the background—the Agora, Athens.*

GREEK RELIGION

It is because we don't know who we are, because we are unaware that the Kingdom of Heaven is within us, that we behave in the generally silly, the often insane, the sometimes criminal ways that are so characteristically human. We are saved, we are liberated and enlightened, by perceiving the hitherto unperceived good that is already within us, by returning to our Eternal Ground and remaining where, without knowing it, we have always been. Plato speaks in the same sense when he says, in the Republic, *that "the virtue of wisdom more than anything else contains a divine element which always remains."*

—ALDOUS HUXLEY, *THE PERENNIAL PHILOSOPHY*

The history of Greek religion is a portrait of man's loss of unity with the Eternal Ground and his efforts to reestablish contact and relationship with the Divine. As we study the ancient evidence, both in stone and words, we are able to see how man has struggled with this loss of intimacy, suffered in that loss, and molded his world in an attempt to remember and regain a measure of intimacy with the god within.

Regardless of our culture and faith, we are indebted to the ancient Greeks for the record they left of their struggles. Their ancient temples and sanctuaries, their lyric poems, their stirring drama are, taken together, an expression of their search for divine company and relationship. It is a characteristic of Greek religion that the divine presence had to be invoked. Divine presence to the ancient peoples was cyclical, like the seasons and the movements of the stars, planets, sun, and moon. Spirit was also related to the forces of impregnation, germination, and growth in nature.

The birth of spirit—as in the stories of the birth of Zeus—had to be protected from the laws of Kronos (time) who ruled the universe. Immortal spirit would survive if not devoured by time, quite literally swallowed as the myths tell it. Mankind had to do its part to keep spirit alive and to nurture it with invocation, sacrifice, and remembrance in the form of festival, prayer, and ritual worship. To forget is to destroy, or to reverse the old saying: out of mind, out of sight. The very existence of spirit at the level of human awareness depends upon will and devotion. It is in this way that mankind "creates" its gods, its myths of spirit.

The law is: if God is not remembered, God dies. To remember means to embody or "to give members to" the idea of God. A god without members or a god unmanifest is a

forgotten god. There are many examples of the dismembered god throughout Greek theology. When the
Greeks made images in their own likeness of the pantheon of
gods, they were remembering the gods of their ancestors,
who in neolithic times lived with their gods as we live with
our technology and our contemporary myths of meaning.

The Greeks were primarily a visual people, and they
remembered their gods in the landscape, in temples, in
sculpture, in drama (much more visual than we may realize),
and in fresco and vase painting. More than other world
religions, Greek religion appears in the landscape, in the
brilliant light as it illuminated the sacred temples, and in the
movements of the nomadic tribes who established sanctuaries along their sacred routes.

Example of rounded hill as a symbol of the Earth Mother,
Hagia Triada, Crete.

THE EARTH SPIRIT

The nomadic tribes, following the herds in season, were
without permanent shelter or formal settlement. They moved
or stayed according to weather and food, completely dependent upon the earth for life. Such dependence instills
worship, that is, exalted feeling based on revealed experience. Without having any religious ideas or rituals imposed,
these nomads understood that the earth ruled them and that
this rule was beneficial when right action was followed.
There was also an extra sense in which the earth communicated its spirit, and there eventually appeared those men
whose special touch of the earth and awareness of spirit set
them apart. We now would call them shamans.

But before the shaman all men took part in the life of the
earth and felt no separation from it. The wind spoke, the

leaves murmured, and the water bubbled up from the rocks, filling the night with meaning. This existence had a rhythm, which was instilled over thousands of generations, gradually developing patterns and formality. The natural patterns were related to human existence: sexual union, generation, birth, nourishment, vitality, decay, and death. Everything had its season (rhythm) and its proper shape (form).

The rhythms emerged in day and night, summer and winter, calm and storm. The forms emerged in the landscape: mountains, rounded hills, horned peaks, gorges, caves, seas, lakes, streams, and springs. At a certain point, probably before the Neolithic Period, this human imagery gave to the earth a dominant feminine likeness. The earth itself acquired female characteristics in both rhythm and form. For example, it is generally believed that during the Stone Age, the cave was seen as the womb where the abundance of the earth was conceived. The early cave paintings, so beautifully wrought in the darkest and most inaccessible parts of caves, might have been prayers of impregnation. The form of the desired birth was painted as a religious act.

The earth, then, became the Great Mother. It was not that a rounded hill *was* a breast to be sucked upon. It was a breast in the mind's eye meant to exalt the feeling of nourishment and dependent love. To keep the hill in view was to worship the earth as mother of mankind, and in Greece the breast of the mother was everywhere. There is also a literal sense, however, that the earth was also a mother, alive, vibrant, productive, protective, nurturing. Thus, there was the reality and the metaphor of the reality.

THE EARTH MOTHER GODDESS

Before polytheism in Greece there was an era of monotheism, of one god who represented the divine idea to men. It is the usual practice of those who see human "progress" in terms of evolutionary change to see man developing in sophistication from a multiplicity of gods and animism toward monotheism, to the One God of our own culture. Such a view ignores the evidence of tradition in most cultures and also suggests that polytheism is a primitive form of religious belief.

First, the complexity of religious belief presented in the pantheon of gods, or "paganism" is far from primitive, and second, the evidence shows us that this complexity grew partly out of the desire for accommodation as cultures mixed during the great periods of migration and partly as an attempt to explain the difficulties of returning to the Eternal Ground. Common to all religious pattern in the Greek experience, however, was a belief in and worship of an Earth Mother Goddess of great power and influence.

In prehistoric times the productive powers of the earth, the facts of birth and death, and of sexual generation created a divinity in which female characteristics predominated. The influence was primarily Eastern. In Mesopotamia, for example, this goddess was variously called Mah, Nintu, Aruru, or Ninmah. In the Aegean islands images of this goddess began appearing before the Bronze Age. Neolithic man made images of this goddess first from stone and then from clay. In Greece she may have had a shape before she had a name. The nourishing breasts, the ample hips, and clearly marked vagina dominate these images. Often, a male child appears as well, giving us an image of an early madonna. Later, the child becomes a man-child, a young god who is both consort and son and who dies each year to be brought to life by the generative power of the goddess.

It is evident that the Earth Mother Goddess, in whose mysterious power life itself resided, was the image of meaning for early man as well as the companion of his days and nights on earth. Other gods and spirits no doubt gradually made their way into the worldview, making their claims of power, expressed in the warmth of the sun, the waxing and waning of the moon, raging storms and devastating fire, but the goddess nurtured and protected as the primary deity of worship.

But as we will learn from Hesiod, intimate contact with the gods ceased to be a constant communion. There came a time when intimacy was lost. In order to recapture the unity, man developed revelatory rituals of feasting, music, dance, and sacrifice, all with the intent of making him feel at one with the mother. Varying from place to place, these practices

Venus of Willendorf, 30,000–25,000 B.C., Natural History Museum, Vienna. Note the exaggerated life-giving features.

involved orgiastic celebration and blood sacrifice as a way to establish contact with the generative power which would result in crop growth, human and animal fertility, and a safe journey for the dead.

Some would say now that the images of the Earth Mother uncovered in the Cyclades and on the mainland during the Neolithic Period were merely primitive attempts at artistic expression and have no sacred intent or function. It is certainly true that the statues have a childlike quality, but perhaps this appearance describes the sacred relationship accurately. The goddess is the true mother as seen by the child.

The primacy of the Mother Goddess and her consort held sway during the Minoan and into the early Mycenaean periods. The record of belief and practice left by these two Bronze Age cultures is unclear, at least in the narrative sense. The record will become clearer in the site discussions for Knossos and Mycenae. It is not until the Archaic Period that the mythology and the meaning behind it become clear.

HESIOD AND THE ARCHAIC MYTH

In the eighth century B.C. Hesiod composed the Genesis of the Greek religion. It is the language and imagery of the Archaic Period of creation and the story of men separated from their gods. The fundamental idea expressed by Hesiod is that the state of mankind has been in decline, that, contrary to the evolutionary view of progress, mankind once lived in a state of grace but fell from it out of foolishness and disobedience—not unlike the tradition of Genesis.

In the epic poem we call *The Five Ages,* Hesiod describes this decline which cannot be located in time. The age Hesiod describes as Golden is a spiritual state and not a physical condition. It describes an article of faith in the human drama, although we can ascribe certain physical conditions to it.

There is in the account of man's early, or prehistoric, state a description of union with spirit, not identity but union, as in a relationship without the separation of selfish desire. All things are provided. The earth yielded its abundance freely, without limit. Tradition and science are together in seeing this period as nomadic. That gods and men sprang from one source is a critical ingredient in the tradition. Mankind came after time (Kronos) came out of chaos, and they were mortal. Their lives passed without strife in their Eden.

Hesiod's description of the Silver Age speaks of a man playing childishly in his own home, isolated from the earth and the spirit he would encounter in moving through the landscape. He thus grows to be a simpleton, devoid of the wisdom of the earth, incapable of living fully or fruitfully in its bosom.

Settlement brings an end to man's unity with the gods. Dwelling in settlement was not in itself evil, but implied separation. Once settled, men had an obligation to serve the blessed gods at the holy altars set up for the purpose of restoring the former unity. Altars became a part of the process of settlement as men selected places on the earth as especially sacred, as sanctuaries.

The next logical step was to endow these special places with holiness, as places where the gods appeared and where human beings purified themselves for the encounter. Settlements, on the other hand, were not regarded as divine but as somehow separate, as nonsacred.

Hesiod's "Brazen Age" marks the complete separation of men from their gods. These men loved war and violence; they took no nourishment from the earth and they depended solely upon the strength of their own arms and armor. The gods took no part in destroying them, but they destroyed themselves. The central image from Hesiod in describing this race is "hard of heart like adamant." The closed heart is one incapable of seeing God. There is no room for the divine; it is shut out of the light. Their destiny was the outer darkness from which there is no return.

In the fourth age, called the Heroic Age, of Hesiod's cosmogony we see the first glimpses of recorded history. The heroes spoken of here are the Mycenaean lords and warriors who, in the 1190s B.C., sacked Troy. They are pictured as noble and "more righteous" than their warlike and hard-hearted predecessors. There is in this mythology an important religious theme emerging. Men must be noble as well as righteous. There is an aspiration to fulfill the possibilities inherent in being human, despite the loss of intimacy with the gods. The way back was to aspire to greatness, the reward for which was immortality in the blessed isles where sorrow had no place, although now "far from the deathless gods."

By the time Hesiod wrote his version of the tradition, the Greeks had little understanding of the Mycenaean way of life, although they may have grasped the true state of man's relationships to the gods. Bronze Age life was very different from Archaic life, as we will see in greater detail in the site discussions of Mycenae. But in religious terms, the *wanax* or priest-king of the hilltop fortresses was the semidivine leader of his people and ruled absolutely. There was, as far as we know, a priest class who served the *wanax*, but its function was to carry out his instruction and his calendar of religious events.

Hesiod brings his story to his own era and to the present time, the Iron Age, when men live in isolation and separation from one another as well as from the gods. Gone is the certainty of authority. And yet some good remains. By this reference Hesiod means that the possibility exists for men to reestablish contact with the gods. He does not speak of a divine spark within man—a concept to emerge more clearly later on—but as long as a certain innocence remains, mankind can be saved from destruction. When Hesiod speaks of human beings reaching the stage when they have "grey hair on the temples at their birth," he refers to a loss of that innocent state when communion with the divine was commonplace. Thus, man will exist as man as long as he believes in and honors the gods.

THE MEANING OF THEOGONY

Hesiod is also the primary source for our information about the Olympian gods and goddesses who came to form the core of the Greek pantheon. The *Theogony* describes the attributes of generations of deities, from the god Chaos to the Earth Mother Gaea to the powerful Ouranos, who with Gaea (or Ge) fathered the race of Titans. This cosmology also reflects the intrusion and imposition of northern and eastern influences. It is supposed that the masculine sky gods came from the north, perhaps as far away as Siberia.

The major feature of this northern tradition is the appearance of Zeus as the central spiritual force, the ruler of heaven and earth. He is not the ultimate creator of the early myths, but he does establish himself as king of the gods and ruler of the spiritual realm. These sky gods still come under a higher law and are not supreme, immortal though they may be. Indeed, Kronos, Father Time, is deposed by his son Zeus and is confined in the western wilderness where he lives with the blessed heroes.

The *Theogony* describes the marriage of the Sky Father with the Earth Mother. Seen by many scholars as a forced marriage in which the goddess is subverted, there is also evidence of a slower and more natural union as migrants from the north assimilated the traditions and customs of the indigenous peoples. The gradual dominance of the Sky Father reflects a maturing process in spiritual matters. As man's consciousness develops, the images of spirituality reflect a growing awareness of maturity and full humanity. Thus, the Olympian gods are both male and female, six each, in fact, and they represent all aspects of the human being. The Earth Mother is gradually subdivided into different female aspects and becomes during the Classical Period aspects of Demeter, Hera, Artemis, Aphrodite, Athena, and Hestia.

The story of the *Theogony* is long and violent. Out of Chaos came the gods, manifestations of consciousness in the cosmos, giving birth through the power of Eros, the force through which all life begins and flourishes and all spiritual knowledge is known. It is the account of the turbulence of the creative forces unleashed out of the primal mystery, some of which are transmitted to man. There are the conflicts of power, the temptations of selfish desires, and the depravity of destructive instincts. Also in the birth of the minor gods, such as Blame and Woe, the powers are released when Blame grows untended by Reason into the Night, enlarged by Dreams into injustice and ruthless vengeance.

Here is a myth of a people who have become aware of their own spiritual condition. The old security has been lost, and men are actively seeking the truth. If we see the truth as spiritual, that is, as being a reality other than that which is to be perceived in the material world, then we can see these stories as attempts to work out the struggle by which man becomes a spiritual being.

The Greeks were aware of living in the conscious plane of the earth, influenced by the Earth Mother and watched by the sky gods. In doing battle with the monsters of experience, man had to please the gods, which he did by being as much like them as possible. The various Olympian gods were seen as aspects of the human *psyche,* or soul. Zeus was the lawful spirit, that which is contained in all souls and is immortal. Apollo was the force of harmony in man, moderating the desires and aligning the soul so that the spirit, or Zeus, could be lord of the whole man. Athena represented intuitive inspiration, the voice of wisdom in the soul. Hades was repressed desire, the destructive tendency to ignore potential destruction. Poseidon was the force which opposed the lawful spirit represented by Zeus. Poseidon is sensual pleasure and perversion as well. Hera, the wife of Zeus and one of the aspects of Earth Goddess, is the willing transformation of desire to spirit, the sublime union of human elements in proper relation.

There is in nature, then, a fundamental impulse to evolve to spirit, toward Zeus, and man possesses the consciousness to undertake this struggle. To be successful, he must conquer or sublimate the destructive elements or monsters of his unconscious nature in favor of the intuitive wisdom of the spirit. And he must also overcome the fundamental guilt arising from the conflict between matter and spirit. To the Greek this task was best accomplished by moderation and recognition of the forces operating within him. As we examine the Olympian gods, we will recognize many of these elements and see in the stories how the Greeks explained through myth the struggles of the spiritual way of life.

THE PANTHEON OF GODS

The twelve major gods of the Greek pantheon were firmly established in Greece by the time of Homer. Although different lists occasionally surfaced, depending on the city and the time, the twelve gods listed below were regarded as the chief gods in the pantheon:

Zeus
Hera
Poseidon
Demeter
Apollo
Artemis
Ares
Aphrodite
Hermes
Athena
Hephaistos
Hestia (sometimes
replaced by Dionysos)

Engraving of the twelve gods of Olympus gathered in the order of the zodiac.

ZEUS

Zeus is king of the gods, lord of Olympus, ruler of the universe. The world is the city of Zeus. Thus, Zeus guards the *polis,* minds the home and the storehouse. In addition, he protects suppliants. The position of one who asks a special favor of one who is in power is vulnerable to arbitrary treatment. Zeus, as king of the gods, is the special protector of those who approach kings in supplication.

Zeus also protects the stranger who seeks hospitality. The traveler in ancient times was especially vulnerable to ill-treatment on the road, and yet he was a special person, perhaps even a god, and so hosts were obligated to provide a warm welcome. Both the *Iliad* and the *Odyssey* emphasize the courtesies due to strangers and the swift retribution from the gods when hospitality is denied.

In the same way Zeus is also the protector of the sanctity of oaths. In Greece, a man's word was the basis of the moral structure of the *polis.* A broken oath brought justice from Zeus in the form of public exposure and shame, the result of which might be banishment. It is Zeus, then, the god of mind and intellect, who sees into the intention behind the spoken word.

The myths surrounding Zeus create for him images of power and generation. The lightning bolt is his special symbol. It is both a weapon for punishment and a flash of enlightenment. Ideas, thought, and inspiration come from Zeus. They are a gift of spirit. If Zeus is invoked before a debate, for example, chances are that the resulting thoughts and ideas arising to meet the situation will be to the point and will represent the truth.

Along with the lightning, Zeus also brings rain to impregnate Mother Earth to bring forth the fruits of the earth. As we trace the first appearance of the Olympians into the Bronze Age and earlier, it is this function of creative energy and generative power that first characterizes Zeus and suggests the sacred marriage of the sky god to the Earth Goddess. In this sense he takes over the functions of his grandfather Ouranos.

On the simplest level, then, Zeus was God the Father to the Greeks. He was the protector and creator in his role as father. He maintained order in the cosmic and domestic households by punishment. On a more sophisticated level, Zeus was the god of intellect and thought. The quality of mind over which he ruled maintained order in the intellectual life. We might think of it as the intuitive power in mind from which springs enlightenment and revelation. At the spiritual level, Zeus was harmonizing spirit as well as the symbol of human consciousness and reason.

In mythology, the birth of Zeus is given special treatment. He was born the youngest son of Rhea (also a goddess of the earth) and Kronos. Because Kronos devoured all of his previous children (keeping them within his manifest nature), Rhea conspired to hide her latest son from his father. She took the babe to a mountaintop cave in Crete and substituted a stone wrapped in swaddling clothes which she gave to Kronos to swallow. Zeus was nurtured by a goat, eventually growing to rebel against his father and to seize control of the heavens, there to rule the gods and men.

*Zeus conquers the Titans,
shown in the mastery of
a four-horse chariot.*

HERA

Hera is one of the earth goddesses, transformed by the Greek culture to an Olympian. Her special manifestation is as the one legal wife of Zeus. As such she represents the lawful marriage of matter to spirit. She was also to the Greeks the ruler of the social order as the patroness of marriage. She was the special goddess of all the stages of a woman's life: virgin maiden, loyal wife, and grieving widow.

Her marriage is celebrated in the springtime, in the month of Gamelion in the Attic calendar, corresponding to our January–February. It was said that the marriage of Zeus and Hera took place on the island of Euboea, to the east of Attica, home of herders. Hera was sacred to cows and oxen, and she was called "ox-eyed" by Homer. She is a majestic goddess, honored by the other gods, and is spotless in her behavior. As such she symbolizes purity in marriage and, indeed, in all sexual matters.

In more psychological terms, what Paul Diel has to say about her is valuable: "The wife of the spirit Zeus is Hera, symbol of the perfect sublimation of desire. Hera represents love, the highest form of sublime aspiration. She symbolizes objectified desire, which goes beyond subjective and physical satisfaction and aspires to the gift of the self to the union of souls. Hera is desire which has surmounted its elemental egocentricity; she becomes the ideal of sublime union between men. On the sexual level, she presides over the right choice of partner and over exclusive and lasting union."

POSEIDON

When the victory over Kronos put Zeus into power, the universe was divided in three parts, with Zeus in the heavens, Hades in the nether world, and Poseidon, the brother of Zeus, in the seas. Poseidon is also the god of horses, and his chariot is drawn with steeds hoofed in bronze and gleaming in gold. As he moves through his domain, the monsters of the deep, some given life out of the original chaos, swarm around him.

Poseidon bears the trident, with the power to stir the oceans to destructive force and to strike rock and bring forth fountains and horses. He also keeps the sea calm for sailors who propitiate his fury with sacrifice. And it is told that when a fisherman finally leaves the sea life, he leaves his net and trident in the temple of Poseidon and there prays for a peaceful old age, free from care.

Earthquakes are the work of Poseidon, and in the Aegean and the Mediterranean his work has left its mark. The palaces of Knossos were continually shaken from their foundations, and the island of Thera was left a shell of itself by an eruption that probably ended the Minoan culture. These manifestations of natural fury are gathered together in this god, who in spiritual terms was also seen as the

representative of insatiable desires. Poseidon was seen as
being opposed to the lawful spirit in Zeus. He is that force in
human beings that is disobedient to the call of the harmonizing spirit.

DEMETER

Demeter was the daughter of Rhea and Kronos and the sister
of Zeus. More than any of the other goddesses in the
pantheon, Demeter signifies Mother Earth and is the direct
link to the Earth Mother of the prehistoric era. Her worship
was particularly strong in the rural areas of Greece, and the
Eleusinian Mysteries belonged to her. She was the goddess
of agriculture and her great gift to man was the art of
cultivation and the annual wonder of fertility and harvest.

Demeter represents the fertile earth and the settling of
man to agriculture. As such, she is a temptation, since the
settling process inhibits man's communion with spirit. Also,
however, these are lawful desires which meet the needs of
man. It is through the art of cultivation that man meets the
goddess in the mysterious ceremony celebrated at Eleusis,
where Demeter was worshipped each year.

APOLLO

With Zeus and Athena, Apollo is one of the three most
powerful gods in the pantheon. He is a latecomer to the
Greeks, and scholarship has theories but no real trace of his
origins. The current thoughts are that he came to Greece
from either the eastern Hittite tradition, where he was
known as Apulunas, god of the gates, or that he came from
the north, perhaps even Siberia. Whatever his source, he
quickly became a central god to the Greeks, who worshipped
him throughout the Aegean and the mainland.

The spirit of art as expressive form is attributed to Apollo,
as is the moral, social, and intellectual principle of moderation in all things. Along with form and moderation, Apollo
represents law and order, particularly as a giver of law and
judge of murder and revenge. His most famous appearance
in court was described by Aeschylus in the *Oresteia,* and
specifically in the *Eumenides,* where he comes to the aid of
Orestes, who stands accused of matricide.

As a guide to human behavior, Apollo is credited with a
series of precepts to the happy life. Some of those include
such wise sayings as "Curb thy spirit," and "Observe the
limit." He also advised against arrogance (*hubris*) before the
gods. And he warned men to "keep women under rule." It is
this latter advice that has prompted many to attribute his
seizure of Delphi from the earlier goddess as the Dorian
imposition of the male deity upon the Earth Mother cult. As
we shall see, the seizure of Delphi had serious spiritual
implications of another sort.

In matters of secular and religious law, Apollo was

Apollo shown with his bow and Daphne transformed into a tree.

supreme. It was left to him to found temples, to establish sacrifices, and, in particular, to rule over the rituals of purification. He presided over the burial of the dead and whatever practices were necessary to propitiate the spirits in the other world.

Apollo was born on the island of Delos, his mother being Leto and his father Zeus. His twin sister Artemis is also one of the twelve. His birth on Delos, beneath the sacred palm tree, makes it fitting that he is the god of light. Light is special to the Greeks. Any visitor to Greece and the Aegean knows about the remarkable quality of the light, a luminous clarity which makes objects stand out from their contexts with sharpness of detail. Light is also spiritual knowledge, and Apollo has the special function of prophecy. It is Apollo who is designated to give to men the word of Zeus through prophetic utterance at his sanctuary at Delphi, where his dictum "Know thyself" is the foundation of spiritual knowledge.

More than any other religion, the Greek expression of divinity is manifest in visual images. From the divine landscape itself with its forms of the Earth Mother to the temples shaped and placed for maximum visual effect, Greek gods are seen more than heard or experienced through ritual. The perfection of their form was most often expressed in the human guise, not from an egocentric arrogance but rather because divinity was an aspiration arising from the human condition and made possible through a conscious expression of that perfection. More than any other god, Apollo represented that perfection. His statues are more beautiful and more celebrated than any in the male form. Long-haired, clean-shaven, muscular, and always young, Apollo was the ideal of the ideal, perhaps most notably expressed by the marble Apollo from the Temple of Zeus at Olympia (in the museum at Olympia).

ARTEMIS

In the wild places of Greece, especially among the gorges and deep forests of Arcadia in the central Peloponnese, running with her favorite deer, is Artemis the virgin goddess. The twin of Apollo and often worshipped in the same temples and cult sites, Artemis joins the other goddesses as an aspect of the original Earth Mother. She guards the wild places and the animals that are untamed. She is also the huntress, however, sometimes outwitting her prey. She retains the purity of the unspoiled earth with memories of life before settlement and agriculture.

Artemis pictured as the Earth Mother—the Artemis of Ephesus.

With her brother, Artemis is also associated with the light, but in her case the less brilliant light of the moon and stars. Thus, she belongs to the night and is often seen pictured with a torch as well as with her traditional bow and quiver. By the Classical Period she was worshipped as goddess of the moon and had a full moon festival in the month of Munychion (April–May).

As a virgin she was the goddess of youth and especially of young girls growing up. Tall and graceful, idealized in full bloom, she was the most popular goddess because she kept guard over the youth. Connected to ancient tree cults, she also had a darker, orgiastic nature. In Sparta, vestiges of this aspect were preserved in the yearly flogging endured by young boys at her altar. The idea seemed to be that Artemis was a guide to proper conduct under the law, and the flailing impressed this conduct on young minds and bodies.

ARES

Reflecting the dark, bloodthirsty aspect of human nature is Ares, god of war. The Greeks understood that the impulse known as war was a part of their character as a people. It is generally thought that Ares joined the pantheon of gods from Thrace in the north, where a more warlike culture evolved, and moved south to join the mix of peoples during the Bronze Age. Ares is joined in his bloody revels by his sister Eris (Strife) and his sons Deimos and Phobos (Fear and Fright).

The violent nature of the war god is joined with sexual passion, and he is paired often with Aphrodite, who in later myths bore Eros from their union. In this aspect, Eros is seen as the infantile creature of passion, playing at the feet of his father or cradled in his arm. In Hesiod, on the contrary, Eros is born of Chaos and is the power by which matter and spirit are joined in harmony. Thus, to see Eros as the child of Ares and Aphrodite is to see him diminished, made a banal image of his more spiritual aspect.

It is not surprising that the worship of Ares was centered in warlike Sparta, where young dogs were often sacrificed at his altar. In Athens his sanctuary was the Areopagus where the high court of justice met to judge crimes of murder. Thus, the spirit of war in Athens was sublimated to the exercise of law as the Council met to make judgments for acts of violence. But nothing is harder to quench than the thirst for war when a culture feels itself threatened and seeks the quick solution to its fears and feelings of injustice.

APHRODITE

Aphrodite is the foam-born goddess, rising from the sea without benefit of a normal birth, spawned in the violent dismemberment of Ouranos by Kronos. In legend she rises from the sea near Cyprus, where she steps ashore to join the Phoenician race as one of the aspects of the Earth Mother Goddess, another symbol of fecundity and generative power.

In addition to her more familiar role as goddess of love, Aphrodite is primarily a nature goddess. Her realm includes the wind and changing sky. She is the goddess of storm, both within man and without. To the Greeks, nature or *physis* included human nature as well as natural phenomena, and Aphrodite controlled the turbulent in *physis*. As such she was powerful and often destructive, a goddess to be respected.

Her powers were exercised in all the elements. In particular she was goddess of the sea and the seafarer. A calm sea fit for safe passage was her work, as was a fair wind for a swift journey. She was also the goddess of plants and tender shoots, of fruitfulness in garden and grove. In human affairs she was recognized in the passion of love, and overwhelming power that drove men and gods alike to irrational behavior.

She is always pictured smiling and ideally beautiful. She carries with her magic charms to induce passion and subdue the will. In her company are her son Eros and the three Graces, Peitho (Persuasion), Pothos (Longing), and Himeros (Yearning). These personifications of the nature of passionate love demonstrate the subtlety and sophistication of the way in which the gods reflected human nature and show

how myth served to explain and, to some extent, manage behavior among the Greeks.

In the most famous myth involving Aphrodite, Paris is asked to choose among Aphrodite, Athena, and Hera as to which of the great goddesses is the most beautiful. According to most versions of the myth, Paris chose Aphrodite over the other two when bribed with the prospect of acquiring Helen as his lover. In spiritual terms the myth represents a test for the mortal Paris. Had Paris chosen Athena, he would have chosen spiritual wisdom of the highest order, a difficult but correct choice for the mortal in his quest for enlightenment. Had he chosen Hera, he would have taken the lawful path in which desire is sublimated properly to the rule of spirit, in this case Zeus, the husband of Hera. But Paris was tempted by the lowest level of human desire and was seduced by personal greed in his choice of Aphrodite in her aspect of sexual passion. His choice causes the Trojan War, the death of Agamemnon, the agony of Orestes, and so on. It is in this way that the myth of Aphrodite helps to inform the struggle between matter and spirit in the human condition.

HERMES

Hermes' name means "he of the stone heap." For anyone who has followed wilderness trails and sought the correct path through forests and mountains, the sudden appearance

Zeus, Hermes, and Aphrodite, in an engraving of the zodiac.

of a stone heap or cairn marking the way is a welcome sight. Hermes is the god of the Sacred Way, the guide on the path. In his more mundane aspect, he is the god of traffic, of roadways, but our interest is in his spiritual function.

Hermes is the son of Zeus and the nymph Maia, daughter of Atlas, the son of a Titan and thinker of mischief. The myth of Hermes emphasizes his precocity and his inventiveness. Born in the morning, by noon he had already invented the lyre and stolen his brother Apollo's sacred cattle. Admitted to the pantheon of gods by nightfall, Hermes became the friend of Apollo and the messenger of Zeus. As such he possessed minor gifts of prophecy and associations with flocks and shepherds with Apollo.

But it is in his aspect as a guide that Hermes is important. His history has been traced back to Minoan roots in cults of mountains and caves. He is associated as well with tree cults, all of which suggests a strong connection in his function as an intermediary between man and god in the task of spiritual realization. Hermes may well be a link back to the Earth Spirit of prehistoric times. The nomadic peoples traced the Earth Spirit through the world, making contact with its powers along sacred paths and in sacred places. Nomadic man moved through the world in a sacred manner, sensing the spirit in the landscape, listening to its voice in nature.

Once man settles, rings himself about with walls and citadels, he loses contact with that moving, informing spirit. The worship of Hermes is an attempt to honor and restore that contact. What Hermes becomes in the mundane functions of his worship is an indication of the loss of that impulse. But the connection remains anyway. He is the god of mining and digging for treasure. He is the god of roads, of the marketplace, and of travelers. Heaps of stones, some marked with directions and inscriptions, marked intersections and doorways. In the fifth century B.C. "herms" were erected outside of homes to protect them from evil.

As a guide Hermes is also the conductor of the dead to Hades, a connection to the original function as a spiritual guide. He is the god of sleep and dreams, another path of spiritual revelation and prophecy. Athletic ability, dexterity, physical beauty, and personal charm are his as well as good memory and an agile mind. In sum, Hermes is closer to mankind than many of the twelve, more so than Apollo and Zeus with whom he is most closely allied. It is in this perception of him as the friend of distant spirit yet the friend of lowly man that Hermes has his greatest appeal and importance.

ATHENA

More than any other divinity the Pallas Athena represents a high order of spiritual development, a fitting symbol of Athens at the height of its glory. The rise of Athens in the order of other Hellenic city-states either reflects the deity who is patroness or is the result of the influence of her presence—perhaps a little of both. In any case, Athena is second only to Zeus her father in the spiritual purity of her being. She is wisdom incarnate, the perpetual maiden or *kore* of the human condition, and symbol of the aspiration of men for wisdom in this life.

The legend of Athena is very old and the story unclear. She is at least as old as Mycenae and probably older. Although not Greek in origin, she quickly became one of the three most powerful gods in the pantheon with her father Zeus and her brother Apollo. She was not born but sprang full-grown from her father's head. This manifestation attests to her identity as Wisdom and Intellect. In spiritual terms Athena possesses a purity which can be attained only with great sacrifice and devotion, so precious is knowledge of her.

Her name, Pallas Athena, means that she is of the clan of the Pallantidae, a name synonymous with nobility in the history of Attica. She is *parthenos,* the maiden, and her home, the Parthenon, is the maiden chamber where she resides. There, represented by the thirty-foot gold-and-ivory statue carved by Phidias, she stood as protectress of the *polis* and defender of the whole country of Attica. In her hand she bore the *aegis* or shield borne as well by her father as the symbol of power. On the shield glared the monster visage of the Gorgon, or Medusa, one glance at which turns men to stone.

That Athena bears the image of the Gorgon is fitting. It is through her wisdom that man is able to overcome the death of the spirit at the sight of the Gorgon. To turn to stone is to die in the spirit, to be nothing but matter, which is dead. In Athena is the wisdom to give spirit its proper place, to turn away from the Gorgon. Athena's gifts also include intellect and understanding. She also gave men the olive tree, the self-sown giver of oil and food. The arts of spinning and weaving are hers, as are health, safety, and security.

Athena is pictured as armed, the defender of Athens, goddess of victory and

Engraving of the statue of Athena by Phidias in the Parthenon, copied from a Roman reproduction, now lost.

peace. She is a mighty warrior, but she fights with a wisdom that defeats Ares in his thirst for blood.

HEPHAISTOS

Hephaistos, "the lame god," the god of fire and of the arts requiring fire, was the son of Hera. Because he was lame and depended upon his genius and the skill of his hands to keep his place on Olympus, he was a favorite of the people and particularly of artisans. Because of his deformity, he was cast from the heavenly company and dwelt nine years in a cavern beneath the ocean. Eventually, he was reinstated but Hephaistos was still associated with volcanoes and turbulence beneath the sea.

This imagery also connects him to Aphrodite, to whom he is married, although unhappily. The marriage is significant, however, in that both gods possess high levels of passion and unruly behavior, much to the displeasure of Zeus. But it is Hephaistos' connection with fire, symbol of consciousness and intellect, that makes him important. Along with Prometheus, who stole the fire of consciousness for mankind, Hephaistos was worshipped at the Academy in Athens, home of philosophy.

In all the legends of the gods where fine metalwork appears, Hephaistos is responsible. These include the great shields of Zeus and Athena and the famous arms of Achilles, so celebrated by Homer. The armor is symbolic of the spiritual strength needed to meet the monstrous destructiveness unleashed in the world. These evils are well understood by Hephaistos, who in his limitations is closer to them.

HESTIA

Hestia is goddess of the hearth, guardian of the home and, by extension, of the *polis* as a social entity. She keeps watch over the family as the stabilizing force of the community. As a goddess she never leaves Olympus, always there to guard it, to preserve the foundation of divinity. Although she is the embodiment of the home, Hestia remains unmarried, refusing the advances of both Apollo and Poseidon. Symbolically, this refusal from Hestia signifies her moderate position between several spiritual forces.

Hestia is the virgin daughter of Rhea, who represents the full joy of life on earth and simple earthly desires. Hestia carries this quality to the center of the home, where she maintains the hearth. Her position in the hierarchy accords her the privilege of being worshipped before and after ritual sacrifice at the temples of other gods. In fact, her name is mentioned before the name of any other gods in prayer and supplication. In great measure the center of religious life in Greece may well have been the sacred hearth of Hestia at Delphi. Here the Greeks kept the stone known as *omphalos* or the world navel, which was the center of the world, the place from which all knowledge flowed.

DIONYSOS

After the time of Homer but sometime before the end of the sixth century B.C., the god Dionysos joined the twelve Olympians, replacing Hestia, in most cases, in the hierarchy. This rise into the establishment of Greek gods was a long process, Dionysos having been an itinerant god of mixed parentage for as long as history recorded the myths of chaos, creation, and conflict.

The god we know as Dionysos came to the Greeks from Thrace, a wild and mountainous country to the north, where his worshippers were known to be rude and boisterous. The cult of Dionysos was firmly resisted in many places and his followers were often expelled, but gradually acceptance of this powerful, magic god overwhelmed the Greek mainland and islands, and moved south to Egypt and beyond.

Before Thrace is fixed too firmly as the original home of Dionysos, we need to give some attention to the other possibilities. The various myths and sources of information suggest that Thebes and Lydia in Asia might also have spawned the god. According to Hesiod, Dionysos was the son of Zeus and the mortal Semele, daughter of Kadmos of the House of Thebes. As happens to most mortals chosen to bear a god's child, Semele was killed by a lightning bolt and Dionysos was hidden away, this time in the thigh of Zeus, away from the wrath of Hera.

This myth affirms several important matters regarding Dionysos. First, Semele has her roots as an Earth Mother, even Earth herself, from whom Dionysos comes in the fire of spirit. He is of the earth and has connections in the underworld as well. He is also a son of Zeus, possessing both power and spiritual nature. Thus it is that he lives in several realms at once: heaven, earth, and underworld.

Euripides in *The Bacchae* places Dionysos' roots in Asia, at least in his travels and birth of the cult. Asia suggests exotic influences and an emphasis upon the mysteries. But Thrace remains the historical source of the Dionysiac religion, which gradually became part of the formal state religion of Athens and famous beyond its rituals for the role it played in Greek drama.

Madness and Dionysos

In his fine work, *The Greeks and the Irrational,* E. R. Dodds helps us to understand the importance of Dionysos to the development and history of Greek religious experience. Dodds describes four types of madness having religious significance: prophetic madness (whose patron is Apollo), poetic madness (which is inspired by the Muses), erotic madness (inspired by Aphrodite and Eros), and telestic or ritual madness (whose patron is Dionysos). Ritual madness is always communal and highly infectious.

Fanciful engraving of prophetic madness, set in the Temple of Apollo, Delphi.

The purpose of ritual madness is essentially cathartic, purging the participants of those irrational impulses which when repressed produce sickness and hysteria. Heads of state and religious officials gradually recognized that to prohibit the expression of this impulse was to repress it dangerously. Transformation, on the other hand, imposed controls on the impulse and organized the madness in a religious form. Such control was deemed necessary just as too much resistance was deemed disastrous.

Dodds also explains why such ritual madness was important. The rational mind resists the impulse to unity with spiritual forces because such unity obliterates the personality or, in another tradition, the ego. The worship of Dionysos had the effect of eliminating the difference and simulating the identity. There was no genuine assimilation to the divine, but the semblance was enough for some. In effect Dionysos seemed to say, "Forget yourself in me and happiness will be yours now." Such immediacy was the basis of its popular appeal.

It was in the rituals of Dionysiac revels that worshippers felt liberated from the restraints of society and self-consciousness. This feeling coincided with the more democratic freedoms instituted in the sixth century B.C. and probably accounted for the rapid acceptance of the new religion. In addition, the new freedoms left the individual without a sense of community, and any ritual that brought a communal experience with it was welcome. The music and dancing helped to erase the sense of isolation that resulted from the new awareness of individualism.

On the negative side of the equation, the figure and worship of Dionysos symbolize our Western view of hell. On one level Dionysos represents the subconscious triumph of earthly desire. He is an image of insatiability. The divine madness produced in worship is nothing but a trap in that the sensation of oneness with the deity can lead to forgetfulness of true spirit. If a man forgets his spiritual nature, he forgets God and clings hopelessly to life.

Dionysos as a God

What then makes Dionysos so important? What makes him a god at all? First, he is an antidote to austerity, to the excessive rigidity of the state religion and the drastic separation of men from the Olympian gods. Dionysos has the touch of mankind about him. He is of the earth and is nurtured by the fruit of the earth. He also died and was resurrected and re-membered. In the myth of his childhood, it is said that he was dismembered by Titans, those forces of destruction, and was born anew after three years in the underworld. This myth connects Dionysos with the nature gods of fertility and seasonal change. It also, of course, connects him to immortality and life after death.

The more immediate quality of his divinity is his love of life and his affirmation of the joys of the earth, the symbol of which is wine. Dionysos is celebrated as the god of the vine. Wine is his special gift to humanity. The wines of Greece, less famous now than in ancient times, were treasured by anyone who could afford them. The great wines were produced in the volcanic soils of the islands, particularly of Naxos, Cyprus, and Lesbos.

The Greeks did not drink heavily. Their northern neighbors did, however, and were judged accordingly by the more moderate south. The Greeks understood the joys of intoxication and were able to use wine as a welcome ingredient in religious celebration. Festival drinking to the point of intoxication was acceptable. What was less acceptable, though, were the nighttime revels of the women in the hills, streaming through the woods with ivy-covered wands, occasionally dismembering an animal in the frenzy of their devotions.

It should be recalled, then, that against the austere purity of Apollo's temple on the slopes of rugged Delphi there lurked the irrational turbulence of Dionysiac revelry. Just beneath the surface of perfect form smoldered the fires of madness. The myths of the Olympian gods and goddesses, reflective of the spirit to which men aspire, also mirrored a nature capable of personal and collective destruction. We have not changed.

As we shall see in the mystery religions, Dionysos is also the friend of mankind and the mythical connection between mortality and immortality. He is of the earth and by the spirit, containing in his nature the source of human salvation.

STATE RELIGION AND FESTIVALS

The tribal or clan structure among the ancient peoples continued to be the source of continuity through three thousand years of turmoil and change in Greek history. By the time of the late Archaic Period, ten noble families in Attica controlled most aspects of society. In religious matters the families controlled worship of the local cults and undertook to legislate the official state religion as well. In order to worship at all—in any official way—an individual had to have the sanction of family membership. To be outside the family was to be unable to worship in the official sanctuaries.

When the tyrant Cleisthenes imposed reforms in Athens and diminished the power of the great families and created the *deme* system, citizens who lived within the *deme* could take part in any function of the *deme,* including religious worship. Thus, every Athenian had a religious home, so to speak. Additional changes took place as further democratic reforms established the rule of law in Athens. Thus, by the time of Pericles, Athens had developed a complicated religious calendar administered by the state and carried out by the principle families.

The idea of a state religion may suggest that Classical Greece had an official religion in the same sense as Rome eventually adopted Christianity. In fact, Greece never had a body of religious belief in a codified form or a sacred book such as the Bible to serve as a standard. In Athens, for example, a series of cults were woven together along with practices and regulations governing the rituals of purification, sacrifice, and burial of the dead. On the Acropolis the cult of Athene Polias (the goddess of the *polis*), the cult of Athene Nike (defender of the *polis*), and the cult of Poseidon-Erechtheus (a hero cult) all existed side by side and yet constituted a whole as a sacred space.

If there was any uniformity in the so-called state religion, it might have been in the generally held beliefs about the human condition and man's relation to the gods. Man's fate, his *moira,* was to exist separately from the gods who ruled his life. The idea of *moira* goes back at least to the Dark Age and means not only fate but portion and share. A man's portion might refer to his family inheritance, the piece of meat to which he is entitled at a sacrifice, or it might mean his destiny as woven by the three Fates who ruled men's lives.

Also, Homer taught the Greeks that the goal of excellence, expressed by the term *arete,* was the meaning of life. Proper respect for the gods throughout one's life might ensure happiness, but in general, suffering was man's destiny and it was better not to have been born at all. Once here, however, it was the task of the noble Greek to seek his *arete,* serving the *polis* as a citizen. His duties were to fight if called upon, to debate the issues of the day, to serve in the assembly or in whatever position the *polis* might assign him, and most of all, to support with his wealth the festivals and honors due the gods.

FESTIVALS IN THE CLASSICAL PERIOD

In the very best sense, festivals were meant to shatter the limitations of time and place, to detach the individual from banal worldliness and from the bounds of body and personality in order to reunite him with the gods and heroes of the Golden Age. They were also meant to recapture the power of deified Nature, to continue uninterrupted the cycle of

*View to the north of
the Panathenaic Way,
Agora, Athens.*

generation, growth, death, and resurrection which formed the basis of man's relationship with the divine.

The Attic religious calendar was originally lunar in structure, with the various festivals becoming fixed on certain days of the month, particularly on the days of full moon. Central to this arrangement was the belief that the influence of the waxing moon caused things to grow and increase, whereas the waning moon brought decrease and decline. Generally, the twelfth day of the lunar month was the best for business as well as for festivals. It is supposed that the calendar regulations emanated from Delphi and was the work of Apollo. In fact, each *polis* had one or two chosen representatives of Apollo who ruled on all matters pertaining to ritual and festival practices.

The table on page 59 shows the Greek calendar and the major festivals celebrated during the year. This calendar, adopted in the fifth century B.C., was based on a combination of lunar and solar influences. The twelve months each had 30 days, making for a year of 360 days. Five extra days were added on as a festival in itself. This system, imperfect as all such systems are, was based on spiritual principles and sacred numerology. So too was the lunar calendar it replaced, which was based on a thirteen-month year of twenty-eight days with one day left over. We shall have more to say in the next chapter about these numbers and their significance as sacred knowledge.

The names of Greek festivals, always given in the neuter plural, expressed the central idea of the feast, not just the god who was being venerated. For example, Dionysia really

Attic Calendar

MONTH	FESTIVALS
Hecatombaion (July–August)	Panathenaia Kronia
Metageitnion (August–September)	Metageitnia
Boedromion (September–October)	Eleusinia Greater Mysteries
Pyanepsion (October—November)	Thesmophoria Pyanepsia Apaturia
Maimakterion (November–December)	Maimakteria
Poseideon (December–January)	Poseidea Haloa
Gamelion (January–February)	Lenaia Gamelia
Anthesterion (February–March)	Anthesteria Diasia Lesser Mysteries
Elaphebolion (March–April)	Dionysia Pandia
Munychion (April–May)	Munychia Brauronia
Thargelion (May–June)	Thargelia Bendidia Plynteria
Skirophorion (June–July)	Dipolieia Skira Bouphonia

means the "Dionysiac things present" rather than a celebration of Dionysos the god. The Lenaia was a winter festival of Dionysos in Attica and celebrated the winepress, the women of the press, and the holy winepress house. And the Anthesteria was the feast of Dionysos celebrating the blossom-giving, growth-promoting aspects of the god. In each case, then, the idea behind the festival was a force usually associated with life-giving energies.

The official state calendar began in the month Hecatombaion at the height of summer with the Lesser Panathenaia, the Greater being every fifth year or third in the case of an Olympiad. As its name implies, this important festival honored Athene as the patron goddess of all Attica. In 446 B.C. Pericles added musical contests to those of chariot racing and athletics. Winners were given wreaths woven from the sacred olive branches plus large vases filled with olive oil. The culmination of the festival occurred on the twenty-eighth of the month, which was the birthday of the goddess. A large procession formed at the Dipylon gate north of the city and wove through the *agora* up to the Acropolis. The procession included many young girls and young men from the noble families, public officials, religious figures, brightly decorated animals for sacrifice, honored warriors, leading citizens, indeed most of the important people of the city.

The purpose of the procession was the adornment of the cult statue of Athena with the *peplos,* an embroidered, saffron robe. Then there followed a sacrifice of a *hecatomb* of oxen. Normally a *hecatomb* meant one hundred, but it came simply to mean a large number. In the case of the Greater Panathenaia, more than a hundred oxen may have been slaughtered. The resulting meat served as the basis of the feasting which followed. It was not, in fact, common for the Greeks to eat large quantities of meat, this having been a northern habit. But on feast days the usual vegetarian and fish diet was set aside.

The feast had a sacred intent. Man and god were present for each another, in the Greek sense of "knowing" one another. This idea of mutual presence is really the concept of the cult experience. The term "cult" for the Greeks meant local and private as opposed to Panhellenic and public in nature. A cult was a sacred relationship between specific people and a particular god.

To share a meal with a god meant that the meat was of the god and was eaten by man, the god taken in, absorbed in the symbolic way of ritual experience. A feast of this kind was always associated with the sky gods and never with the gods or spirits of the underworld. In the latter relationship, food and blood were offered to the chthonic powers but never

Engraving of a priest and a priestess pouring a libation at an altar.

shared by the living. No joining or "knowing" was desired in these cases because the souls being "nourished" existed below in limbo and the living were not meant to contact them.

Such a distinction points out a principle of Greek festivals, including their sacrifices and feasting. The intent of festival was to attract the god to his or her sanctuary, to be present there for the worshippers. The focus was on this world, the world of the living, and not another, invisible world. These are the gods of human existence, affecting life now and events in the living future.

When these festivals were motivated by the reality of the idea behind them and were not merely excuses for holidays, the Greeks believed that the possibility existed that the forces being celebrated might not appear again the next year if proper rituals were not performed. Such a fear made certain that human beings were a part of this cycle and were not self-consciously outside of it in some existential way. The original idea and the loss of its vital center were expressed by the legendary King Alcinous of the Phaeacians, with whom Odysseus found shelter in his wanderings. He said, "For the gods, at least until now, always appear clearly to us when we sacrifice glorious *hecatombs*, and they banquet with us, sitting where we sit."

MYSTERY RELIGIONS

The so-called mystery religions were a spiritual oasis, a place of vitality and nourishment in the relative desert of the official state religion of the Classical Period. Here we are able to identify a set of beliefs and a tradition both familiar and continuous. The essential idea of these mysteries was that the human condition included a divine element or potential which could, through knowledge, ceremony, and grace, be realized. Man was not, in this view, completely separate from the gods living in isolated splendor on Olympus.

There was not only a common source, as Hesiod claimed, but there was a common element in every human being. Those involved in the mystery religions possessed secret knowledge which was transmitted through the special bond of membership from generation to generation. Indeed, we are able to trace the essentials of the knowledge to our present time.

In the Aegean, the roots of the mystery religions were sunk in Cretan soil. The Minoans were the mystics of early Hellenic culture, celebrating the esoteric discipline of prophecy in the caves of Dikte and Idha and conducting initiations into the chthonic mysteries in their palace labyrinths. Since the secrets of the Minoan mysteries remain hidden, let us consider the better known and understood practices surrounding the cult figures of Orpheus and Pythagoras.

ORPHEUS

Orpheus was both a man and a legend. He was born in Thrace during the time of the heroes. Some place him as a contemporary of Herakles. The legend, fostered by the Orphics who claimed his name as founder, gives Kalliope, one of the Muses, as his mother. He was a poet and musician, and his lyric gifts soothed not only the gods themselves but men, animals, and trees. Part of the legend places him aboard the *Argo* as it sailed with the Argonauts and Jason to seize the golden fleece. His powers of music, god-given and spiritual in nature, kept the destructive voices of the Sirens at bay.

The central event in his life involved his beautiful wife Eurydice, who died of a serpent's bite and went to the underworld. Orpheus followed her there, charmed Persephone with his music, and won his wife's release on the understanding that on the way back to the light he would not look back at Eurydice, who was following him. He was unable to refrain from turning to look at her and as a result lost her forever. Some time later he was dismembered by Dionysiac Maenads, whose orgiastic celebrations he offended. He was subsequently reborn by virtue of the cult which bears his name.

Orphism

Early in the sixth century B.C. the Orphic movement gained in prominence throughout Greece, but particularly in Crete and in Athens. It came upon the religious scene as a mystery cult, which meant that the knowledge of its rites was secret and that a ceremony of initiation was required of its members. There is evidence that the cult may have come to maturity in Crete many years before as part of the Mother Goddess worship and Dionysiac celebrations there, and that in fact its rites were not secret.

From the sixth century B.C. onward, Orphism refined its beliefs, taking the earlier myths of Orpheus and combining them with philosophical tenets emerging from the East. Orphism recognized the unity of God from many manifest gods; thus, the worship of many gods was possible. Knowledge of God came gradually, which meant that the divine mysteries had to be taught in stages.

The Cosmology of Orphism

The Orphic cosmology was based on the principle that man contained an element of divinity. The myth working out the truth was different from the Olympian tradition and began when Zeus fathered a child with Persephone, queen of the underworld. The child, Dionysos-Zagreus, was a threat to the Titans, the immortal gods who always opposed Zeus for control of the cosmos. Dionysos-Zagreus was deceived by the Titans, captured, and devoured. Zeus responded to this outrage by destroying the Titans with a lightning bolt, reducing them to ashes. Out of these ashes Zeus fashioned humanity. In the nature of humanity, then, there resided the ash of the immortal Titans and, most important, an element of Dionysos, son of Zeus the spirit. These two immortal elements, which might be called the *daemon* of Zeus and the *psyche* of Titanic immortality, form the basis of man's immortality.

The initiation ritual of the Orphics remains a mystery in its detail, but must have involved purification with water and, according to several sources, a covering of mud and water which symbolized the birth of humanity from ashes. Certainly the initiation imparted knowledge of the *daemon* existing within the individual and of the various practices within the brotherhood which helped to realize this immortal nature.

Plato mentions the Orphic idea in an analogy: lack of knowledge of man's true nature was like preparing for a rite of purification by carrying water to the bath in a sieve, always running out before the moment of purification can occur. Plato's philosophy was indebted to the Orphic cosmology.

The idea of water and purification is well expressed in one of the few extant tablets containing Orphic doctrine. Known as the Petelia Tablet, it was discovered in Lower Italy near Sybaris. The poem was written on thin gold leaf, rolled up, and placed in a cylinder hanging from a gold chain. It was presumably hung around the neck of a dead person as an amulet.

The Orphic Petelia Tablet

Thou shalt find out to the left of the House of Hades a Well-spring
And by the side thereof standing a white cypress.
To this Well-spring approach not near.
But thou shalt find another by the Lake of Memory,
Cold water flowing forth, and there are Guardians before it.
Say: "I am a child of Earth and of Starry Heaven:
But my race is of Heaven alone. This ye know yourselves.
And lo, I am parched with thirst and I perish. Give me quickly
    the cold water flowing forth from the lake of memory."
And of themselves they will give thee to drink from the holy Well-spring
And thereafter among the other Heroes thou shalt have lordship.

The Lake of Memory symbolized to the Orphics and later to Plato the true path of spiritual knowledge. The idea is that through memory we are able to re-member our divine nature, to assemble again what the Titans tore apart when they devoured Dionysos. To the Orphics, then, Dionysos is the god who is remembered by sacred practice and whose element is mingled in human nature if only we are able to remember it.

Transmigration of Souls

Through a process of purification, which included abstaining from the eating of flesh, an individual could be reunited with

Zeus. However, the process involved several embodiments. This suggestion of the transmigration of souls or reincarnation appears throughout Orphic fragments. In particular, we have an ode of Pindar dated in 472 B.C. which speaks of soul migration.

"In the presence of gods high in honor, whoso took delight in keeping oaths has his portion in a life free from tears; while the others endure pain that no eye can look upon, and all they that, for three lives in either world, have been steadfast to keep their soul from all wrong-doing, travel by the high-way of Zeus to the Tower of Kronos, where the Ocean airs breathe about the Islands of the Blest."

These elements, then, speak of specific practices which lead the individual to liberation and the attainment of divine status. Such a belief is very different from the orthodox beliefs of most Greeks, who suffered in what they perceived as complete separation from the gods. The received tradition saw humanity in a degenerate age and condition in isolation from the gods, who, if they existed at all, treated mankind with disdain and arbitrary cruelty. For those Greeks, however, who followed the Orphic tradition, the Golden Age of Hesiod was possible now in that an individual could, through knowledge and practice, be reunited with Zeus.

THE PYTHAGOREAN MYSTERIES

The seafaring race called Pelasgians settled in Greece before the Bronze Age and worshipped the Earth Mother Goddess. According to their legends they were born from the teeth of the serpent Ophion in union with the goddess. As a young man Pythagoras studied with the Ionian philosophers and traveled widely, particularly to Egypt where he studied with the temple priests. He returned to Greece only to find an unfriendly climate for his work. He settled for a time in Crotona, Italy, where he taught and founded a community.

In the early fifth century B.C., in the atmosphere of democratic reforms, his community was destroyed and Pythagoras fled to Metapontum in Italy, where he died in 504 B.C. As a result of the upheavals, his followers dispersed and founded other communities, thus spreading his beliefs to a wider area, including mainland Greece. Based primarily on the study of number, the Pythagorean cult developed a cosmology and spiritual practices devoid of the traditional mythology. Because his mysteries were very close to the secret doctrines of the temple priests (see Sacred Architecture), Pythagoras was in disfavor among the religious elite of his time.

There are strong similarities between the Orphic beliefs and the Pythagorean doctrines. Common to both schools of thought was man's essential divine nature. Contemplation and devout practice produced the purity necessary for salvation. The doctrine of the transmigration of the soul was also important to Pythagoras. The love of wisdom, which is the purpose and meaning of philosophy, was the reason for existence, and all of human life could be properly understood from such love. His community lived in a strict daily regimen, including spiritual exercises and a careful diet, which excluded meat. One exercise in particular which gives us a glimpse of his principles involved having students at day's end report exactly everything which had taken place during the day. This exercise helped the memory in its work of recalling deeper and more hidden facts of existence, such as the relationship to the divine.

The Octave and Sacred Number

The most famous aspect of the work of Pythagoras was his discovery of the mathematical properties of the octave. This discovery was of great importance because it demonstrated the relationship between number and actual experience, and thus the relationship between divine principle and human life. Pythagoras discovered the mathematical relationship between the sound of a plucked string and its octave, the ratio of 1:2 and 2:1. When a string is halved, it vibrates exactly twice as fast and produces an exact octave. This demonstration of sound proved to Pythagoras that the cosmos functioned on the level of number and thus principle.

The Golden Verses of Pythagoras

No actual writings from Pythagoras have come down to us. His students, however, Lysis in particular, collected both sayings and prayers in a sacred document known as the Golden Verses of Pythagoras. For the most part merely wise sayings for the virtuous life, there are several verses which breathe a richer air. The following lines indicate the depth of these sacred writings:

> Begin thy work, first having prayed the Gods
> To accomplish it. Thou, having mastered this,
> That essence of Gods and mortal men shalt know
> Which all things permeates, which all obey.
> And thou shalt know that Law hath stablished
> The inner nature of all things alike;
> So shalt thou hope not for what may not be,
> Nor aught, that may, escape thee. Thou shalt know
> Self-chosen are the woes that fall on men—
> How wretched, for they see not good so near,
> Nor hearken to its voice—few only know
> The Pathway of Deliverance from ill.

Here we witness a whole series of thoughts far from the orthodox religion of the Classical Period. The verses end with a ringing affirmation of the message central to all the mysteries:

> And if at length
> Leaving behind the body, thou dost come
> To the free Upper Air, then thou shalt be
> Deathless, divine, a mortal man no more.

THE ELEUSINIAN MYSTERIES

The site section on Eleusis examines the full range and detail of this important cult. However the Mysteries need to be placed in the context of Greek religion, for they attracted a high level of participation and were prominent in the Athenian religious calendar.

The ancient Earth Mother cult maintained its power at Eleusis right in the face of Olympian dominion. The goddess of veneration at Eleusis was Demeter and by extension, her daughter Persephone, or Kore. In religious terms the mysteries at Eleusis met the fundamental need of human beings concerning life after death. Part of the appeal in completing the year-long initiation process was the promise of an eternal existence, albeit unclear and cloudy in detail. It would seem that the inclusion of this cult in the state religion and the extensive fame of this celebration throughout the known world reflected a deeply held belief in cyclical patterns of life and death for all creatures and the promise of immortality which was central to the ritual.

Some scholars believe that the climax of the nine-day celebration was the symbolic marriage of Zeus and Demeter, resulting in the birth of the savior Dionysos. This different interpretation of the coming of Dionysos indicates an Orphic influence upon the Mysteries and shows the connection between the various mystery cults throughout the ages. If man was to be cured of the impulses which keep him from God, then he had to be absolved and cleansed so that union with the divine was again possible.

RELIGION AND PHILOSOPHY

In general the expressions of human beings seeking to understand the nature of the truth changed dramatically from the Archaic to the Late Classical Period. Early expressions of the love of wisdom took the form of myth— narratives of human experience and aspiration in figurative language. Later, the Milesians ventured into new territory by expressing their knowledge in words free of petrified imagery. ·

In the fifth century B.C., the height of Greek culture and achievement in so many areas, philosophy took a turn to the secular except for the thinking of Socrates, whose thought is contained in the dialogues of Plato, his student and follower. Socrates developed a sacred path not based on ritual or religious practice. His method of philosophy was based on self-knowledge and reminiscence. The individual had to be carefully led to remember knowledge deeply imbedded in the soul. Guided by "the God," the seeker cleared away the impressions of the moment and the ideas and opinions of others to arrive finally at the still center where truth resided. Socrates himself taught nothing except his method. He asked questions which exposed falsehood and revealed truth, if the student was willing and adept.

The dialectic was Socrates' unique contribution to philosophical inquiry. Not exactly a technique or method, the dialectic was really philosophy itself, the love of wisdom working itself out in human expression. The best way for human beings to express their love of wisdom was in conversation, the interaction of minds aspiring to the truth and willing to allow a higher law than ego to rule the process. In dialogue after dialogue, mostly led by Socrates, who represents not only the mortal man but also the inquiring soul, Plato leads the seeker to understanding and then knowledge in the company of other seekers.

We find in Plato's dialogue entitled *Meno* an example both of the dialectic and of the purpose of philosophy. Socrates and Meno explore together the meaning of philosophical inquiry:

> Socrates: I have heard from certain wise men and women who spoke of things divine that—
> Meno: What did they say?
> Socrates: They spoke of a glorious truth, as I conceive.
> Meno: What was that? and who were they?
> Socrates: Some of them were priests and priestesses, who had studied how they might be able to give a reason of their profession: there have been poets also, such as the poet Pindar and other inspired men. And what they say is, mark now, and see whether their words are true— they say that the soul of man is immortal, and at one time has an end, which is termed dying, and at another time is born again, but is never destroyed. And the moral is, that a man ought to live always in perfect holiness . . . The soul, then, as being immortal, and having been born again many times, and having seen all things that there are, whether in this world or in the world below, has knowledge of them all; and it is no wonder that she should be able to call to remembrance all that she ever knew about virtue, and about everything; for as all nature is akin, and the soul has learned all things, there is no difficulty in her eliciting, or as men say learning, all out of a single recollection, if a man is strenuous and does not faint; for all inquiry and all learning is but recollection.

Here, then, clearly stated, is the purpose and method of philosophical inquiry. Rather than filling the mind with information or acquiring a belief system passed on by the culture, Plato urges those who wish to know the truth to listen to the soul, the aspect of being which resides within and which knows the truth from prior experience. All of Plato is but the exercise of individual recollection. The participants in his dialogues remember through the discipline of rediscovery, a peeling away of the layers of acculturation to find the core of reality beneath.

AFTER SOCRATES AND PLATO

It is worthy of note that the influence of Plato and his Academy lasted formally in Athens until A.D. 529. Aristotle was one of its early students, studying there for twenty years and eventually starting his own school, the Lyceum. Aristotle extended the philosophical realm to natural science in one direction and to the true "essence" of things in the other. His greatest contribution was in the field of general knowledge, extending and defining the process by which human thought is properly organized and codified.

Aristotle was mainly concerned with the "substance" of things. He began with substance and went back to essence, whereas Plato began with essence as ideal form and regarded the substance as an illusion. For example, Aristotle described the soul as the form of the body. Beyond form is prime matter which is expressed as potential. This approach to the mind and to philosophy does not lead so much to a standard of truth as it does to rational understanding and the birth of metaphysics—the process by which we begin to build various systems of ideas about things. Aristotle gave mankind the freedom to become self-realized individuals, but there was a price to pay. Through his thought, mankind became isolated in a personal rather than a universal struggle for wisdom. Each individual found his own knowledge, struggled with his own self-realization. We were alone at last.

In the second and third centuries A.D., the Neoplatonists focused on a single characteristic of Plato's philosophy: the concept of God as unity, with the other gods thought of as *daemons* in an intermediary stage of spiritual reality. The idea of the One, coming from Pythagoras, was combined with the Orphic spiritual practices and evolved into a continuity of vision. The works of Plotinus (A.D. 205–270) and his disciple Porphyry (A.D. 232–304) represent a culmination of the Platonic tradition in ancient times.

It is Plotinus who rendered many of the visionary ideas of ancient times into clarity for modern readers. He expressed the idea of the world soul, which anticipates later thinking and the concept of the *nous* or universal mind which is a vision of how the unity of the One achieves multiplicity. Although man is captured in the single body, he possesses universal mind which allows liberation through contemplation upon the One. This line of reasoning later came to be known as the Perennial Philosophy and entered the modern philosophical tradition through the Gnostics of the Early Church and later mystical traditions.

SACRED NUMBER AND GEOMETRY

And wise men tell us, Callicles, that heaven and earth and gods and men are held together by communion and friendship, by orderliness, temperance, and justice . . . Now you, as it seems to me, do not give proper attention to this, for all your cleverness, but have failed to observe the great power of geometrical equality amongst both gods and men: you hold that self-advantage is what one ought to practice, because you neglect geometry.

—PLATO, *GORGIAS*, 508a

Modern man is Callicles, neglecting geometry in favor of self-interest. We have forgotten the lawful relation between heaven and earth, between spirit and matter. We might be able to remember with the help of the Greeks the connection through geometry, not the discipline and drudgery of school exercises, but rather the relationship between the communion Plato speaks of and the power of geometric equality which leads to the religious idea of unity.

The important requirement for study at the Academy of Plato was an understanding of the principles of geometry as a basis for the study of philosophy. In the history and the work both of Plato and his mentor Pythagoras, the study of geometry was a sacred devotion in which number and geometric form revealed the laws of the universe. How this came about takes us deep into the past not only of Greece but of Egypt and of Northern Europe as well.

THE BIRTH OF GEOMETRY

Before the first stone structures and before archaeology uncovered the first signs of structural geometry, there were signs and symbols scratched and painted onto cave walls all over the world. Of all the shapes created by early human hands the most important was the circle, almost certainly expressive of the sun and the moon. Since we also know that these neighbors in space were worshipped as gods, we know that the circle was a symbol of divinity. It had power to invoke divinity and to be the first expression of our desire to commune with the gods.

The circle was whole, unending, complete, perfect. It was absolute and unchanging. It was the symbol of light, warmth, and life itself. It also had duality in that it represented both the sun and the moon, each of which accumulated attributes and powers as the pantheon of gods grew in response to human need and understanding.

Within the circle there began to appear a cross, dividing the circle into four parts, four directions, four seasons. The cross was the first sign of the manifest world. The ancient lunar calendar may have developed from the crossed circle when it was discovered that connecting the lines of the cross, thus making a square within the circle, produced an image of a span of time (month) divided into four units (weeks) of seven days each. These seven days (times four) gave thirteen months of twenty-eight days, which in turn gave a 364-day year with an extra day. Laying such a divided circle on the ground connected the actual movements of the sun and moon to the symmetry of the circle and square.

The relation of the sun and moon to the circle and its natural divisions is one of the great discoveries of early cosmology. First, the simple circle, so expressive in its unity, represents the sun and moon, in themselves objects of power and awe. Then, divisions within the circle are discovered which, when drawn, express divisions within the year and events in the heavens such as the summer and winter solstices. Thus, early Neolithic formations of stones following these patterns have given evidence of early man's desire to understand and predict seasonal events.

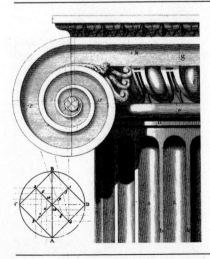

Engraving of an Ionic column with geometric patterns for the forming of a perfect spiral.

GEOMETRY AND STRUCTURE

Soon, specific structures began to appear in which the geometry of circle and cross developed as an expression of human understanding of the movements of the sun and moon in relation to the earth. The most famous of these structures is Stonehenge, completed by the brilliant Druids before 1850 B.C. As we now know, Stonehenge served as a solar and lunar calculator and most likely was also a temple. There were connections between these early geometric formations and Greek culture. Bladud, tenth king of the Druids, long after the generation that constructed Stonehenge, was a student of Pythagoras and founded a Druid center for the study of astronomy and geometry in Bath, England, and actually imported philosophers from Athens to teach there.

Similarly, in early Egypt, where the depository for all sacred knowledge was the temple, the temple priests possessed and controlled access to these same principles. The Egyptian priests understood the basic laws of the universe and embodied them in their structures, both temples and pyramids. Egypt became the source of esoteric knowledge and the school for the transmission of that knowledge throughout the Mediterranean.

PYTHAGORAS

It was the secret knowledge of cosmic number and form, plus the relationship between matter and spirit that Pythagoras learned in the years he spent in Egypt. By then, of course, two thousand years after the construction of the Great Pyramid but still within the active years of the great temples, the esoteric knowledge held in close secrecy by the priests was no doubt more loosely held. By the sixth century B.C. writing had opened the doors of hidden sanctuaries throughout the world.

For example, during the years when Pythagoras lived (570–500 B.C.), Confucius, Lao-tzu, and the Buddha were also teaching the esoteric knowledge, and their words were being written down for a much larger following than could be reached by oral tradition. So it was with Pythagoras and sacred geometry. The secrets were emerging into the light, not without some danger to their integrity, however, and probably to their effective power.

Pythagoras said (or one of his students reported) that "All things are numbers." Such a statement taken seriously means that the creation—all that may be perceived and understood—is number. That idea is usually understood in symbolic terms, that a number can come to be symbolic of or a metaphor for an object or concept in the world. Pythagoras, however, went beyond symbolism to law. He said that a thing (object, state, thought) is as it is because it operates out of the Law of Two or Five or Nine. Thus number is the same as law, and these laws can be stated and are useful guides to an understanding of Greek form.

SACRED NUMBER

The Law of One

The One, the Eternal, the Absolute: indivisible, all-knowing, all-embracing. The All, the Greek *nous* in its broadest conception. The Monad, the Fire, the first cause. Unity. Universal Being. The Point which makes possible the circle. One. The idea of One does not consider the existence of zero, of negation or absence. The beginning is One, identity and unity.

The Law of Two

Self-awareness creates Two, polarity, the opposite. One becomes Two. In nature there is opposition: positive, negative; active, passive; male, female. The Duad. Duality. Two points making a line. Two is the first feminine number. Eve. The other.

The Law of Three

The synthesis of thesis (1) and antithesis (2). The resolving or holding of tension. The third point which forms the triangle, the first plane. Surface. The Pythagoreans posited that the cosmic order manifested itself in Three. Inspiration is the third force by which the artist (1) meets the medium (2), the mysterious force out of which comes the manifest world. Inspiration, desire, *eros,* is the third force. Balance is possible in the order of Three. The third point makes the triangle. The triangle establishes hierarchy. Like all odd numbers, it is male.

The Law of Four

The world is manifest in Four. The fourth point makes the solid. The articulation of the principle molded into sentences, expressions of law. Four is material; it is substance, the artifact created out of the One, Two, and Three. The Pythagoreans called Four the Eternal Principle of Creation. There are four directions, four seasons in nature, four regions in the sky. Four is Two and Two, showing the double aspect of duality itself. Four is Three and One, God in Man, and thus soul, the first step in spiritual awareness and the first step in initiation into mysteries. As we begin to understand God by understanding the world, so we begin with Four, the square, the solid, manifest world in which our senses play. We know God by knowing the presence of the soul within.

The Law of Five

Five is the Law of Life, the union of Three (male) and Two (female). Five is Spirit arising from matter, thus often connected to the resurrection of Christ. If Four is the manifest world, Five comprehends that world. It is understanding. Five is the measure of the pentagram whose dimensions lead to the Golden Proportion, the geometric symbol of regeneration and rebirth. Because Five is a spiritual number, it also represents the potential of creation and the principle of eternity, although not eternity itself. If Four is the cube, Five is the sphere. Finally, as we shall see later, Five is the central number in the Pythagorean diagram of number, the Tetractys. In its position it relates to the One and is half of the Divine Decad or Ten.

The Law of Six

The Law of Six is a creating number, a partial resolution which proceeds to the divine Seven. Six is the feminine number of love and completion, Aphrodite's number. Six doubles to twelve and hence to the major time frames of creation. It relates to space in the same way, the hexagram emerging from the circle into ideal forms. Since it suggests a measure of completion, the number Six anticipates the desire to unite with the divine perfection. Thus, we often see temples with six columns on the narrow side. Here, the even number is both practical—allowing for the central door—and ideal, expressing the measure of earthly wholeness which aspires for eternal perfection in another order of experience.

The Law of Seven

In the number Seven the combination of numbers making up seven helps us to understand its laws. Six, the number of earthly completion, plus One, the Divine Monad, equals a new stage in spiritual evolution. In Seven we experience a new understanding, a growth in divine knowledge. Creation took seven days, six of creativity, the seventh of rest. On the seventh day there arises a new order. Seven is also the sum of Three, the sacred Triad, and Four, the Principle of Creation. Thus in Seven, there is a union of spirit and matter.

The Greek word for Seven is *septos,* which also means holy, divine. Plato equated the Universal Soul with Seven, as having been generated from its laws. In the Pythagorean system Seven was the most sacred of the numbers, presumably because its combinations and active principles were the core of spiritual work. In geometry we see the principle of Seven most often expressed in the relationship of square (4) to triangle (3). One such sacred relationship, of course, is the pyramid with its square base (the manifest world) and triangular sides rising to a point (divine principle and aspiration).

The Law of Eight

When we reach the numbers beyond Seven, we enter a complex world of principle and law because these numbers, as we saw in Seven, have their life in combination with the lower integers. Eight, for example, is seen most often as twice Four, as the physical world but at a new level. Eight is the octave. It vibrates with the One and is a new note. Thus, Eight suggests beginnings, but with divine sanction. In the Christian numerology, Eight is seen in the octagonal shape of baptismal fonts and often with the number of steps descending to baptismal waters.

Eight is manifestation in its fullest development, regenerated from the primitive Four to a higher order. The association of Eight to the Goddess is an expression of perfection of the feminine. The eight columns fronting the Parthenon, consecrated to Athena, is an example of this relationship. The Earth Mother is Eight, breathing in and out in cycles, spiraling out and back in the figure eight form (of later cultures), and embodied in the serpent that cures in the darkness of sleep.

The Law of Nine

When the human being has reached the culmination of his or her journey, reached the point of fulfillment, it is said that the Law of Nine is operating. The best expression of this culmination is the symbol of the enneagram, a universal symbol which, according to the ancient traditions, is an expression of all human knowledge. This large claim signifies the strength and breadth of the Nine as a law. Before we look at the enneagram, we might note some of the facets of Nine the sum of $8 + 1$, $7 + 2$, $6 + 3$, $5 + 4$. Expressed here are all the number laws in relation to Nine, all in odd and even combinations. Also, we see that in multiplying factors of Nine that $9 \times 2 = 18$, and $8 + 1 = 9$. So too, $9 \times 3 = 27$, and $7 + 2 = 9$, and so on through any number multiplied by nine. Thus, any multiple of Nine can be reduced to Nine again when the integers are added together.

The significance of these arithmetic truths means that as a law, Nine expresses a point of completion for the human

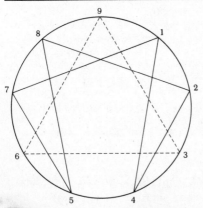

Fig. 1. The enneagram, showing the number configuration aligning geometry to number symbolism.

cycle. From this point the only upward movement is to the Decad or Ten, the Divine Reality. Thus, Nine is the number of Initiation.

The enneagram is a geometric expression worked out within the laws of a circle divided by Nine and expressing the Triad (see Fig. 1).

The Law of Ten

The Pythagorean system finds its completion in the Decad. The final number, which is really a beginning or a return to One $(1 + 0 = 1)$. Ten completes the Tetractys and expresses the return to the source which is the aim of all human aspiration correctly understood and pursued. And yet the Ten is also more than One. It expresses the cycle of action and manifestation. It is the perfect circle and the One whose sum is the One. The circle is the journey—the separation, the initiation, and the return. In the enneagram it is the circle which contains the Nine, which gives the Nine its form and meaning. Without the circle the other points fall into chaos or align themselves in an arbitrary order. Without the circle, nothing. That is why the architects of sacred temples and sanctuaries always began with a point and a circle, out of which grew the manifestation in form: the line, the triangle, the square, and so on.

The Sacred Tetractys

The Pythagorean numerology is expressed in the Sacred Tetractys, which is an arrangement in a pyramid of the numbers from one to ten (see Fig. 2).

To understand the system of ten is to understand the relationships of the numbers as they appear in this simple configuration. For example, the One is at the apex of the form; it is the source and the unity. The Two, or Duad, appears beneath, and it forms a small pyramid; thus it is also Three. The form shows the Three as the One and the Two,

Fig. 2. *The sacred tetractys, a number pyramid from Pythagoras, key to his theory of number relationships.*

but it also shows the Two as two points, or a line. The Three is the next level. It, too, creates a larger pyramid made up of the Six, which is also a resolution in the creation. The final row or the Four makes up the full perfection of the form and comprises the Ten. This pattern, then, begins to show us the relation of the sacred numbers to one another and to the principles of geometry we now will explore.

SACRED GEOMETRY

Behind the outward appearance of the art created by the Greeks stood immutable laws of number and form. These laws were expressed as geometric principles, two of which in particular are embodied in the pottery, sculpture, and structures created by the Minoans, Mycenaeans, and Greek peoples.

The structural laws are based on the relationships which were brought from Egypt, first by the Minoans and then by Pythagoras, and applied to the circumstances of a new culture. In geometry, the basic forms begin with a point, which produces a circle, a square, and so on out to more elaborate figures.

Two principles in particular are relevant to the Greek experience. The first may be called the Circle and its Square, the second the Golden Proportion. The Circle and Square is a simple enough principle and is based on the prehistoric relation of circle and cross described earlier.

First, a point is established and a circle inscribed—on the ground if the resulting form is to be a structure such as a tomb or temple. Then, working from the center (the point) a cross is drawn, from which an external square is constructed (see Fig. 3). In sacred terms, the point is the One and the

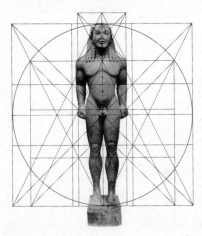

Fig. 3. Circle and square imposed on Archaic kouros, *showing the geometric basis of design and universality of the human form.*

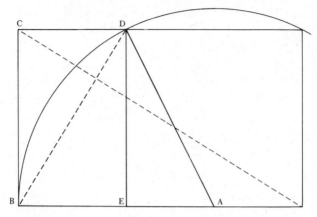

Fig. 4. *Constructing the Golden Proportion. From point A (bisected side of the square) inscribe an arc, which falls on point B to form the Golden Rectangle, forming a smaller rectangle (BCDE), which is also a Golden Rectangle.*

resulting circle is an extension of that unity out into space and is the basis of the square which is the basis of the resulting manifestation.

The second major principle of geometric form is the Golden Proportion, a form which was sacred to the Greeks and the Egyptians because it expressed a unique idea. The Golden Proportion was regenerative, that is, it described a set of laws which returned to the One or to unity from multiplicity. Thus, as a principle it expressed the idea of returning to the source or uniting again with divinity. The Golden Proportion also produced an aesthetically pleasing shape, one which had an immediate and compelling appeal to the eye.

The Golden Proportion is created by establishing a relationship of two particular points along a line. The proportion can be arrived at in several ways, but one pattern involves the construction of two squares within a circle, a diagonal (which corresponds to the square root of five) and an arc which corresponds to the original circle, which in turn creates the so-called Golden Rectangle.

The importance of this rectangle is that it creates an image or illustration of a return to unity. It does so because the geometric relationships always create the same proportion, one which embodies itself in every smaller or larger form. The principle can be shown in the spiral form which is created by the evolving pattern (see Fig. 5).

The Greek philosopher Protagoras said: "Man is the measure of all things." This law expresses two related principles. First, it affirms that the role of man in the universe is to express the laws as perceived through the human instrument. Second, it states that the laws which

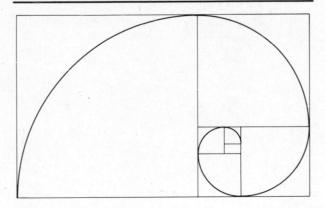

Fig. 5. *The Golden Proportion, with spiral which follows and forms a series of Golden Rectangles.*

make up the universe are expressed in microcosm within the human being, both in body and in mind. To understand and to express those laws is to know the creator of the universe.

In this way sacred geometry, particularly as it is expressed by circle and square and the Golden Proportion make manifest the laws by which matter appears from spirit and by which matter returns to spirit. In the Greek culture, these proportions were expressed clearly in pottery. Minoan and Mycenaean pottery show the Golden Proportion as the ruling form in the work. Later, the Archaic and Classical shapes of the amphora show the same laws. The measure here is based on the principle that working from this form and perceiving it when manifest is a sacred act. It is a prayer as well as a sacrifice made to the gods who revealed the form in

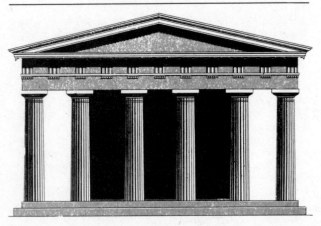

Engraving of the Temple of Hephaistos, the Agora, Athens.

the first place. The Greek artist did not sign his work, did not claim it as his creation as the modern artist does. The work came from a higher source and was an exercise in revelation expressed in form. The artist was merely a willing instrument.

GREEK TEMPLES

Similarly, in the Greek temple as built in Greece and surrounding areas during the Archaic and Classical Periods, the laws of sacred geometry ruled every line, angle, and shape. Whether laid out by the principle of circle and square or the regenerative laws of the Golden Proportion, they expressed in the landscape the power of form to transform matter to spirit. We say that these temples demonstrated the characteristics of the gods they represented. Indeed they did, but in geometric terms, they also reminded the Greeks that the gods were lawful aspects of themselves which, when properly aligned, could bring benefit as well as knowledge through the geometric solid within which the law was being celebrated.

SACRED
ARCHITECTURE

Architecture is harmony, rhythm, melody, and form in space. And in the case of the ancient Greeks, the harmony emerges from the desire to recover lost communion with the gods and to invoke the power that those gods possessed. Elements in the composition were the female forms of the landscape, the forms of nature, and the ideal form of the human being. The Greek architectural creation was always harmonious, the effect never lulling nor exciting to passion.

As we saw in the overviews of history and religion, the ancient Greek peoples developed their culture from their relationship to the landscape as goddess. The Earth Mother lay across the land in the hills, valleys, gorges, and caves. Her shape and nature nurtured and protected early inhabitants as they followed the herds along sacred pathways worn in the body of the earth. The sacred places in this landscape emerged after a time as sanctuaries, where altars were erected, usually oriented to a particularly dominant feature of the goddess-landscape.

THE SACRED LANDSCAPE

Eventually, in the time of settlement, the Minoans selected building sites according to these same principles. Some valuable work on sacred architecture and landscape has been done by Vincent Scully, the art historian from Yale University, who has studied the relationship of the Earth Goddess to palaces and temples throughout the Mediterranean. In his *The Earth, the Temple, and the Gods* Scully sets the stage. "From roughly 2000 B.C. onward, a clearly defined pattern of landscape use can be recognized at every palace site. More than this, each palace makes use, so far as possible, of the same landscape elements. These are as follows: first, an enclosed valley of varying size in which the palace is set; I should like to call this the 'Natural Megaron;' second, a gently mounded or conical hill on axis with the palace to north or south; and lastly a higher, double peaked or cleft mountain some distance beyond the hill but on the same axis. The mountain may have other characteristics of great sculptural force, such as rounded slopes, deep gullies, or a conical or pyramidal massing itself, but the double peak or notched cleft seem essential to it. These features create a profile which is basically that of a pair of horns, but it may sometimes also suggest raised arms or wings, the female cleft, or even, at some sites, a pair of breasts. It forms in all cases a climactic shape which has the quality of causing the observer's eye to come to rest in its cup. Though there are many overlaps in shape and probably many unguessed complexities in their meanings, still the cone would appear to have been the earth's motherly form, the horns as the symbol of its active power."

Scully's text describes these features of the landscape as they appear throughout Greece and as they relate to the later functions of temple siting as well. The important point is that as a result of this influence we cannot look at these sites isolated from their natural context. The architecture and the landscape are a unity. The so-called "natural megaron" in which a palace or temple sits is as the name suggests: a sacred enclosure in which religious ritual takes place.

Without considering the function and power of the landscape, the ritual invocations at the palace altars or temple

The Palace at Knossos in Crete, resting in its sacred landscape.

sanctuaries become too abstract, too psychological in nature. To know that the whole community was being held in the protection of the goddess meant that the activities and devotions taking place there were controlled by her rhythms and a structure greater than personal desires or thoughts. The goddess was a context within which the entire life of the community was motivated and carried out.

The landscape also had aesthetic value. Temple design

was influenced by setting. Scully is adept at sensing the aesthetic considerations involved in design and placement. For example, he speaks of the Temple of Hera at Paestum (in Italy) "which was intended to sit in deeply shadowed heaviness upon the plain." This is in contrast to the Parthenon, which was designed to lift upward, to suggest in its design the wisdom of Athena, her spiritual nature in contrast to Hera's more physical influences, even though these two goddesses both shared characteristics of the earlier Earth Mother Goddess whose landscape held these temples.

ARCHITECTURE AND NATURE

The earliest examples of architecture in the Greek context are Minoan and Mycenaean. The palace remains at Knossos and the Lion Gate at Mycenae both reveal an early use of the column. The evidence shows that the column was initially simply a tree trunk, cut and trimmed to serve as a support for roof, porch, or second story. Too often considered simply phallic, the function and symbolism of the column is more properly related to the goddess because it suggests growth, fertility, protection, and fruitfulness more than it does generative, sexual power. Scully elaborates: "It might be argued that the column, thus enclosed, as later by lions at Mycenae, may have been considered especially expressive of the goddess since it joined to its tree symbolism a specific description of a female state of being. Thus the whole palace became her body, as the earth itself had been in the Stone Age."

Later, the column was fashioned in stone and later still in

The Hall of the Colonnades at Knossos, showing early use of the column, originally inverted trees.

Fig. 6. *Hopi Indian spiral and matching Minoan coin showing the image of the labyrinth.*

marble. At Knossos we note how the stone column maintained the tree shape of the wooden columns used earlier. Trunks were cut and then reversed so that the narrow portion of the trunk served as the column base. The idea seemed to be that reversing the trunk prevented the tree from sprouting again and allowed water to run off the column without gathering at the base, thus preventing rot. Also, as we shall see in the Ionic and Corinthian orders, the natural imagery of the tree evolved the voluted and leafy capitals, emphasizing the symbolism of fertility and fruitfulness.

From the earliest remains we find the labyrinth as an important architectural feature. The labyrinth is a fundamental symbol of life, death, and fertility. The labyrinth is, by definition, a maze of twisting and turning paths designed to disorient and confuse the mind. Its sacred purpose was to shake the mind from its illusions of place and certainty to prepare it for a sacred experience. The labyrinth has been expressed as a spiral motif in nearly every culture. For example, the spiral labyrinth is an Earth Mother symbol to the Hopi Indians of the American Southwest (see Fig. 6).

TheMinoan palaces were built on the principle of the labyrinth, the palace as the Earth Goddess within which the people lived and worshipped. Coming and going through passages, passing from darkness into light and back to darkness, shifting from level to level, turning and suddenly emerging within sight of the sacred symbols of the goddess, the architecture was the substance of life and meaning worked out in ritual movement and form. Later, we will find approaches to temples retain a sense of the labyrinth as a ritual and architectural element.

THE ARCHITECT IN ANCIENT GREECE

The architect in Greece was the *arche,* or head, the leader of those, called the *techne,* who would actually build the temple. The architect worked with simple tools, the compass and straightedge and line, sized according to the task on the ground. Without knowing exactly how this secret process worked, we can speculate from tradition and from myths just how a temple was designed. As it was a sacred process, it must have had its beginnings at the altar, the location of which was established many hundreds or even thousands of years before.

The architect selected the exact spot from which the temple would be generated. According to specific ritual, a stake was driven into the ground at that spot, thus fixing the spirit of the god to the site. A circle was drawn, symbolizing the god and the abundance of spirit to be celebrated. From that circle either another circle was constructed to form the Golden Proportion or a square was constructed following the Squared Circle principle. The symbolism of the square was the recognition that this temple was a manifestation of the celebrated god.

THE FEATURES OF TEMPLE DESIGN

As an expression of human form and natural law, the temple specifically symbolized the imperishable spirit emerging from matter. The temple was not meant for human habitation and was used only in a limited way for worship. It was an expression of the divine nature which inhabited it. Joseph Campbell, in his crucial book *The Hero with a Thousand Faces,* speaks of the purpose of sacred architecture when the hero (all of us) enters the temple . . . "where he is quickened by the recollection of who and what he is, namely dust and ashes unless immortal."

The entrance to the temple was always articulated in terms of an equilateral triangle formed from the roof peak to the floor, or stylobate, at some point. The triangle always expressed spiritual aspiration, a rising of matter (expressed as the base line) to the point of spiritual unity at the peak. The entrance, then, became an aspiration for such unity with the god whose temple the worshipper entered.

The temple appears in Greece in the twelfth century B.C. Temples were Olympian in nature, celebrating the new gods in their marriage to the earlier earth deities. In many ways the temple represented control over the sometimes chaotic forces of nature and the underworld. In some of the Bronze Age sanctuaries, the forces unleashed there were unpredictable and frightening. The temple served to fix the deity to the laws of form as expressed in the actual temple design. At the same time there was the impulse to unity, to establish human communion with the gods on a regular, predictable basis. The temple was not only linked to landscape but was also connected to movements in the heavens. Usually oriented to the east, the temple faced the sunrise and might have been, as well, designed to fix the movements of the morning star as a guide to the festival days for the enshrined god.

Scully describes eight principles of temple design and function. In brief, they are as follows: (1) most temples are oriented to the east, the exceptions being made for special landscape features or site requirements; (2) the function of the temple was to bring the human being to the divine point of view, or as we have said, communion; (3) the temple brought to a resolution the natural enclosure of the site; (4) each temple created a complex inner landscape for the purpose of worship; (5) the temple was a sculptural entity reflective of the god enshrined there; (6) the temple was a complete expression of art in its own right; (7) the later temples were forced to reassert the principles of enclosure rather than depending on their relationship to the landscape; and (8) the character of the temple changed according to two factors: the landscape and the deity enshrined.

Temple Nomenclature

Before describing some further principles of temple design and construction, it would be useful to define a few constituent parts. We will begin with the various ground plans for temples, including the names, some in Latin and some in Greek, that are traditionally used to describe various features. Then, we will look at the three basic orders of Greek temple design.

Temples are generally described according to the arrangement of columns in relation to the walls. In Figures 7–11, solid walls are drawn as double lines with shading. In general, doors were placed in all openings. The platform or temple base is pictured as a single line.

Fig. 7. *The simple temple* in antis.

The phrase *in antis* refers to the projections of the temple walls beyond the enclosing walls. *Antae* are the extended walls beyond the basic rectangle of the inner section. The sacred enclosure or inner room of a temple is known as the *naos* in Greek or the *cella* in Latin. The *pronaos* is the porch or entranceway to the *naos*. Also, there sometimes was an additional room inside called an *adyton,* which was an inner sanctum where only the priests or priestesses were permitted.

In the Prostyle temple design, there are no *antae* and the

Fig. 8. The Prostyle temple design, typical of simple treasuries.

Fig. 9. The Amphiprostyle temple design.

Fig. 10. The Peripteros temple design.

Fig. 11. The Dipteros temple design.

naos is fully enclosed with a simple *pronaos* formed by a row of columns.

Figure 9 illustrates the Amphiprostyle design with columns at the rear, but no rear entrance.

The Peripteros design is the most common of all Greek temples. Peripteros describes a temple in which the *naos* is designed *in antis* and is surrounded by a single row of columns supporting the roof element.

In the Dipteros design the *naos* and *pronaos* are surrounded by at least two rows of columns, creating the illusion of a forest. There are also numerous columns at the front and rear of the temple.

These basic designs also vary in the number of columns in front, or which cross the width of the temple. The number is always even, so as to provide for a central door, and varies from four to twelve columns. The usual, or six-column front, is known as hexastyle.

The Doric Order

The first so-called order of column and entablature design was the Doric, named for those peoples who migrated to Greece in the twelfth century B.C., bringing with them this temple design with elements as shown in the illustration.

Thus, in the nomenclature, the column is the vertical post with all its features. In the Doric order the column has no base. The entablature refers to everything above the column, including the roof elements. So, when we speak of the vertical elements we are speaking of the column and its features, and when we speak of the horizontal elements we are speaking of the entablature and its features.

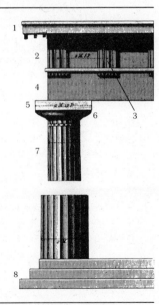

The Doric Order
1. *Cornice*
2. *Frieze*
3. *Triglyphs*
4. *Architrave*
5. *Abacus*
6. *Echinus*
7. *Shaft*
8. *Stylobate*

The Ionic Order

The Ionic order is later than the Doric and is attributed to the Ionians, also late settlers into Greece. This order has a greater elegance and more organic quality and was used either alone or in conjunction with the other orders. The major differences with the Doric are the spiraled *volute* and the elaborate column base with *torus*.

The Ionic Order
1. Cornice
2. Frieze
3. Architrave
4. Capital

The Corinthian Order

The late addition of the Corinthian order, seen sparingly until Roman times, introduces a new capital design featuring small volutes at each corner and elaborate leaf designs from the acanthus plant, common to Greece. The illustration shows the major contrast to the other orders.

The Corinthian Order
1. Cornice
2. Frieze
3. Architrave
4. Capital

THE DYNAMICS OF TEMPLE BUILDING

As the concept of the temple evolved, there developed principles of construction based on the relationship of key elements, namely the vertical and the horizontal forces involved. The vertical columns rose organically to a point of union with the heavy horizontal forces pressing down. This point of union became the focus of construction.

The Doric order evolved to a point of ultimate expression in the Parthenon. The architectural expression of the vertical and horizontal union results in a column which has a slight bulge or *entasis* as it descends from the point of union above. The capital has a slightly flattened look, as if the top of the column had been spread by the weight. The resulting effect is one of balance and stability and yet a certain springy sense as if the entablature might rise rhythmically only to fall back into place. The effect is one of dynamic balance.

The Ionic order presents a slightly different, more organic sense of union. Here, the weight of the entablature actually curls the top of the column down to a point of stability. As a result of this image of curling—either of vegetation or of water, the column itself is not affected in the same degree. Thus, the Ionic column is generally thinner, shifting the sense of union to the capital.

In the Corinthian order, a fine example of which can be seen in the museum at Epidauros, the effect of union is more mystical in that the leaves do not appear to carry any weight at all. The sense of weight disappears in the upward thrust of vegetation, with only a slight curl in the volutes. In this order the union of vertical and horizontal is hidden or ornamented away, more suggestive of miracle than of tangible interaction.

As we proceed, now, to discuss the various sites in Greece, we will encounter specific examples of these principles. The variety of articulation within principle speaks to the exuberance of the Greek imagination and the sensitivity to each context. We can say, then, that the Greek experience expresses itself in the lawful application of principle to individual context with sacred intent.

2
THE
PALACE
CULTURES

CRETE AND THE MINOANS

When we speak of the palace cultures in ancient Greek history, we refer to those archaeological sites called Minoan or Mycenaean where the remains are predominantly from what we call the Protopalatial and Neopalatial periods, the years from 2000 B.C. to 1200 B.C. In the two most important of these sites, Knossos and Mycenae, the palaces were relatively undisturbed by later construction. In both cases, indeed, only minor traces of later Archaic or Classical temples remain and in neither case do these traces obliterate major evidence of the earlier architecture.

It should be remembered that many other sites in Greece offer some evidence of Minoan or Mycenaean remains, but as we see on the Acropolis in Athens, for example, nothing of the earlier settlement is left for us to examine. We have evidence only of prior occupation in the form of isolated walls or pottery or inscriptions discovered as the archaeological teams penetrated the layers of history down to bedrock.

The palace cultures which remain for us to examine reveal a remarkable record of human culture and achievement. Here were cultures in which a priest-king ruled a tightly organized hierarchy which was communal in structure. All the elements which make up culture were present in one complex, a palace made up of royal apartments, connecting living quarters for the ranking members of society and their retainers, shrines and altars, storage areas, courtyards, public meeting halls, even grave sites in the case of the Mycenaeans. There were, of course, separate dwellings outside the palace complex, but the culture was still defined by the palace.

Living as we do now in separate and private dwellings, isolated from those who govern and those who conduct our religious rituals, we can have no clear idea what communal existence was like. For the palace culture, secular and religious life were integrated in the person of the priest-king. Service to this monarch and to the gods and goddesses of the culture defined daily life. We might even speculate that private thought was of a different order. So integrated were these cultures that even individual consciousness as we

The author in front of the Horns of Consecration at Knossos, Crete.

know it might have been different in some way, more collective, perhaps.

The only experience we can have of this life is to visit the palaces and attempt to move through the space with our attention focused on the elements before us. There is the landscape which frames the palace, and the overall shape and design of the rooms and courts. The understanding which comes to us from our movement through the complex might in some small way allow us to pass over the stones and through the doors as our ancestors might have done.

KNOSSOS

Knossos is one of the great treasures of the world, and what remains today for the modern pilgrim to experience offers enough to make certain that a visit to the island of Crete and a full day on the site forms part of an itinerary. Overnight cruise ships leave from Piraeus for Iraklion, the major city of Crete and site of the ancient port of Knossos. The cost of passage with room and bath for this voyage is about the same as a night in a Class A hotel, thus providing a saving for those counting their drachmas. But for those who prefer the convenience of flight, Olympic Airways goes into Iraklion on a regular basis from Athens, and the flight is both short and reasonably priced.

Although the cruise ships throb with the rhythm of powerful engines, the traveler still rides on the waves under the clear Mediterranean sky to land on Crete as the Minoan sailors did in the third millennium. It is exhilarating to experience those things that never change, such as the movement of the sea and the feeling of solid ground under the feet after a voyage.

THE PORT OF IRAKLION

Iraklion is an unusual city. It is still ringed by ramparts built by the Venetians who ruled Crete from A.D. 1204 to 1669. It is named for Herakles, the mythical hero whose twelve great labors included (number seven) capturing the mad bull of Crete and transporting it alive to Mycenae. Herakles is usually pictured in late mythology wrapped in skins and carrying a huge club with which he subdued most of his enemies, and to this day the youths of Iraklion roam the streets of the city on New Year's Eve bopping each other over the head with air-filled plastic clubs. It is a rather poor honor for the great hero.

The city offers a full range of hotels and easy transportation to the ancient sites. Finding a good restaurant in Iraklion isn't easy, but the sidewalk cafés offer fresh local produce and the winding streets hide numerous shops. Crete is one of the agricultural centers of the Mediterranean, and the countryside boasts miles and miles of olive and orange groves as well as fertile valleys which furnish fresh vegetables for the mainland.

THE SETTING

The palace of Knossos sits on a small hill called Kephala, just over 3 miles (5 km) south of Iraklion. The site can be reached by city bus or taxi. Kephala Hill is surrounded on three sides by ridges and is dominated to the south by Mount Jouctas, a mountain sacred to the Minoans. To the north the valley forms a gentle bowl which opens out and down to the sea, visible in the distance from the upper floors of the palace. The location of the palace is ideal from the point of view of living conditions. The site is protected from winds, the Kairatos River flows nearby on its way to the sea, and the fertile valley provides ample grazing and rich soil for cultivation.

More than any of the later Archaic or Classical sites, the Minoan palaces on Crete seem ideal expressions of man's harmony with nature. These structures appear to have literally grown like organic matter into the hillsides on which, over many generations, they spread. There is no such thing as a final palace, a culminating structure which can be shown. That is why an artist's rendering of the palace should not really be made, although some attempts have been admirable. We can have no sense how the complex looked at any given moment in time, but we can appreciate the concept behind the changing details.

Knossos is a microcosm of the landscape in which it sits. The Central Court is the valley of the Kairatos River. The

Mount Jouctas, sacred mountain of the Minoans,
south of Knossos, Crete.

surrounding two- and three-story chamber complexes are the ridge lines to the east and west of the palace. The great Horns of Consecration and the propylon to the south are the images of Mount Jouctas and the Lower Gypsades hill, which rises gently in the foreground. The original wide, sloping ramp to the north (now a much narrower ramp) is the gradual incline to the sea. The palace, then, is man's construct of the sacred land where he founded his culture and took his place in the cosmic scheme.

To what extent this analogy was a conscious articulation on the part of the priest-builders of the past is a modern question without an ancient answer. Our sense of what constitutes "conscious" in 2000 B.C. cannot be measured in the framework of the late twentieth century A.D. It might best be said that the planning of the palace was "natural," meaning in harmony with nature and the gods whose power was sought and heard and felt in every undertaking.

HISTORY

NEOLITHIC TIMES

The story of Knossos begins in the seventh millennium, B.C., the Neolithic Period. The earliest evidence of a settlement in Crete is found on Kephala Hill. It is assumed that these early peoples came to Crete from the south and east, and there is enough similarity to Egyptian culture to support that conclusion. Beneath the floor of the Central Court excavators discovered at a depth of 20 feet (6m) tools and pottery detailing the history of neolithic settlement and suggesting the worship of an Earth Mother Goddess.

Part of that worship was related to the presence of Mount Jouctas, the peak visible to the south of Knossos on which Neolithic cult remains and Minoan sanctuary buildings have been found. There is precious little evidence anywhere concerning Neolithic religious belief or practice in relation to either landscape features or cult figures, so that conclusions must be based on the few finds at various sites and on the general theories held as to the importance of the Mother Goddess in the pre-Bronze Age Mediterranean.

What the archaeological record shows is that prior to the Bronze Age, the Neolithic settlement at Knossos was one of the largest and most prominent settlements in Europe and that the palace culture followed with little apparent upheaval. Thus, the palace culture which developed later on the site was not a wholly new thing but was, rather, a continuity of religious belief and practice.

"MINOAN" MIGRATION

Some time in the third millennium B.C. the peoples we commonly call Minoan came to Crete to intermingle with the earlier immigrants. Most scholars believe that this race came either from Egypt and points south or from the Near East. There is no evidence that these new migrations took the form of conquering invasions. As the new population began to build its palaces, the same locations and values as the old seemed to serve the new. The difference was that this new race exhibited extraordinary artistic knowledge and skill.

As outlined in the Historical Overview, the Minoan Period in Crete coincides with the beginning of the Bronze Age in 3000 B.C. In the period known as Early Minoan (roughly 3000–2400 B.C.), evidence has been found of two- and three-story rectangular dwellings made of sun-dried mud brick and plaster. All of these dwellings were leveled when palace construction began in the Middle Minoan Period. There are a few of these early remains well to the south of the present remains and at the bottom of the walled pits in the West Court.

PALACE CONSTRUCTION

Current dating procedures place the first palace construction in 2000 B.C., or the period known either as Middle Minoan IB or the more current term, Protopalatial (sometimes assigned the dates of 1900–1700 B.C.). It is to this period that we assign the construction of the Central Court, the West Court, and the Theatral Area, plus scattered buildings no longer in evidence. Monumental wall and foundation remains from this period throughout the site suggest that the broad outlines of a concept of design for the palace as a whole were already in place. In the period called Middle Minoan II, the palace assumed its monumental proportions. From 1900 to 1700 B.C. the fundamental forms of what now

The West Porch of Knossos, showing multistoried construction.

remains were erected. To this period we can assign the development of the palace as one connected series of elements. Any later additions and repairs, including the modern reconstructions which greet visitors today, were imposed upon the forms erected during these two centuries of development.

The main features of this design included the enclosure of the Central Court by multistoried structures, the development of the Grand Staircases on the western and eastern sides of the Central Court, the elaborate magazine for storage to the west, and the royal living quarters to the east. Also included were the cult areas to the north and south, including the Lustral Basins, the Shrine Rooms, and the general processional passages which were used to approach the Central Court and the sacred life of the palace.

PALACE DESTRUCTION

Between 1800 and 1700 B.C. a disaster, probably an earthquake, destroyed the early palace, marking the beginning of the period known as Middle Minoan III or Neopalatial. From this time down to 1450 B.C., when all the palaces on Crete were destroyed, Knossos saw constant remodeling of the major features. Much of what we actually see today comes from these two or three centuries of construction. Also, the history of the palace in these times is complicated by the arrival of the Mycenaean overlords who assumed control of the palaces and made changes according to their own vision of culture. The important construction of the Throne Room and attached rooms to the west are attributed to this period.

The date 1450 B.C. is given in the history of the Mediterranean for the great volcanic eruption of Thera, the modern island of Santorini. There are Minoan remains on Santorini at the ancient town of Akrotiri which give silent witness to the disaster which occurred. Beneath the volcanic dust of Akrotiri archaeologists have uncovered priceless frescoes (now in the Archaeological Museum at Athens) depicting details of the Minoan culture. The theory that the Cretan palaces were destroyed by this volcanic eruption would be more generally accepted if there were definitive evidence of layers of volcanic ash or similar direct connection to the eruption at the Cretan sites. But there might also have been associated earthquakes and massive tidal waves which could have destroyed the palaces. When the palace was first excavated there was evidence of sudden destruction rather than a more gradual deterioration from a declining culture. Someday we may know the full story.

Historically, the end of the Minoan culture on Crete in 1450 B.C. marked the close of the Eastern influence in ancient Greek history. From this point on the influences on culture are mostly northern and "European." Although Eastern influences may be dimly perceived until modern times, the dominant themes of culture are hereafter Western. Thus, the preservation of Knossos to the present affords a rare opportunity to explore the connections to the mysteries of ancient Egypt and the sacred worlds of the East.

MYTHOLOGY

... Knossos, the great city where Minos, who spoke with the great Zeus, was nine years king.

—HOMER

Myths are the tales of truth masked in the drama of the human condition. They explain the histories of races, tribes, and individuals in their struggles to know and understand destiny and the meaning of life. The myths involving Knossos are some of the most intriguing ever told. They tell the stories of Minos, the legendary priest-king; of his wife Pasiphae, the moon goddess; of the Minotaur; of the artist Daedalus and his unfortunate son Icarus; and, finally, of Theseus and the lovely Ariadne.

EUROPA AND ZEUS

The story of Minos, the founder of Knossos and of the race which bears his name, begins in Asia Minor in the land now

Engraving of Europa being carried off by Zeus as a bull.

called Israel, where the fair Europa lived with her father, King Aganor. As often happens in the sacred myths of human experience, this story begins with a dream, in which Europa is visited by two goddesses in the form of continents, rival Earth Goddesses, who inform Europa that she is to be visited by Zeus, Bright Consciousness, who will plant his seed in her. The girl is frightened and seeks peace and forgetfulness with her friends in the nearby hills sacred to the goddess.

Zeus descends from Olympus in the form of a splendid bull with delicately curved horns and majestic head, and he grazes near where the girls are picking roses on a gentle green mound. Europa is induced by the beauty and gentleness of the bull to climb upon its back, whereupon the bull moves swiftly down to the sea and swims to Crete. Europa is left, frightened and alone, on the shore. Soon, however, Zeus appears as a handsome stranger and takes Europa to wife. The union of Zeus and the Princess Europa produces three offspring, one of whom is Minos, future king of Crete.

MINOS AND THE MINOTAUR

Minos lives in the Greek memory in several vivid myths and in an utterance from the Delphic Apollo. Found in the works of the third century A.D. philosopher Porphyry, this oracle of Apollo cites the greatness of the philosopher Plotinus and says that his soul had returned to the heaven of Plato and Minos and all the choir of love.

That Minos should be included in the company of Plato in heaven and that Apollo should single out his soul as having attained such heights are an indication of Minos' reputation as a sacred figure in the mythology and history of the Greeks and the Romans. In legend, Minos was a son of Zeus and himself possessed oracular powers. When he claimed the throne of Knossos, he prayed to Poseidon to send a sign that he had a just claim to the throne. Poseidon immediately sent a sacred white bull from the sea as a fitting sign and as a suitable sacrifice to himself.

Minos was so struck with the beauty of the bull that he kept it rather than sacrificing it to Poseidon. This affront to the god was an act of spiritual greed, keeping for oneself what was due the gods. Later, when Minos married the beautiful Pasiphae, worshipped in her own right as a moon goddess, Poseidon caused Pasiphae to fall in love with the white bull, which still roamed free as part of the king's herds. Pasiphae confessed her lust to Daedalus, the Athenian artist living in exile in Knossos, who agreed to fashion for Pasiphae a likeness of a cow into which she was able to receive the bull. From this union came the monster Minotaur, half man, half bull, which Minos confined to the darkest recesses of the labyrinth.

MYTH AND SPIRIT

In this myth are all the elements of man's relationship to divinity. Knossos itself, the palace and its environs, is the stage upon which man acts out his role in the cosmos. Poseidon, god of the sea, is the dark mystery of divinity, responding to the prayer of a noble son of Zeus, Bright Consciousness, to assume his proper place in the hierarchy. The prayer is answered with the sacred (white) bull, symbol of prophetic power.

When Minos refuses to sacrifice the bull, to relinquish power to the gods where it belongs, he is guilty of greed and arrogance (*hubris*). Pasiphae, who represents the powers of the subconscious as symbolized in myth by the moon, seeks union with the bull, acting out an inappropriate desire made possible by the greed of Minos. The result is the birth of a monster, a deep flaw in the social structure of the culture.

The role of the labyrinth is crucial to the drama. The Minotaur is confined in the subconscious of the culture, in the darkness where greed and desire flourish and are repressed and nurtured. In these circumstances the development of consciousness is inhibited. Minos cannot aspire to his proper relationship to the gods while the Minotaur—his repressed nature—remains in the dark of the labyrinth.

All of these relationships are evident in the landscape at Knossos. Poseidon's mysterious sea is visible to the north, at the end of the long valley. Mount Jouctas, a mountain expressive of the horns of power and the authority of the gods, lies to the north, exactly in line with the important passages of the sacred procession and the Central Court where the bull myth is acted out. The palace sits on a raised mound, the stage where man acts out his role in the cosmic drama. The dark passages of the labyrinth—the subterranean Shrine of the Double Axes—are where the destructive powers of the underworld must be met, propitiated, and transformed.

That Minos should eventually succeed in transforming this destructive power and attaining the status of a wise man is a measure of his struggle as a man and of the story of the evolution of a soul. The light and sun of the Central Court mark the place in the open where the struggle of the soul is manifest. The rituals of the Minoan religion most likely culminated in the Central Court, where the bull leaping and other symbolic actions acted out the human aspiration for unity with the gods.

In a fragment of a play by Euripides, *The Cretans*, we learn that when the Minotaur is born and confined in the depths of the labyrinth, King Minos sends for the Idaean Daktyls, who were priests and medicine men who lived in a sanctuary on Mount Idha, the mountain sacred to Zeus on Crete. The Daktyls are called upon to purify the palace and to bring peace and moral order back to the culture. It is interesting that a special priesthood is sought out to bring their particular powers and understanding to this crisis. Because we have only a fragment of the play, we do not know the outcome of the purification, but doubtless many of the sacred processions and rituals relate to these acts of purification.

THESEUS AND ARIADNE

The hero Theseus was in legend the founder of Athens. When he became king, he united the families and tribes of

Attica under the leadership of Athens and became its wisest king. When his father Aegeus was king, Theseus sailed to Crete with thirteen other Athenian youths in payment of a tribute to Minos. (Some say the tribute was seven boys and seven girls, others just seven youths.) The youths were sacrificed to the Minotaur every nine years for crimes against the Cretans by Athens. Theseus pledged that he would destroy the monster and end the tribute.

Before leaving on the ship for Crete, Theseus sought the council of the Delphic oracle who pronounced that he should perform sacrifices to Aphrodite before he embarked. Having done so, Theseus and the other Athenian youths set out in a ship rigged with black sails, symbolic of the mourning associated with the payment of the tribute to Crete. King Aegeus, however, also put aboard the ship a white sail and urged Theseus to hoist it upon their return if Theseus met with success.

In Crete, Theseus appeared at Minos' court and took part in the games which formed a part of the rituals of sacrifice. So noble in form and manner was Theseus that he captured the love of the beautiful princess Ariadne, who gave him a magic sword and a skein of sacred thread to find his way in the depths of the labyrinth. With these gifts Theseus killed the Minotaur and with Ariadne escaped from Crete and sailed for home. On the island of Dia (according to Homer) Ariadne was claimed by Dionysos as his bride, causing Theseus to return to Athens in mourning, thus forgetting to hoist the white sail of victory. King Aegeus, seeing the black sail, assumed the worst and threw himself into the sea, named for him in memory of the tragic error.

The other myth, later in time from the Homeric version,

Engraving of Dionysos and Ariadne riding off in triumph. Centaurs are typical participants in myths of Dionysos.

has Theseus abandoning Ariadne on the island of Naxos and setting sail for Athens. The mourning princess is then saved from despair by Dionysos. Theseus is thereafter, as king in Athens, obliged to honor the memory of Ariadne and to proclaim special festivals in Athens to Dionysos to propitiate his guilt.

THE JOURNEY OF THE HERO

In Theseus' long and illustrious history he undergoes all the trials necessary for spiritual development. In Crete, Theseus meets the terrors of the underworld in the form of the Minotaur in the labyrinth where we may become lost in our journey. We might think of the labyrinth as habit, doubt, repressed desires, and submersion in the world. Theseus is given the simple tool of the skein of linen thread with which to find his way out of the maze. Giving his love and promise of escape to Ariadne brings him this tool. Hers is the gift that ensures success in the search.

By abandoning Ariadne after his escape from Crete, Theseus fails to understand the nature of his victory. Thus, he sails back to Athens under the black sail of darkness, which results both in the death of his father and the animosity of the god Dionysos. It is only in dedication to proper duty and sacrifice to the god that Theseus learns from his suffering to be obedient to powers greater than that of his own personal mastery of the world.

It is in these myths of Minos and Crete that we learn much of why Knossos has lived so long in the Greek imagination as a place of mystery and power. Knossos is synonymous with man's attempt to build a palace of human dreams and aspiration and to risk the wrath of the gods by exceeding the powers proper to human life. We are in awe of the attempt and of the gods whose powers brought destruction to the dream.

RELIGION

Very little is known of rituals and the names of the gods of Minoan religion. We can only speculate from a wide variety of sources what may have constituted the patterns of Minoan belief and practice. The main elements of the religion were the sacred pillar (column), the tree cults, and the bull. Various images from frescoes, rings, seals, pottery, and the famous sarcophagus from Hagia Triada suggest that the relationship of these elements had to do with the shedding of bulls' blood (the *mana* of life of the bull) at or on the pillar which represented the power of the goddess in the renewal of life and the growing cycle of the year. It was the province of the goddess to renew the life-giving powers each year.

In this way, we can connect the reverence for the bull with the importance of the living tree as a symbol and the pillar as a symbol of the goddess. The bull was always netted or snared by the foot, so as to make certain that no blood would be spilled prior to the sacred ceremony during which, bound and still alive, its throat was cut, permitting the blood to drain into sacred vessels. This sacrifice recognized the life force of the bull and the divine connection with that force to growth in nature. As we visit the site, we shall see the images of bull and pillar in their relationship to one another in the architecture of the palace. Minoan religion was bound up in the rites of purification at lustral basins, the movements to and within the palace along sacred processional ways, and festival occasions when the community gathered to sing and dance in honor of their divinities.

THE SITE

Those looking for the famed labyrinth at Knossos need look no farther than the palace itself. The pre-Hellenic word *labrys* means double ax, which no doubt gave rise to the word labyrinth being connected to Knossos. But myths have a way of speaking more truth than simple etymologies can explain. The palace itself is a labyrinth, a maze of connecting rooms and passages which penetrate the darkness, emerge into light, and articulate the story of the Minoans and their culture. The visitor enters the labyrinth at the West Porch entrance to the palace. But our visit really begins at the modern entrance to the site.

THE ARCHAEOLOGICAL RECORD

At the entrance to the site is a bronze bust of Sir Arthur Evans, the famed British archaeologist who in 1900 began excavations here. Evans was present in 1935 at the unveiling of the bust, having just completed work on a four-volume account of his work at the site. Although minor excavations in 1877 had uncovered storerooms and various walls, it was Evans who first began extensive digs. He had been keeper at the Ashmolean Museum at Oxford and there developed an interest in the ancient scripts found by Heinrich Schliemann at Mycenae. The theory at the time was that the site at Knossos was most probably the source of the Mycenaean culture. Few realized just how important were to be the discoveries on Crete. A new culture was to be revealed.

Having purchased the land around Knossos and signed an agreement with the Greek government, Evans hired diggers and began work. Within two years he had uncovered most of what we see today. At the time, little remained intact. The volume of rubble was awesome, all the various floors having fallen into a single mass. Evans and his colleagues determined that if the proper relationship of levels and supporting columns were to be understood, some form of reconstruction would have to be attempted. As well, many frescoes were found in the rubble and their location in the palace had to be determined. Most of the restoration of these frescoes was finally accomplished by the Frenchman Jules Gilliéron under Evans' watchful eye.

What we see today is a compromise of archaeological principles. Without any reconstruction, we would see little but outlines of walls and column bases at the lowest levels of the palace. Only models, similar to the ambitious wooden reconstruction at the museum in Iraklion, would reveal the complexity and beauty of the original. What Evans attempted was a partial rebuilding of the palace as he understood the evidence uncovered. For example, only a few of the wooden columns remained and these had been charred by fire, but some remaining pigment showed that the columns were painted white, red, or black.

It became clear that the Minoans had mastered the technique of multistory construction, using stone walls and columns for vertical support and logs and plaster for ceilings. In addition, hewn logs were used as door frames and lintels, giving the entranceways a graceful, modern look. Evans made every attempt to reproduce Minoan masonry and decoration, even using the same materials except for the decision to use concrete rather than wood for columns and ceilings.

Purists may decry the results of Evans' attempts, pointing out justifiably that early important remains were obliterated by the modern reconstruction, but the result for the contemporary visitor is a rare opportunity to step back in time to share the beauty of a very special place. Careful observation will permit the visitor to distinguish original construction from Evans' reconstuction. A visit to the palace at Phaestos will reveal a more disciplined example of archaeological research, still in progress.

The West Court

The modern entrance to the site is from the west across a bridge beneath which we can see the ancient ramp leading up to the West Court. Elements of an early retaining wall are still visible as are foundations of houses which would have been outside the original Middle Minoan palace (before 2000 B.C.). Several striking architectural features are immediately evident.

The Minoans built raised walkways through their courtyards. From their placement and proximity to altars, it is clear that these were designed for processions. Since religious and secular life were fused in one ceremonial vision of life, we have come to call these walkways Sacred Ways or Processional Ways. Their narrowness suggests that the processions were single file and moved along a route which permitted large crowds to view the participants.

Two altar sites in the West Court and the Processional Ways slicing through the open area seem to indicate that this western court was always an important sacred area for the Minoans. And the remains are some of the earliest at the site, further suggesting a long and continuous ritual history.

The Walled Pits

Also from the Middle Minoan II period (2000 B.C.) are three walled pits which were used by the Minoans as places to deposit refuse from ceremonies and sacrifices. As we have seen from later Greek depositories, arrangements were always made for the used ceremonial items to be disposed of properly. Sacred items could not be left around or simply thrown down an embankment. A careful examination of the walled pits, particularly the two nearest the Processional Way, reveals the foundations of houses from the Prepalatial Period. Still evident are the red plaster floors and walls indicative of fine workmanship at this early period. Evidence of such early remains is rare at the site.

Ancient Road and Theatral Area

Rather than plunge right into the palace at this point, visitors might approach the complex from the north by the ancient Royal Road, which is found by turning left from the West Court and walking to the stepped platform or stage known as the Theatral Area. This stepped court seems to have been used in later periods (Late Minoan I) as a place of reception, perhaps a kind of reviewing stand from which processions might be observed. Earlier the whole area was organized as a large courtyard similar to the West Court. The present raised position would have provided a dramatic stage from which the king might have held court outside the palace, among the people, and yet still very much in command.

The ancient road, or Royal Road as it is sometimes called, has a reputation of being the oldest road in Europe. Certainly

The Sacred Way leading to the Theatral Area at Knossos.

most of the paving stones are original and date from the third millennium B.C.. The height of the modern side walls indicates the extent of the digging needed to reveal the original stones. The occasional breaks in the wall expose some of the old houses and shrines which lined the road in ancient times. It may be that this road was a short connection to the Little Palace, the remains of which (not open to the public) have been excavated on the other side of the modern road, or it may have turned north and gone all the way to the sea. To date, no remains have been discovered beyond its present state of exposure.

The North Lustral Basin

Just beyond the Theatral Area, to the north and at the end of the palace complex, sits the reconstruction of the North Lustral Basin. Its location here suggests that the area served as a point of purification for those about to enter the palace. We can see and experience the ritual by descending the sixteen steps to the basin, which is approximately seven feet square and fed by the natural level of water in the palace system. That is, the bottom of the Lustral Basin corresponds to the level to which the water rose in its natural course through the palace. The lustral basins were probably not used for bathing but rather for purification, which meant more a ritual pouring of water over the body combined with prayers and other ritual devotions.

The Processional Way

Once purified the visitor entered the Processional Way at the Theatral Area and moved south along the western side of the palace. Altars to the right and then to the left may have been

The North Lustral Basin, Knossos, where visitors may have purified themselves before entering the palace.

stops along the way as the single line approached the West Porch. Traces of blackened gypsum, evidence of the fire that destroyed the palace for the last time, can still be seen along the way.

The West Porch is significant for several reasons. First, a single column is placed right in the middle of the doorway. Its position commands attention and causes the procession to move around it. The column was a symbol of the goddess, of her strength, her support of the world, and her fecundity. This one in particular lines up precisely with Mount Jouctas to the south, reminding us of our proper relationship to the gods as we move into the palace.

The West Porch also featured wall frescoes relating to the bull leaping which formed such an important part of the sacred life of the Minoans. The images of bull leaping, the presence of the column and mountain serve to draw attention to the sources of power which give this palace its reason for being.

The Corridor of the Procession

The way narrows now as we continue south. This long corridor was decorated with frescoes of the procession itself. Life-sized figures of men and women, elaborately dressed, carried gifts and ceremonial vessels for libations. Similar frescoes have been reproduced on the walls of the Great South Propylon. Our own artistic traditions tell us that these frescoes served to elevate the procession to an art, to remind the worshipper of the heritage as well as the beauty of this action. That the frescoes tended to mirror the procession itself suggests that their purpose was, as well, to serve as an example of how to move and look.

The way then turns left and our attention is drawn to the floor of the corridor. The procession moved along carefully laid gypsum slabs, raised slightly to control and direct its movement. On either side of the raised walk was inlaid a greenish schist, a crystalline rock having a closely foliated structure.

The actual route of the procession from this point is speculative. The evidence provided by fragments of frescoes makes it appear that one route took the celebrants into the South Propylon, up the Grand Staircase and into what Evans called the Piano Nobile or the main story where Evans located the state apartments and the ceremonial halls. Another, more direct route for the procession to the Central Court makes its way past the South Propylon and then left directly to the court. Since there were no doubt many kinds of processions, we do not have to make a choice of routes.

The Great South Propylon

Certainly the most impressive entry into the palace is through the Great South Propylon. The Minoan, Mycenaean, and Greek cultures all emphasized the importance of the entrance. Most of the sites in this book feature monu-

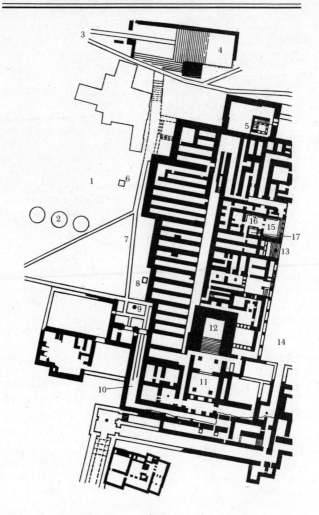

Fig. 12. Knossos, Crete
1. West Court
2. Walled Pits
3. Ancient Road
4. Theatral Area
5. North Lustral Basin
6. Altar
7. Processional Way
8. Altar
9. West Porch and Column
10. Corridor of the Procession
11. Great South Propylon
12. Staircase to Piano Nobile
13. Staircase to Central Court
14. South Procession Corridor
15. Outer Throne Room
16. Throne Room
17. Lustral Basin

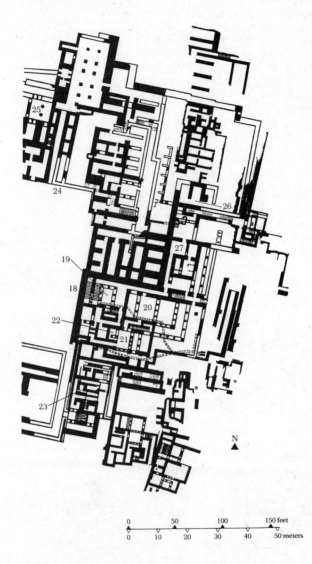

0   50   100   150 feet
0   10   20   30   40   50 meters

N

18. *Grand Staircase*
19. *Hall of Colonnades*
20. *King's Megaron*
21. *Queen's Megaron*
22. *Queen's Bath*
23. *Shrine of the Double Axes*
24. *North Entrance*
25. *West Bastion*
26. *Giant Pithoi*
27. *Workshops*

mental entrances, places where attention is focused, energies are gathered, prayers offered, and greetings extended.

The sacred importance of this area is emphasized by the presence of the large sculptured Horns of Consecration, which have been restored and placed where the original fragments were discovered. The horns represent those of the sacred bull, symbol of the power beyond man's control. They are placed so as to frame the peak of Mount Jouctas, with its own suggestion of horns. At the time of writing a young cypress tree presumes to interrupt the direct line of sight.

The procession into the Great South Propylon passes through a gateway, past a great column and the frescoes on the wall to the left, up two steps, past two square columns, then two round columns to the Grand Staircase. There are twelve steps in this staircase as there are in all of the major staircases in the palace. This uniformity was certainly conscious, although the reason for it is not clear. It could be that twelve steps is the proper height for a story. It could be that twelve marks a calendar division, or a multiple of the threes and fours that seem to dominate other architectural features of the palace.

Twelve represents a certain spiritual fulfillment, such as the twelve labors of Herakles. Twelve are the signs of the zodiac, the tribes of Israel, the loaves of bread in the tabernacle. In many traditions twelve represents achievement and resolution, as well as initiation and spiritual transformation. We shall see twelve reappear elsewhere in the palace.

The Piano Nobile

Once at this level in the palace, our procession moves past a

The Great South Propylon at Knossos, with frescoes of the sacred procession.

single column to a vestibule, through double doors (note the marks in the floor for doors), into a central lobby and then through double doors once again into the Tricolumnar Hall. This impressive room, with its sets of three circular and square columns and various doors to adjoining rooms, must have been ceremonial in nature. It suggests a point of arrival, a place where ceremonies can be held. Support for this view was found in an adjoining room called the Treasury where Evans found many ritual vessels of superb quality, such as those pictured in the processional frescoes.

As Figure 13 indicates, the Piano Nobile contains a multitude of rooms and corridors which are connected to this major line of procession. To the left is a great hall which covered the lower level of magazines used for storage. The so-called Great Hall overlooked the West Court, and the presence there of an altar along with the connecting Sanctuary Hall (so named from the remains of sacred subjects in wall frescoes), points to an area devoted to religious ceremony.

The goal of the procession is the Central Court, reached by the staircase which takes us to the right and down to the court. The staircase, again with twelve steps, was covered, the roof being supported by the single columns whose gypsum bases we can see on our way down.

The Central Court

The Central Court was the focus of life at the palace. Its broad expanse, 180 feet, 6 inches (55 m) by 92 feet (28 m) insures generous light and air to most areas of the palace and strongly asserts the palace's public or participatory qualities. Such an open area at the center of a complex of connected rooms and passages means that the Minoans treasured and maintained an open society within a contained, sacred environment.

There is no evidence to suggest that the famous bull-leaping ritual occurred at any place other than in the Central Court. Most likely, the ritual was a culmination of religious festival and procession. As we learn from frescoes, the ritual involved both young men and women, who, with great skill and courage, seized the horns of a lunging bull and swung up, landing in a flip on its back, and then leaping to the ground. No doubt some were killed or seriously injured in the attempt.

It is interesting that the frescoes show young men and women with both light and dark skin. The explanation has been given that the late mixture of the original Minoan stock (dark) with the Mycenaean (light) is reflected here.

The function of the bull-leaping ritual was most likely related to the symbolism of the Horns of Consecration and the Shrine of the Double Axes. The bull was divine power, both a gift and a danger to man if ignored or treated with arrogance. In the ritual the youths seized the horns as symbolic of this power and with great faith, skill, and attention used the natural power of the bull's charge and goring reflex to fly through the air and land safely. Accomplished as part of a broader religious ceremony, bull leaping, followed by the ritual sacrifice of the bull with the double ax, united the participants with divine power and renewed the strength of the society for another year.

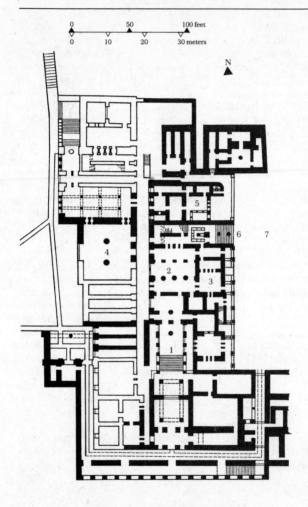

Fig. 13. *Piano Nobile, Knossos, Crete*
1. Staircase
2. Tricolumnar Shrine
3. Treasury
4. Western Hall
5. Terrace Rooms
6. Staircase
7. Central Court

The Throne Room

To the left of the stairs down to the Central Court are located the anteroom and so-called Throne Room of the palace. Since the actual royal quarters and reception areas appear to be located in the eastern half of the palace, this western Throne Room may well have been the ceremonial province of the priest or priestess of the labyrinth. Here is where the speculations become fanciful. This Throne Room did contain a number of sacred vessels and other signs of religious function when Evans uncovered it. Since the Minoans unified the functions of priest and king, priestess and queen, this room may have been used by either monarch in the role of religious leader.

At the time of writing, the room has been closed to the public in order to preserve the original gypsum throne—the oldest throne in Europe—from further wear. Gypsum is a very soft stone as is evident from the water erosion affecting other exposed gypsum throughout the palace. From the barrier, however, we are still able to see how this room was laid out and perhaps how it functioned.

Against a wall decorated in frescoes the throne faces a supporting column, symbol of the goddess as upholder of order. Thus the occupant of the throne acknowledges the power that sustains it. The fresco is balanced in red and white, in horizontal line and vertical waving plants, in red-and-white waves that remind us of the natural patterns of the sea close to the shore when the tidal sand is stirred. Flanked by mythological griffins, the eagle-lions of insight and power, the throne is ringed with benches upon which lesser authorities sat during ceremonies. The throne itself is a graceful seat, delicate yet solid, flowing and yet firm. It is

Exterior of the Throne Room, Knossos.

The Throne Room,
with the oldest throne
in Europe, Knossos.

not a seat which suggests consummate power. It seems to recognize a higher law and a respect for natural forces.

Behind the column, down six steps, is a private lustral basin, perhaps open to the sky, where ceremonies of purification may have taken place. Also, in the western wall of the Throne Room there is a door leading into another small room called by Evans the Inner Sanctuary. Here the evidence suggests that preparations for ceremonies took place. This entire section of the palace is a late addition, perhaps constructed in the Late Minoan II period, when the palace was ruled by the Mycenaean overlords. As a result the images of the griffin and the single column are reminiscent of the famous Lion Gate at Mycenae.

The Frescoes

Above the Throne Room, up a spiral staircase to the left, Evans reconstructed a terrace and a room to house several reproductions of frescoes found in the palace. The so-called Miniature Frescoes are significant because they show ceremonial scenes in which crowds of celebrants fill the court or Theatral Area. These illustrations come as close as we may get to a look at the actual style of ritual celebration. The arms flung skyward suggest an ecstatic moment in the ritual. Another fresco portrays dance as part of ritual, while a third illustrates the bull-leaping ritual.

Before crossing the Central Court to the eastern complex, the visitor might walk south toward the Procession Corridor. This entrance to the Central Court may have been used for the bull-leaping ritual. The reproduction of the priest-king fresco on this wall indicates just where the original was

The priest-king fresco of Knossos. Much of what is known of Minoan royalty has been gleaned from this fresco.

found at the time of excavation. The original sections are now in the museum at Iraklion. The king holds a rope in his left hand, on the other end of which may be a bull, a griffin, or possibly a sphinx. (See illustration, p. 138).

The Royal Labyrinth

Across the Central Court, in the eastern part of the palace, we find the depths and complexity associated in legend with the labyrinth. We have no physical evidence of official procession in these rooms and corridors, but since we do find ceremonial rooms and evidence of shrines, initiatory rituals involving mock burial or the journey to the underworld may have taken place here. Part of the purpose of such rites was to be exposed to the forces of death in order to be reborn as a member of the community. No better place exists to celebrate such a rebirth than in this maze of rooms and halls.

Diodorus, the first century A.D. Greek historian said, "The rite of initiation at Eleusis, which is perhaps the most celebrated of all, and the rite of Samothrace, among the Cicones, whence came Orpheus, its inventor, are all imparted as mysteries; whereas in Crete at Knossos, from ancient days it was the custom that these rites should be imparted openly to all . . . who wished to know such matters."

The linking of Minoan ritual to the Mysteries at Eleusis and the rites of Orpheus means that initiatory ritual was part of the Minoan culture, and the linking of that ritual to the palace and its mazelike structure led to the myths of the labyrinth. Did the rituals grow out of the structure? Did the structure make manifest the rituals and beliefs of the inhabitants? The latter seems most likely in a culture where the presence and power of the gods were a part of every action and filled each moment with meaning. The palace is a construct of myth. Ritual created it. What we are able to see here is the same as a ritual, and that is why we can descend into this labyrinth in a sacred manner.

The Grand Staircase

The Grand Staircase of the east wing is a monumental accomplishment. The gypsum staircase has four sets of twelve steps connected by landings and sets of three steps, making two full stories down from the Central Court. Again, we see the pattern of threes, fours, and twelves which greet us throughout the palace. Such a pattern may have been practical (counting steps as one descended in the dark) or symbolic. One can imagine hymns or chants linked to movement up and down these steps.

In daylight the stairs were lit by an adjacent light well supported by columns all the way to the bottom. At the first level is the Upper Hall which features frescoes of the great figure-eight shields. These cowhide shields were made with the backbone of the hide down the center, shown as a brown band, and the rest of the hide scraped clean for lightness. From the shapes of early Cycladic goddess figures we can see the possibility that these shields were images of the Mother Goddess in her protective aspect. At the bottom of the staircase is the Hall of Colonnades. From here we can proceed along the corridor adjacent to the stair landing, to the Hall of the Double Axes or the King's Megaron.

The King's Megaron

Masons' marks on the wall to the right gave the name to this room. The glass cover on the north wall protects what is left of the spot where a wooden throne sat. The eroded gypsum presumably fell to this spot from above. One of the special features of this room is the system of doors and partitions which controlled air flow in summer and winter and provided privacy when needed. Note the holes in the floor where doors swung open or closed. The doorjambs are constructed in such a way that the doors folded away to make flush pillars opening up the two halves of the megaron.

Decorating the King's Hall is the spiral motif seen throughout the palace but particularly evident in the eastern quarters. This spiral, which also appears on Minoan coins, symbolizes the sacred snake as well as the maze design of initiatory ritual. At the center of the spiral is the rosette design, also featured everywhere at Knossos. The rosettes usually have twelve outer petals and twelve inner rays or petals radiating from a central point. In most cases in these rooms, the rosettes form patterns of twelve around doors, with six across the top. The designs are closely connected to the actual heights and widths of doors, which suggests that the decoration was planned with the architecture and not simply added later.

The Queen's Megaron

Opposite the door from the north corridor is another door which leads by several turns into the Queen's Quarters. The main hall, decorated with dolphins and rosettes, (see illustration, page 9), opens out to two light wells, one of which is decorated with frescoes of dancing women. The ceiling features spiral designs, giving the entire room a wonderful feeling of movement and lightness.

A system of connecting corridors and small rooms fill out the Queen's Quarters. The first room contains a plaster reproduction of the queen's bathtub. The next little room is the toilet, so arranged with plaster piping to provide running water from a cistern above. The water system was quite elaborate, running through the eastern portion of the palace to a drain outside on the eastern slope and hence to the river below.

The corridors connecting the Queen's Quarters to the rest of the living area are so constructed as to allow the curious wanderer to explore a multitude of routes through the complex of rooms. Indeed, if several of the corridors and stairways were not now blocked off, even more possibilities would exist. The visitor can now return to the Hall of Colonnades or leave at the lower level to explore the southeastern extension of the palace.

Beyond the Queen's Quarters, farther south at the same level, is the Shrine of the Double Axes. The present remains are from a very late period in the history of the palace, but the area may always have been the location of a shrine. Found here were several small sets of horns with holes providing a place to set the image of the double ax, plus a clay figurine of the goddess and several smaller figures. This shrine seems to have been connected to the Royal Quarters and may have been a private area of worship.

The North Entrance

We can now return to the Central Court and examine the North Entrance to the palace, passing out to the Lustral Basin and the Theatral Area once again. The outstanding feature of this entrance was the ramp which approached the Central Court from the large Pillar Hall or Custom House as Evans called it. The hall must have served a ceremonial purpose for this entrance to the court. In the Protopalatial Period the ramp was wide and open, leading up to the Central Court. It may have been an access to the court for the bulls and all the attendants involved in the bull-leaping ritual. At a later time, the ramp was narrowed and contained on both sides by bastions.

The West Bastion supports the bull fresco-relief which pictured a bull charging from the north. Combined with the image of the priest-king fresco of the South Entrance, we may have here a complete history of the ceremony beginning in the west corridor of the Processional Way. The bull is pictured charging in an olive grove. This representation may

The West Bastion, with bull fresco, showing an exterior scene and not a ritual of the Central Court, Knossos.

represent the capture of the bull outside the palace or it may symbolize the vitality and fecundity of the bull as reflected by the ritual.

The Domestic and Artistic Remains

Visitors with additional time to look at the hundreds of rooms which remain might explore the area to the northeast of the court. Here were pottery stores, the magazines of the Giant Pithoi, the East Bastion with elaborate ramps and drainage pipes, which by their clever design help to control the flow of water down the slope. In this section as well there is evidence of the artistic life of the palace, where artisans worked to fill the constant demands for pottery and ritual items.

The Hills Beyond

When the site closes at the end of the day, the visitor can take a picnic and, turning down the narrow paved road to the little village of Makrytichos to the north, cross the Kairatos stream, and hike up the dirt road into the olive groves above the palace. Here the remains of the Royal Villa become visible, a beautiful Minoan structure which seems to have been a private dwelling for the royal family. The villa is not open to the public.

Above the palace, on the hillside, the grass is soft and the view magnificent. One is able to see just how well this palace is located in the landscape, protected on all sides and yet open as well. Continuing excavation has revealed the extent of the Minoan city beyond the palace. Ruins have been uncovered along the river to the south and on the opposite hill to the west.

In these relaxing moments it is possible to assemble

impressions into some sense of the whole. The total effect of Knossos is one of complex clarity, massive ease, random order—in effect, a paradox of architectural vision and construction. The frescoes add to the effect by relieving the right angles and sense of bulk with graceful line, colors of sea and sky, images of plant life, and human and animal beauty. One has the sense that the occupants of this palace did not run up and down the halls or stairs. Movement in this space was measured, directed.

Henry Miller best expresses the mood at this moment. At Knossos, he said, "I do not pretend to know, but I felt, as I have seldom felt before the ruins of the past, that here throughout long centuries there reigned an era of peace."

PHAESTOS

At Phaestos it is possible to touch the sky. So claim many ancient visitors to this magnificent site in southern Crete. It is not that Phaestos sits so high on its acropolis, only two hundred feet off the Mesara Plain. Rather, the site seems to float at the end of one of the largest and most beautiful valleys in Crete, surrounded completely by high mountains, snowcapped in winter. To the east, down the long stretch of the Mesara Plain lies Mount Dikte, sacred as the birthplace of Zeus and a center of oracular power. To the north, behind the surrounding ridgeline, is the Idha Range, with the twin-peaked Mount Idha, also sacred to Zeus and famous for the great Kamares Cave, where the beautiful pottery bearing its name was first discovered. The mouth of the cave is visible from Phaestos.

The journey to Phaestos from the north rivals the visit to the site. The trip from Iraklion is not a long one, although it may be delayed by stops at several points to admire the dramatic landscape. Also, in transit, the visitor will want to pause at Gortyna, the ancient Greek site famous for the Classical remains of the Code of Law. These original stones were under water for two thousand years until 1884. They were revealed when the marsh was drained and are now displayed at the site, which also features Roman remains and a charming sixth century A.D. basilica.

The approach to Phaestos is over a ridgeline and a winding road down into the Mesara Plain and then up once again to the site. Standing above the palace and absorbing the sweep and power of the landscape, one is struck with the sense that the first settlers back in Neolithic times comprehended the power and sacred harmony revealed to them on this modest hill above the plain.

SACRED LANDSCAPE

Vincent Scully was the first to articulate fully the details of the relationship of sacred landscape to palace and temple siting in Greece. His analysis of the features of landscape as symbols of the Earth Goddess and the resulting orientation

The palace remains of Phaestos from upper terrace, including the Grand Staircase.

and structure of Minoan palace sites is most vividly seen here at Phaestos. First, the fertile Mesara Plain forms a natural enclosure within which the palace hill is held. Second, the twin peaks of Mount Idha to the north, with its cave sanctuary, rises behind the intervening rounded hill. Idha presents the sacred horns of power and the sacred cave of the goddess in her capacity as the deity of birth, fertility, and death. The shape of the mountain is echoed by the twin-pillared northern entrance to the Central Court leading to the royal apartments overlooking the mountain.

All of the Minoan palaces on Crete (Knossos, Phaestos, Mallia, Gournia, and Kato Zakros) display similar relationships to their physical contexts. And like Knossos, Phaestos is a microcosm of its setting. The reason the palace looks as it does can be read in the landscape surrounding it: the Central Court as plain, the structures to the north and west echoing the adjacent hills. Our understanding of this site depends on the widest possible attention to context as we pass over the remnants of a civilization whose importance emerges from our sensitivity to its elusive genius.

HISTORY

Like Knossos, the hill and surroundings of Phaestos revealed extensive Neolithic settlement. Between 2000 and 1900 B.C. the Minoans arrived to begin building their palace. The same disaster which destroyed Knossos leveled Phaestos some time after 1700 B.C. and marked the beginning of the Protopalatial Period and the construction of a new palace. The destruction of 1450 B.C. brought an end to Minoan-Mycenaean culture, although the site continued to be inhabited.

The historical record shows that Phaestos took part in the Trojan War and that it continued to be a city into Greek times. The record also shows that in 180 B.C. Phaestos was conquered by Gortyna and came under its domination. Such a continuous history indicates that the study of the site has been complicated by the overlays of many cultures. What we see today, with few exceptions, is the Minoan site.

The history of the site also includes ample references to Phaestos as a center for Minoan standards of weights and measures. In terms of its sacred history, these random bits of information also suggest that Phaestos was a center of oracular law and revelation for the entire Minoan culture. Indeed, as the myths of the site reflect, its kings were often credited with attributes similar to those associated with Moses and other lawgivers to the tribes of Israel.

MYTHOLOGY

The ancient sources link Phaestos with Rhadamanthys, who was brother to Minos and the second child of the union of Zeus and Europa. Other myths connect Rhadamanthys with Herakles, no doubt at the time the great hero came to Crete to remove the sacred bull from Cretan shores. In another account Rhadamanthys is the son of Hephaistos, who as the god of fire and craft—and by extension to volcanoes and earthquakes—was confined in a cave for nine years to fashion works of art for the gods. The reference to the number nine suggests the Sacred Tetractys (see p. 75) and the communication with the Gods through revelation. Thus it was part of the myth of Rhadamanthys that he retired to the cave of Mount Dikte for nine days every nine years and returned with the Law. It is in this way that Phaestos is connected to revelation in the myths surrounding the Minoans.

THE SITE

In 1894 the American Institute of Archaeology began excavations at the site. In 1900, at the same time that Evans began his dig at Knossos, Pernier and the Italians began an extensive dig at Phaestos. Pernier's work continued on and off for thirty years and included some restoration work as well. Starting in 1949 Levi resumed excavations which have been continuous to the present. The archaeological record shows that the site was occupied from Neolithic through Hellenistic times.

When Henry Miller arrived at what was the visitor's pavilion, just before the Second World War, he found there Kyrios Alexandros, guide, caretaker, and lover of Phaestos and all it stands for. Alexandros polished Miller's shoes and offered him a meal, including a bottle of sweet wine from

Samos called *mavrodaphne*. Miller was overwhelmed by the surroundings. "Stone and sky, they marry here. It is the perpetual dawn of man's awakening. At the very gates of Paradise the descendants of Zeus halted here on their way to eternity to cast a last look earthward and saw with the eyes of innocents that the earth is indeed what they had always dreamed it to be: a place of beauty and joy and peace. In his heart man is angelic; in his heart man is united with the whole world."

The first task before entering the excavation is to orient the site with the surrounding landscape. As has already been noted, the palace both echoes and absorbs the landscape elements of the setting. To the north, Mount Idha presents her twin-peaked summit as the dominant feature of the Idha range and marks the center of the island of Crete. Down the valley to the east Mount Dikte rises in the distance, the dominant mountain of Eastern Crete. The southern range is the Asterousian, the coastal range with the Libyan Sea beyond.

The Upper and West Courts

At the first level, or Upper Court, the ancient road came from the north and descended to the West Court. Most of the stone foundations remaining in this upper area date from Hellenistic and early Christian times, but there are vague traces near the long staircase of a Minoan Protopalatial Processional Way. The stairs bring us to the West Court, where early remains form most of what we see.

The Theatral Area reminds us of the ancient road at Knossos where the narrow paving divides and the steps provide a place for ceremonial viewing or religious ritual.

The ancient road leading to the Palace and Theatral Area, Phaestos.

The nine steps of the Theatral Area may have sacred numerical significance. We have already heard that nine years and nine days appear in the mythology of Phaestos and in the patterns of revelation involving Rhadamanthys. Nine in the Pythagorean symbolism—which the Minoans might well have absorbed from earlier Egyptian sources—denotes man's struggle to unite with the divine, to return to the source.

Early Propylon

Although the natural movement from the Theatral Area would be to approach the Grand Staircase, we can also follow the ancient road as it moves southeast from the Theatral Area toward the early or Protopalatial entrance to the palace and Central Court. As the plan notes, this entrance turns left (east) and enters the palace approximately at the middle of the court. A long corridor leads straight ahead at this point. Nothing remains now of this entrance, but we can speculate that a proper entrance and walls lined with frescoes led the procession on its way to the court.

Grand Staircase and Propylon

Returning to the northern entrance via the Grand Staircase, we now enter the Neopalatial remains of the palace, those which replaced the earlier structures after the disaster of 1700 B.C. These grand steps, 40 feet wide (12 m), number twelve, again reminding us of the sets of twelve steps throughout the palace at Knossos. As the procession made its way up these steps, the participants faced, directly ahead, a single column whose base suggests an oval shape, the

The magnificent Grand Staircase of Phaestos.

symbol of the goddess and an echo of the rounded hill due west of the site. The extensive propylon continues into three more chambers before turning right (south) to descend another flight of steps to the Central Court.

Central Court

The Central Court is oriented on a north-south axis on Mount Idha. The northern gate to the royal apartments presents a massive entryway leading to a wide corridor. The entrance reminds us of the northern ramp at Knossos, but in this case the corridor leads to the North Court and the royal apartments. No other series of chambers in the palace appears to indicate a separate Throne Room. This absence has led archaeologists to conclude that Knossos may have been the seat of a form of central government where the kings of the other palaces gathered under an overlord.

Royal Apartments

The area now covered to protect recent excavations reveals details of the royal wing of the palace. This series of rooms, corridors, and courts provides a spacious and dignified living area and one suited well to ceremonial functions. The north corridor from the Central Court leads into a wide court which is framed by a foundation wall belonging to the Protopalatial palace. Another corridor to the right leads north to the apartments to the left. First, we encounter a double-columned room with terrace which may well have been the queen's quarters. Farther along a complex of rooms shows the main entrance to the Royal or King's Megaron. The floor paving is still apparent, as are the walls showing

Northern gate to Royal Apartments, Phaestos. Mount Idha lies due north from this entrance.

window frames and door supports. To the north we see the remains of a porch or portico which leads to the left and a lustral basin area.

This whole area, revealing a complex of rooms and sacred areas for ritual and purification, show us the nature of the life of a priest-king. The chambers are connected and fluid in their arrangement. They face north in the direction of the sacred mountain which signifies power and protection. The rest of the palace spreads out to the south and includes its ceremonial entrances, its magazines for the storage of the riches of the culture, and the central court where much of the life of the community took place.

The Northeast Complex

To the east of the royal apartments, there remain Protopalatial buildings which must have served both a religious and an artistic function. Of course, in Minoan times, the religious and artistic life of a palace was integrated into a single purpose. The goddess was being served by priest and potter in the same way. These rooms to the northeast show this function. It was in the first series of small rooms that the mysterious Phaestos Disk was discovered. This clay disk, eight inches (20 cm) in diameter and half an inch thick, has successfully defied decoding for years. We still do not know what it means. It may be a great sacred key or a toy or a guide to economic development. That it is a sacred key is more likely than not, but, so far, efforts to explain its spiral form and forty-five different symbols have been inconclusive. The disk may be seen in the Archaeological Museum in Iraklion.

Eastern and Southern Sections

To the east, off the Central Court, we find a sequence of interesting rooms which were probably dedicated to religious

Phaestos Disk, eight inches in diameter, found in northeast storehouse.

ritual. From the corridor to the court from the northeast corner, we can explore the rooms which connect and lead to a lustral basin at the southern end of the complex. The rooms seem to have accommodated a ritual of purification which took place in various stages. The only information we have of these rituals lies here in the shape and artifacts of these ruined shrines.

At the southern end of the Central Court we see that the hillside has fallen away, perhaps in the disaster of 1450 B.C. but more likely at a later date in a more local geological event. Over the fence to the south are the remains of the houses which surrounded the palace hill and formed the outlying community. Last, at the very southern tip of the site, beyond the remains of the southwest apartments, lie the foundations of an Archaic temple of Rhea. Rhea was the daughter of Ouranos and Gaea and is usually called the mother of the gods. Her worship here in Archaic times would signal a recognition by the Greek settlers of the importance of this site to the Earth Mother. It was here on Crete, in a cave on Mount Dikte or on Idha, as various legends have it, that Rhea gave birth to Zeus, father of humanity.

HAGIA TRIADA

Only a few minutes by road to the west of Phaestos toward the Libyan Sea lie the remains of a small palace called Hagia Triada, which is named for the fourteenth-century Church of the Holy Trinity which overlooks the site. Very little is known about the site and various scholars have speculated that it might have been a summer villa for the kings of Phaestos. Its proximity to Phaestos argues that it is unlikely to have been a separate entity, either politically or economically, but it may have had a unique ritual function. In any case, the little palace is a gem as an archaeological find and possesses some fine examples of Minoan architectural design and construction.

What we do know about this small palace has emerged from steady excavation by the Italians which continued throughout the twentieth century. Notable finds at the site have included the unearthing in 1911 of a large number of inscribed Linear A tablets, the discovery in 1938 of a seascape painted on a floor and dated to the Late Minoan Period, and the discovery in 1962 of Minoan figurines and votive remains nearby. The history of occupation of the site reveals that it was built in the Middle Minoan III Period, was important in Late Minoan times, and later became a cult site and was occupied through Hellenistic and Roman times.

The assumption that it was important as a cult site is not surprising given its location and relationship to the sacred landscape. Mount Idha appears clearly in the distance to the north, directly in line with the major staircase which must have served as part of the Processional Way. Also in the

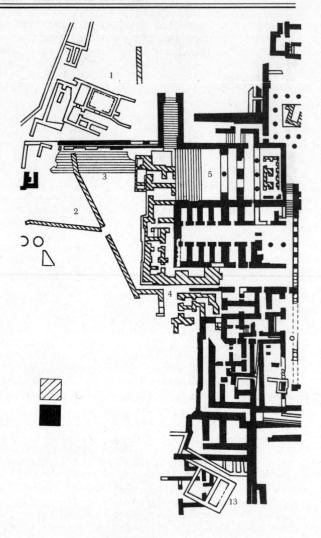

Fig. 14. Phaestos
1. Upper Court
2. West Court
3. Theatral Area
4. Early Propylon
5. Grand Staircase and Propylon
6. Central Court

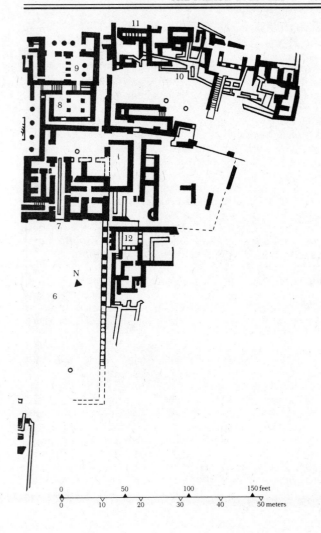

7. North Corridor
8. Queen's Apartments
9. King's Apartments
10. Northeast Complex
11. Archives (Phaestos Disk)
12. Sacred Area
13. Archaic Temple of Rhea

middle distance appears a perfect conical hill which is echoed in the stonework and column construction of the main palace.

Worked carefully into the hillside so that it would orient itself to both Mount Idha and the sea, the palace first took shape in its western section and culminated in the main hall at its western extreme. In later times, under Mycenaean influence, the northern addition filled out the present design. The Mycenaeans also built a megaron over existing Minoan structures in the western section. An interesting feature of the northern addition is the presence of an *agora* or market-place as part of the Mycenaean period. The *agora* suggests that this site in its later period was used year round and served as a village as well as palace.

There are two arguments about the function of this site. The first is based on the absence of two of the major ceremonial features of the Minoan palace sites—the central court or theatral area. The absence of these features has led to the conclusion that this "villa" was devoted to pleasure and relief from the hot summers at the central palace at Phaestos. The other argument is that this small palace was ceremonial in some unique way not including the functions of a central court and theatral area. Enough ritual items have been uncovered here to suggest use of the site as a cult center of some sort.

A visit to the museum at Iraklion will reveal several major finds from the Minoan periods which have added significantly to our understanding of burial cults. The major find was the painted stone sarcophagus showing, on one side, a procession or processions perhaps relating to burial, but perhaps also relating to worship of Dionysos. Pictured in the procession are seven figures, three with libations and musical instruments, approaching a shrine decorated with columns, double axes and sacred doves, and the second showing four figures in a sacrificial ritual within the palace. More will be said about this interesting piece in the section devoted to the Iraklion Museum.

MALLIA, GOURNIA,
AND ZAKROS

For those with the time and interest to explore the other Minoan sites in Crete, a trip to the eastern half of the island will provide the opportunity to visit Mallia, Gournia, and the latest gem in the Minoan crown, Zakros. These sites contain the familiar landscape elements so important to palace siting and reveal unique features which add to our appreciation of the richness of Minoan culture.

MALLIA

The palace at Mallia is only a short drive east from Iraklion, too long perhaps for a taxi drive but accessible by bus. The site was first excavated in 1915 by the French, who continued until the 1930s and picked up again after World War II. In addition to the palace site, archaeologists uncovered two large houses, an underground crypt west of the palace, and an extensive burial enclosure north of the palace.

The palace itself is oriented on a north-south axis, with the sea to the north and the sacred Mount Dikte to the south, with its sacred cave dedicated to the goddess and connected in later myth to the birth of Zeus. Although Mallia does not possess the same full landscape elements because of its proximity to the sea, the palace itself was so constructed as to contain within it the necessary ritual elements.

The Central Court is entered from either north or south and is approached on the Sacred Way in the West Court. The south entrance is the most direct and ends at a Theatral Area in the southwest corner of the court. The north entrance features an ancient flagstone walkway, a main entrance hall and a north courtyard. A long corridor leads to the Central Court, at the north end of which is a ceremonial pillared hall. This interesting hall is entered through a narrow door, "guarded" by a single pillar. A right turn reveals the six-pillared hall.

Two items in the Central Court are of particular interest. First, a sacrificial pit was uncovered at the southern end of the court, near the Theatral Area. This pit is the only such

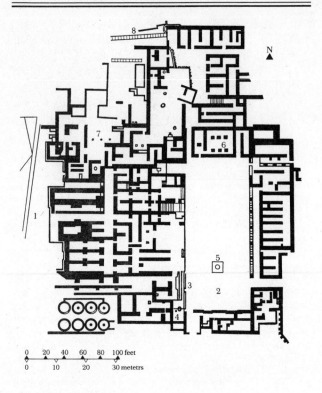

Fig. 15. Mallia
1. Sacred Way—West Court
2. Central Court
3. Theatral Area
4. Kernos
5. Sacrificial Pit
6. Pillared Hall
7. Royal Apartments
8. North Entrance

ritual element discovered at a Minoan palace. It may have been located at this place because the theatral area was constructed within the enclosure rather than outside. This particular configuration of ceremonial elements may relate to the unique placement of the palace in the landscape. Thus, Central Court and Theatral Area were combined in their sacred functions.

The other item of interest is the *kernos,* or offering table, near the ceremonial stairs. This round stone is placed toward Mount Dikte in an axis to the stairs. The stone is unique in its design and mysterious in its function. A central cup, ringed with a shallow depression, is surrounded by thirty-three smaller cups or depressions and one larger cup extending from the circle. This stone may have contained offerings of grain and produce from the area or blood from animal sacrifices. The center hole may have held a post or column with the double-ax symbol, as pictured in the Hagia Triada sarcophagus.

Of special interest at the site are the two giant *pithoi,* or storage jars, which tower above the visitor. The detailed rope designs in the terra-cotta are obviously decorative, but may also have been functional. They show the pattern by which these huge containers were roped so that they could be moved or tipped.

GOURNIA

Further along the eastern coastline from Mallia at the Gulf of Merabello is the Minoan site called Gournia. Although this site is clearly Minoan, it is less clearly a palace. It is valuable to archaeologists as an example of an early (1600 B.C.) town. The site covers a ridge and shows evidence of royal quarters— a small palace perhaps—on the top of the ridge, with the rest of the town spreading out below. To the south of the palace, linked by what may have been a ceremonial staircase, is the *agora* and a courtyard.

The archaeological value of Gournia is the suggestion that it makes of a secure, integrated culture. The central shrine, located on the north slope, the palace, and the *agora* fit into the enclosed landscape to form a nurturing whole, where the population is held in the embrace of the goddess. One has the impression of a secure world, where distant kings kept foreign powers at bay and life consisted of daily ritual and work woven into one activity. Finds at the site have included large numbers of ritual elements—figurines of the goddess, tripods, and double axes—and work elements—carpenter's tools, weaving tools, mortars and pestles, knives, saws, and tools for producing olive oil. It is at Gournia that one feels the close relation of work and worship, that at one point in time the two were one activity.

ZAKROS

Finally, far to the east, facing the Near East and the probable roots of the Minoan culture, is the newly uncovered site of Zakros. The name of the site comes from the nearby town of Zakros, which is at the end of the main road from Sitia and Palaikastro to the north. High mountains separate this palace from the rest of Crete, and in ancient times this city must have been isolated and accessible only by sea. Zakros was certainly an important trading port throughout its history.

When the city was destroyed—in the great conflagration of 1450 B.C.—the site was abandoned abruptly and completely, never to be reoccupied. Therefore, when the site was excavated fully beginning in 1961, it revealed valuable treasures of the Minoan culture. Discovered were Linear A tablets, frescoes, sacred vessels, plus household materials, and tools left behind as the inhabitants fled.

There was also evidence of volcanic ash, suggesting that the general destruction of the Cretan palaces may have been related to the great Thera eruption. But intriguing questions remain. Why weren't the sites ever reoccupied? Could the destruction have been so very complete? Was a tidal wave involved? Could it have struck Phaestos to the south and Zakros, too, hidden behind mountains to the east?

IRAKLION:
THE MUSEUM

It is not the purpose of this section to provide a comprehensive guide to the Archaeological Museum in Iraklion. What is offered here are highlights from the twenty galleries and a few interpretive suggestions. The museum has several complete and colorful guides to the museum and its holdings. Since most of the pieces have come from the major palace sites in Crete, a logical step might be to visit the museum first, particularly to study the frescoes, which give a fragmented but vivid introduction to the sacred life of the Minoan culture. Finally, this guide will not cover those items in the collection which date from the period after 1100 B.C., the generally accepted date for the end of the palace cultures.

GALLERY I

The first gallery in the museum contains representative items from Neolithic sites in Crete, dating from 5000 B.C. to 2000 B.C. and the beginning of the palace cultures. In Cases #1 and #2, for example, there are examples of the figurines we suppose to be Earth Mother Goddesses from this period. The earlier the figures the less distinct the female features, leading to the caution that they may not be sacred figures at all, but the later examples leave little doubt as to their religious function.

An interesting figure in Case #12 (#4676) is the clay sculpture of a bull with male and female figures clasping the horns. The image expresses the complexity of the sacred nature of the bull and the myths and rituals associated with it. Case #13 contains Mother Goddess figures and human figures in gestures of worship. The folded arms indicate the formal position seen in many Minoan illustrations of ritual activity. The stone seated figure from Tekes is particularly striking. He sits, back straight, head held high, arms folded across his chest. The position is relaxed but formal; it gives us an image of the king on his throne, full of authority and yet not threatening.

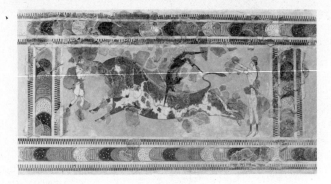

The bull-leaping fresco, restored from scant fragments, Knossos.

GALLERY II

In Case #19 we see the Goddess Vase from Mallia, most likely used in votive ceremonies. The liquid poured from her breasts. In Case #23 we begin to see the fine examples of the Kamares-style pottery. These delicate pieces were so named because they were first discovered in the Kamares Cave on Mount Idha. We know from their location that they served a sacred purpose.

In Case #25 are the so-called Town Mosaics, which were no doubt inlays for wooden boxes or decorative panels. The glazed earthenware figures show various architectural features of Minoan houses or sections of palaces. We are able to see two- and three-story construction, flat roofs, door and window beams, and floor construction consisting of rows of small logs bound together and plastered over. Also in Case #25 is a pictograph of a standing man, spear in one hand with his left hand touching his heart. This, too, must be a position of either worship or salute to a leader.

In Case #24 we find the model of the Tricolumnar Shrine. This religious figure shows three columns—a typical Minoan configuration—supporting a roof element and three doves. The addition of birds in such models or frescoes suggests an epiphany of the goddess, thus an idealized sacred theme.

GALLERY III

This gallery features finds from Phaestos in the Middle Minoan Period, from 2000 B.C. to 1700 B.C. The effect of these assembled pieces leaves us with an appreciation of the very special quality of work from this palace. The people of Phaestos enjoyed a unique relationship to nature and to their gods, one of openness, playfulness, and imagination.

The central treasure in this gallery is the mysterious

Phaestos Disk (Case #41). This round clay disk (p. 128), about 8 inches in diameter, was found in the palace ruins of Phaestos and has baffled scholars ever since. The majority opinion now is that the disk has a sacred intent, perhaps as a hymn or as a guide to ceremony. What we do know about it is that it was made by pressing damp clay with seals corresponding to some symbolic or linguistic meaning. There are 45 different seals, used 241 times on both sides. Each side is generally made in a spiral form, but the figuration is not quite a spiral in that the outer ring of twelve sections is broken by the spiral as it turns to reach the outer edge.

The presence of twelve segments on the outer ring suggests a calendar function, perhaps related to festivals. On both sides there are 49 figures in the outer ring. Other interesting features include the inclusion of the eight-leaf rosette design, which is sacred to the Minoans as well as the later Greeks, and the circle with seven dots arranged in a circle of six with one in the center. We are reminded that for Pythagoras seven was the most sacred of numbers, and it may have held special meaning for the Minoans as well. But at best these are merely vague clues to a mystery still very much unsolved.

This gallery also contains fine examples of Kamares pottery, beautifully inscribed with geometric designs fluidly intertwined with images of nature. The unique vase in Case #43, with its attached rosettes, suggests the fecundity of nature and the exuberance of growth as these flowers grow out of the vase as they do out of crevices in rocks. In Case #33A a unique design features a sea scene sculpted around a post. Dolphins sport among the seashells and seaweed in a balanced image of great beauty.

GALLERY IV

The Bull's Head Rhyton (p. 142) in Case #51 is one of the treasures of the museum. Made of black steatite (soapstone), with eyes of rock crystal and jasper, this libation vessel was used in sacred rituals at Knossos. The vase was filled through a hole in the neck and emptied from the nostrils. The horns were probably gilded wood, although the present horns are a restoration made to give the appearance of gold.

Also important in this gallery, in Case #50, are the two glazed earthenware goddesses. The snake goddess in particular gives us a vivid sense of the chthonic aspect of the Earth Mother Goddess in Minoan religion. The snake cult combined images of the renewal of life, of curative powers, and prophecy. The statues also tell us a great deal about the dress of the time—the constricted waist, and breasts left bare, the heavily embroidered flounced skirt.

Interesting sacred vessels in this gallery include the alabaster lioness head in Case #59 and the collection in Case #58. In particular, note the shell vessel on the top shelf as an example of the superb craftsmanship of the period. Case #56 contains the ivory bull-leaper. The famous fresco upstairs will show the daring routine of these leapers as they transformed the charging power of the bull into feats of daring and agility.

GALLERY V

Featured in this room are items from the so-called Palace Style of the Late Minoan Period, just after 1450 B.C. In the room are a variety of items from Knossos. In Case #62 are examples of Egyptian and Near Eastern art, demonstrating the wide-ranging trade of the Minoans and their Mycenaean overlords. In Case #66 is a stone vase found by Evans in the throne room at Knossos. In #70 is a fragment showing the capture of a bull with a net, a method of capture which prevented injury to the bull and the premature spilling of its sacred blood.

Case #70A shows us a good deal about the architecture of a Minoan house. The model reveals the use of wooden columns, the cross beams, and the use of small logs tied together to form the roof. Case #69 illustrates some of the many examples of Linear B script found at Knossos. The numerical system of lines and circles permitted the tabulation of items into the tens of thousands. The phonetic signs were both ideograms (signifying specific objects like figs, men, wheat, and wheels) and numerals.

One interesting example of the symbolism of phonetic signs is the figure for *ka*, the circle with cross. The crossed circle is one of the earliest forms inscribed by human beings to express the cosmos. Linear B may well have an extensive internal symbolism similar to its Egyptian counterpart.

GALLERY VI

These Late Minoan artifacts from Knossos, Phaestos, and Archanes feature attractive ritual dancing motifs, such as the clay figures in Case #71. Four men in a round room (*tholos*) perform a sacred dance, as evidenced by the inclusion of horns of consecration. Dance was one of the important features of the Minoan religion, reflecting the rites and rituals of fertility which must have been associated with seasonal festivals.

In Case #87 are several rings, one of which, the famous Isopata Ring has intrigued scholars for decades. Engraved on the gold are four female figures engaged in an ecstatic dance. They are without heads and from their necks appear to come beads or drops. The assumption might be that some brutality is being pictured, but more likely is the theory that the symbolism suggests a state of ecstasy in which all interfering thought (the head) is gone and a state of freedom and unity has been reached. The ring also contains symbols which appear to float in the space around the women, one of

Large amphora showing the famous double ax. Noteworthy is the fusion of the ax into the natural imagery of plants.

whom also appears to float above the ground. The symbols include an eye and two organic images suggestive of growth and fertility. The eye may indicate spiritual vision achieved in the dance.

GALLERY VII

This room contains several fine examples of steatite carving, three of which are particularly striking. In Case #94 the Harvester's Vase illustrates a sacred procession from the grain fields. A priest leads the file of celebrants as they joyfully return laden with the harvest. The successful harvest is, of course, the culmination of the ritual year. A rich harvest provides food, security for the winter months, and affirmation of the nurturing protection of the goddess.

The vase in Case #95 shows two male figures, one clearly a king or leader and the other making a presentation. This illustration gives us a more accurate picture than the more formal frescoes. The images are impressive and quite handsome. In Case #96 is a vase with scenes from the games, including the bull-leaping ritual. The bull is shown charging at the leapers, a reminder of the danger and difficulty of this ritual act.

Twoother displays in this room deserve attention. Case #100 contains two potter's wheels. Note the double-ax carvings on one of the wheels. Also, in Case #101 are examples of gold jewelry, one in particular being significant. The gold bee pendant has a delicacy and balance that remind us that to the early Greeks and perhaps the Minoans as well the bee was an image of spirit, a buzzing presence producing nectar which to the Minoans was a sacred medium.

GALLERY VIII

The finds of this gallery are mainly from Zakros, the most recently excavated site in Crete. The stone vessels stand out as superbly crafted pieces. In Case #109 the rock crystal vase with gilt ring and a delicate handle of beads was carefully assembled by the museum staff from hundreds of fragments. In Case #118 a stone amphora illustrates the high quality of attention and workmanship of the Zakros artists.

Bull's Head Rhyton, a libation vessel found at Knossos, Case #51, Iraklion.

GALLERY IX

The collection in this room dates from Late Minoan culture in Eastern Crete. In Case #123 several items of sacred importance stand out. The two figurines, one male, the other female, show postures we have come to associate with religious ritual. The female stands erect, right hand resting on her left shoulder, left hand resting on her right hip. Similar poses are typical of women in attitudes of worship. The male figure stands with his arm across his chest.

In Case #122 is an ox-shaped rhyton, very naturalistic in rendering. Careful examination reveals a faded decoration which looks like a net. As mentioned earlier, the bull was captured with a net so as not to spill its sacred blood until the sacrificial moment. Thus, the net was seen to be sacred as well, being a critical part of the ceremony. The net on a sculptured bull would mark it as worthy of devotion.

GALLERY X

The Late Minoan III collection in this gallery features several interesting goddess figurines, hands held aloft, eyes closed. In Case #133 is figure 9305, the Poppy Goddess. She is crowned with opium poppies in her function as bringer of sleep, dreams, revelation, and death. Her posture evokes images of her sublime state, her stillness and serenity. The contrasting state is seen in Case #132 where we see the ecstatic dancers with lyre player.

One of the most popular figures is the female swinger in Case #143. Discovered at Hagia Triada, this lovely piece is also sacred, as we know from the rituals of swinging which formed a part of festivals welcoming the arrival of spring. The posts supporting the swing relate to the tree cult and are crowned by the representation of the goddess in her form as a bird.

GALLERY XII

Before going upstairs, pause to admire the wooden model of the palace at Knossos, constructed by Z. Kanakis in 1967. The care lavished on this model reflects a personal interpretation of the latest information available as to the appearance of the palace. Of course, since the palace remains do not permit us to know exactly what the structure looked like at any given moment in time, what we have here is a composite picture.

GALLERY XIV

The second floor of the museum holds the display of the frescoes and the larger pieces deserving of greater viewing space. Close attention to the mounting of the fragments recovered from the palace sites reveals the sometimes daring interpretations by scholars and artists as they extrapolate from fragments to original works.

In Gallery XIV one of the major pieces is the bull-leaping fresco from Knossos. Roughly one-third of the original was recovered and then pieced together. The reconstruction was aided by the presence of fragments at crucial points in the action of the scene. What we see, then, is a representation of the sequence of a leap. The leapers, both male and female, are in the key positions of the acrobatic leap. The first grasps the horns of the rushing bull and is tossed back over the bull's head; the second leaper is pictured springing from the bull's back, having flipped over the head; the third lands with arms raised, under perfect control to complete the leap.

Questions have been raised often about the depiction of the leapers as white and red. In most frescoes the distinction is that white figures are women and red are men. In a few cases, there appear red women as well, leading to the speculation that since these frescoes are Late Minoan, the red figures might be Minoan and the white Mycenaean. But since these exceptions are rare—and perhaps in error—we may accept color depictions as follows: women are white, men are red, gold objects are yellow, silver vessels are blue, and bronze vessels are red.

Some have speculated that the bull-leaping ritual was initiatory, meaning that every youth attempted the feat at some point as part of the rite of passage to adulthood. Such a conclusion ignores the extraordinary difficulty of this feat and the probable function of the performance as part of a seasonal ritual relating to the renewal of Nature's power each year. The feat was probably undertaken by a select few athletes, both male and female, as a vivid and nearly magical expression of human mastery of powerful life forces as embodied in the sacred bull.

The other major piece in this gallery is the Hagia Triada Sarcophagus. Mention of this important piece has been made in the section on Hagia Triada. The scenes painted on the stone of this piece have intrigued scholars for half a century. Some scholars conclude that the scenes are exclusively dedicated to the worship of the dead, as might be fitting the function of the sarcophagus. On its four painted sides are scenes of procession and sacrifice. What we can say about this extraordinary piece is that all of the decoration taken together gives us more information about Minoan religious practices than we find from any other single source.

First, the scenes are framed by the common sacred border decorations of spiral and rosette. The flux and cycle of natural life are expressed by the spiral motif, which is held at the center by the rosette, which expresses the unity and symmetry of universal law. Throughout our journey in Minoan culture we have seen these symbols giving order to existence. In the case of the sarcophagus the decorations are framed by straight lines in red, white, blue, and gold. Here are the columns, the upholders of the culture, and the beams, protecting and supporting human life.

The scenes depicted on the sarcophagus may relate exclusively to burial ceremony but they may well represent human worship of the gods related to death and resurrection. On the long side devoted to processional themes, we see a figure without arms or legs "standing" with a symbolic tree and receiving the sacrifices appropriate to his attributes. In this case the god must be Dionysos, the dis-membered god of death and resurrection, receiving his tribute in a moon-shaped boat and in the form of two young, vibrant bullocks.

On the other side, a bull is sacrificed and trussed, but very much alive, on a sacrificial table. Surrounding it are priestesses in various poses of worship and sacrifice, reaching out to touch and to receive the power from this bloodletting ceremony. The blood of life and divine power will be symbolically and literally joined to the sacred tree-column as an affirmation and a prayer for a renewal of the growing cycle and for the journey of the soul after death of the body.

GALLERY XV

Our knowledge of various Minoan ceremonies is enhanced by the presence of several miniature frescoes discovered at Knossos. In the first, #25, we see a ritual dance being performed in a sacred grove, perhaps in the West Court of the palace. We see in the forms and gestures an Egyptian influence. These scenes depict the public nature of religious ceremony and the ecstatic nature of the experience.

Attention is also drawn in the gallery to the decorative relief from a Knossos ceiling. The spirals and rosettes form an orderly sky as yellow rosette stars float in blue waving clouds and swirls of air. Such symmetry and color remind us of the image of the palace as the context where human beings play out their earthly drama, where architecture transforms sky, earth, and underworld to a vision of human understanding and belief.

THE MAINLAND AND
THE MYCENAEANS

The identity of the peoples who by 1550 B.C. would establish the culture we call Mycenaean is uncertain. The migrations which began in 2000 B.C. introduced a new race with a new language (a form of archaic Greek) to the mainland. Homer referred to them as Achaeans, Danaans, and Argives. The extent to which these peoples had contact with the already stable Minoan culture in Crete and beyond is documented by changes in pottery design. There are artistic and architectural connections which indicate strong Minoan influence. The accepted theory now is that those who came to be called Mycenaeans were Indo-European and entered Greece from the Balkans or from southern Russia.

Engraving of a cross section of a Mycenaean tholos *tomb, Mycenae.*

We can follow their tracks down from the north around the Black Sea. They rode horses, made gray pottery (called Minyan), wore armor, and conquered their enemies with bronze weapons. Their men were bearded and were fearsome warriors. Excavations at Troy VI (one of the levels of habitation) show that these peoples occupied Troy in 1900 B.C. We can also assume that they made contact with the Minoans as well, resulting in a gradual fusion of so-called Minyan and Minoan culture on the mainland.

The major ruins associated with the Mycenaean culture are centered in the Argive Plain, at Mycenae, Argos, and Tiryns. More recently, the remains of the famous palace of Nestor at Pylos in the western Peloponnese has been extensively excavated.

MYCENAE

Soil of my fathers, Argive earth I tread upon,
In daylight of the tenth year I have come back to you.
All my hopes broke but one, and this I have at last.
I never could have dared to dream that I might die
In Argos, and be buried in this beloved soil.
Hail to the Argive land and to its sunlight, hail
To its high sovereign, Zeus, and to the Pythian King.
                                    —AESCHYLUS, *AGAMEMNON*

From the acropolis of Mycenae, north in the Argive Plain,
the fertile valley opens out to the west and the mountains
and to the south and the gulf. On a recent mid-January
afternoon, on the day in myth and history that Agamemnon
landed in Nauplia and returned from Troy to his palace, a
cold wind blew across the hill, and through the black clouds
to the west the sun streamed in piercing rays. As the clouds
scudded to the south, the sun swept across the god-shaped
mountains like a searchlight.

Mycenae broods. Henry Miller said, "I feel the approach of
the cold breath from the shaggy gray mountain towering
over us." Behind the citadel the chasm of Chavos drops away
to dizzying depths. This is no Knossos, redolent with the
buzzing, fragrant life of its surroundings. Instead, Mycenae

The Argive Plain from the citadel of Mycenae.

is cyclopean walls and overhanging mountains and deep gorges and the remains of conspicuous wealth, all speaking of its glorious and violent past.

HISTORY

The story of Mycenaean culture has been pieced together from excavation, epic poetry, written history (all much later), pottery, and from the deciphering of Linear B script. The tablets found in Mycenaean sites reveal in the accounts of their economy a glimpse of the culture. In many ways, it is as if the history of our own culture was to be assembled in A.D. 5000 from a scattering of sales records, inventory lists, and news magazines salvaged from a fire and buried for three thousand years. The difference is, of course, that in the case of Mycenae, we are working with a small palace with limited population and many fewer cultural "elements" to catalog and analyze.

By the time writers such as Homer and Plutarch sought to describe the Late Bronze Age, there had intervened a dark age in which most of the traditions and values of the earlier time had dissolved into memory and filtered through an entirely new social and political system. Thus, our study of Mycenae begins from a perspective best described as the Heroic Tradition. We carry with us from our school days Homeric images of heroes and kings courting the gods and gaining fame for themselves in monumental battles fought over questions of personal honor. Shifting attention slightly to the daily lives of these superhuman figures reveals a unique and historically significant time in the sacred and secular history of the Mediterranean world.

THE DIVINE STATE OF KINGS

Linear B tells us that the king, the sole power of the culture, was *wa-na-ka* (*wanax*), the chief priest, commander in chief, regulator of events, and supreme judge. The *wa-na-ka* was surrounded by a hierarchy of officials and minor lords whose duties overlapped and who also lived in the palace. As a result the culture was highly centralized. Wealth in the form of gold, silver, bronze, agricultural produce, and herds was carefully controlled and allocated according to the wishes of the king.

The power of the *wa-na-ka* was supported by a warrior class whose task it was to control access to the territory ruled by the palace and by a class of scribes whose task it was to record taxes and to master the details of a complex economy. In addition, there was a priestly class who carried out the rituals of worship and gave prophetic utterance when asked, and, presumably, sometimes when they weren't.

A part of the mythology of Mycenae includes a story of the rivalry between Atreus and his brother Thyestes. Each claimed the right to rule Mycenae, and the test of rule involved a knowledge of astronomy. Such knowledge was necessary for proper rule by the *wa-na-ka,* whose responsibility it was to set the calendar for festivals and to regulate the cycle of planting and harvest. Rule, then, was not based on force or fear, although both must have been commonplace enough, but rather on knowledge of natural cycles and on the wisdom to use that knowledge well.

By 1500 B.C., when the Mycenaean culture dominated Greece, there were at least 320 citadels under the general leadership of the *wa-na-ka* of Mycenae. Domination of the rest of the mainland and the Aegean was complete. The great northern sky gods now ruled, with Zeus supreme among them. For over three hundred years all was Mycenaean.

DECLINE AND DESTRUCTION

By 1100 B.C., when the era was over, only forty citadels remained. By that time Mycenae itself was reduced to a minor town as Greece slipped into the Dark Age from which it gradually emerged three hundred years later. No record remains of the social changes and political revolutions of this period. By the beginning of Classical times the story of Mycenae emerges once again in a minor way as a result of the Persian invasions. A small band of Mycenaeans stood with Leonidas of Sparta at Thermopylae in 480 B.C. and again at Plataea in 479 B.C. Their brief resurgence at this time resulted in destruction in 468 B.C. at the hands of the more powerful Argos, by then an expanded city-state. By the time of the Roman era in A.D. 200, when the Greek traveler and geographer Pausanias passed through, Mycenae was an abandoned ruin. Only the Lion Gate, some outer wall, the chamber of Atreus, and the suggestion of a grave circle were in evidence.

Although it is not possible to know what caused the decline and eventual disappearance of the Mycenaean culture, it is possible to speculate from the later Geometric Period when conditions in Greece were heading toward the establishment of the Classical city-state. Increase in population, increased trade, and contact with the east and south, far-flung military campaigns such as the conquest of Troy, all these must have contributed to a lessening of the centralized power of the *wa-na-ka.* It must have been impossible after 1100 B.C. for the king to command absolute obedience and to maintain the same degree of religious authority. Those citadels such as Argos and Athens which were able to overcome their physical limitations and change their vision of political and religious rule survived the revolution and evolved successfully into a new age.

The culture that had so completely controlled the mainland of Greece and had ventured to the islands and Crete could not withstand the pressures of the migrations that swept into their lands like an avalanche. Not only Dorians but many different peoples, most of them speaking dialects of Greek, invaded or simply migrated to the south, no doubt responding to pressures from the north as huge population shifts took place. The Mycenaeans who survived fled mostly to the east and to Asia Minor where they became immigrants or seized control of palace cultures similar to their own. Eventually, what was distinctly Mycenaean blended into the Oriental landscape and for thousands of years all that remained was the haunting monument of the great Lion Gate protruding like a tombstone from what was to become only a minor village in Archaic, Classical, and Hellenistic times.

MYTHOLOGY

The myths of Mycenae are the stories of Perseus, who was the legendary founder of Mycenae, and of Tantalus and Pelops, who were the ancestors of Agamemnon, Orestes, and Electra. Also involved are those connected by marriage and alliance: Clytemnestra, Menelaus, Helen, Odysseus, and the other heroes of Troy.

These myths took early form in hymns and dance and later in the epic poems of Homer and the tragedies of Aeschylus, Sophocles, and Euripides. They acquired religious sanction in the decorations of pottery and the friezes of Archaic and Classical temples. They became the education of all Greece and the foundation of moral philosophy and law. Only the myths of Oedipus rival the stories connected to Mycenae, where, even today, shepherds speak of encountering the spirit of Agamemnon on the slopes of Mount Euboea, where he is said to wander seeking rest from the foul murder at the hand of his wife.

PERSEUS AND THE MEDUSA

The sacred founding of Mycenae is attributed to the hero Perseus, son of Zeus and Danae. Like many heroes, Perseus begins life under the cloud of a prophecy linking him to the death of a progenitor, in this case his grandfather Acrisius. These myths all express the natural cycle of fathers and the sons who seize power in the natural course of events. Informed of the prophecy, Acrisius confined his daughter Danae and her baby son Perseus in a wooden ark and put it to sea, hoping they would die. Like the child Moses and the Egyptians Isis and Horus, Danae and Perseus are saved, and Perseus sets out on his heroic journey.

As a young hero, Perseus must accept his spiritual heritage as a son of Zeus and overcome the temptations of destructive earthly desires, in his case represented by the terrible

Medusa, whose face turned all who looked upon it to stone. This stone was a symbol of spiritual death or the permanent sleep of the soul. Guided by Hermes and inspired by the wisdom of Athena, Perseus overcomes the Medusa by seeing her only in the reflection of his sacred shield. Seeing earthly desire only as a reflection of a greater reality permits the hero to awaken the soul to its proper destiny. Such is the nature of the sight of the soul. So Perseus was able to conquer the Medusa, acquire the love of the beautiful Andromeda, and became a king and noble leader of his people. After his adventures—here only briefly touched upon—Perseus became the king of Tiryns and founded Mycenae with the help of the Cyclops, who built the huge walls of the citadel.

TANTALUS AND PELOPS

The other major myth attached to Mycenae involves the figure of Tantalus, whose destiny it was to live in human memory as the most brutal of men. Tantalus was so close to Zeus (spiritual reality) that he was invited to dine with the gods on Olympus. In return, seeking to please the gods or, in other versions of the myth, to show his superiority over them, he sacrificed his son Pelops by cutting him up as a meal for the gods. Only Demeter, the Earth Mother, partook of the meal before the other gods discovered the sacrilege. As a punishment, Tantalus was eternally "tantalized," left hanging from a tree over water he could not drink and fruit which winds blew from his outstretched hand whenever he reached for some.

The myth of Tantalus and Pelops has been variously interpreted as the fall of man from divine grace and as the ritual dismemberment of the year-god in the cycle of seasons. Pelops was saved by the gods and restored to life with their divine protection. In this resurrection he echoes the myths of Dionysos, also dismembered and restored to life. Pelops became a consort to Zeus and eventually returned to earth as king of the Lydians and Phrygians near the Black Sea. His contribution to the myths of Mycenae was as father of Atreus and Thyestes, two brothers who were always rivals for the right to rule Mycenae.

ATREUS AND THYESTES

The great House of Perseus came to an end when his descendant Eurystheus went off from Mycenae to fight a war and was killed. The nobles of Mycenae chose Atreus as the new king, thus ushering in a new dynasty. Atreus and his combative brother Thyestes had sought sanctuary in Mycenae from Elis where Pelops was busy with intrigues of his own. The essential myths surrounding Atreus involve his efforts to solidify his claim to the throne at Mycenae against the efforts of Thyestes to dislodge him.

One such myth, coming to us from Apollodorus, reminds us of Minos and the white bull of Poseidon. Atreus had sworn to Artemis to sacrifice the finest sheep in his flock. Knowing of this oath, Hermes planted a horned lamb with a golden fleece among the herds, knowing that Atreus would be tempted to keep the lamb for himself. Once again we see a hero tempted to claim what rightly belongs to the spiritual realm. Atreus compromises by sacrificing the meat of the lamb but keeping the fleece for his own pleasure.

Thyestes stole the fleece and claimed kingship on the basis of its control. The fleece was a necessary element in the important rainmaking rituals conducted by the king. Whoever controlled the rain controlled the kingdom. Atreus countered this deception on the part of Thyestes by demonstrating control over even more elemental forces than rain. Atreus reversed the movement of the sun so that it set in the east. Such awesome control was seen as proof of his right to rule the kingdom. Thyestes was banished.

Myths involving the shift of the sun's path occur in many traditions. In the Hebrew Old Testament, in 2 Kings 20:1–11, Yahweh reverses the movement of the sun as a sign of His love of King Hezekiah and His intention to extend the king's reign for fifteen years. Such myths seem to relate to the reign of kings in the natural cycles of growth and decay. It is natural for kings to serve for a time (nine years is often the figure) and then to give way to their sons or to younger men. In this case Atreus righted a wrong by demonstrating his astronomical knowledge and power and thereby regained control of the kingdom.

THE HOUSE OF ATREUS

The myths of the House of Atreus take us through the darkest labyrinths of the human psyche and finally into the light of a new order of justice and divine mercy. It is a tale which haunts the stones of Mycenae and finds its resolution on the sunlit acropolis of Athens, where Orestes is cleansed of the blood of his ancestors.

The essential story begins with the birth of Agamemnon, son of Atreus and Aerope, who also bore Menelaus, future king of Sparta and husband of the beautiful Helen. Also in this story is Aegisthus, the incestuous son of Thyestes. It is Aegisthus who will seduce Clytemnestra, war bride of Agamemnon and mother of his four children: a son, Orestes, and three daughters, Electra, Iphigenia, and Chrysothemis.

The myths of Atreus and his descendants are linked as well to the famous judgment of Paris, the divine beauty contest won by Aphrodite and resulting in the abduction of Helen to Troy and the disastrous Trojan War. It is this campaign to regain Helen that forms the basis of Homer's epic poems and much of the subject matter of Classical tragedy. It is to Aeschylus and his famous trilogy, the

Oresteia, that we owe most of our understanding of these myths.

The Death of Agamemnon

There was never love between Agamemnon and Clytemnestra. Theirs was a marriage of power politics and war. It was made in violence and it ended in betrayal and death. Agamemnon, as king of the most powerful citadel in Greece, was chosen to lead the expedition against Troy. In order to gain favorable winds for the journey across the sea to Troy, Agamemnon sacrificed his daughter Iphigenia upon the altar of his own ambitions. It was this outrage that Clytemnestra cited to the people of Mycenae as justification for the assassination of her husband when he returned after ten years to sit once more on the throne.

But deeper than Clytemnestra's claim of revenge lay her lust for Aegisthus and his vengeful intrigues to seize power in Mycenae. After the fall of Troy, Agamemnon sailed home, preceded by signal fires set on a string of mountains to announce his arrival. He landed at Nauplia and took the ancient road to Mycenae, there to be greeted by his wife. Led to a warm bath and fresh garments, he was snared by a net and killed with the sacred double ax. The myth makes clear the parallel of the death of the king to the sacrifice of the sacred bull in Minoan ritual.

After the death of Agamemnon, Clytemnestra and Aegisthus ruled in Mycenae under the cloud of murder and the realization that the young Orestes had escaped and might someday return to avenge his father's murder. His sister Electra remained behind, crying out to the gods for *dike,* (dee-kay) the justice that must be done. Eventually, in the gods' good time, Orestes returned, disguised and guided by Apollo whose command was to kill his mother by stealth and deception.

Orestes and Electra lured their mother with the false news of the death of Orestes. Unaware, Clytemnestra welcomed Orestes, who after revealing himself to her, struck her down. The same fate awaited Aegisthus.

The Trial of Orestes

Rather than being able to assume the throne in Mycenae in his turn, Orestes was driven out by the avenging Furies, whose wrath descended upon him for the murder of his mother. Orestes sought shelter in the Temple of Apollo at Delphi, where the god sheltered him, but the Furies continued to sting him with guilt and retribution. Driven to Athens, Orestes was brought to trial as a matricide, and Athena resolved an impossible quandary by voting to absolve Orestes of his guilt. The cycle of death and vengeance was at last broken.

It is fitting that the myth of the House of Atreus ended outside the walls of Mycenae and that the citadel was left with the memory of the carnage which characterized its history. Soon after the death of Agamemnon, the Mycenaean citadels were burned and abandoned as centers of power. Certainly at their best, these outposts produced a heroic age that glorified the human capacity to achieve monumental results. That the age also produced monumental crimes of the spirit speaks to the loneliness of humanity once severed from its gods.

THE SITE

THE ARCHAEOLOGICAL RECORD

The story of excavation of Mycenae begins with Heinrich Schliemann and his vision of the Bronze Age as told by Homer in the *Iliad*. Schliemann was a German industrialist, whose financial success permitted him to spend his later years searching for the sites made famous by Homer. His successes at Troy and Mycenae make him the father of prehistoric Aegean archaeology. After Schliemann's world-famous discoveries at Troy in 1871, he turned his attention to Mycenae in 1874, and within two years he had excavated most of Grave Circle A, again with world-shaking results. His finds included the famous gold masks now on display at the National Museum in Athens.

It was not difficult for Schliemann to discover Mycenae because the site had always been known. Even in Classical times the Lion Gate was visible, enough exposed to reveal the monumental construction so typical of Mycenaean architecture and engineering. So awed were the later Greeks with these visible remains that they credited the construction of the gate and walls to the mythical Cyclops. We still refer to this type of construction as cyclopean.

In 1886, after Schliemann, B. C. Tsountas began his long-term work on the site, clearing most of the citadel and discovering over seventy chamber tombs. In this century, work was begun by the British School in 1920. In 1950, after the interruption of World War II, the British resumed work and discovered many more grave sites dated in the Late Helladic and Geometric periods. The Greek Archaeological Society began work at the same time, resulting in the discovery of Grave Circle B in 1951. Major discoveries were made under the supervision of George Mylonas beginning in 1958. Of particular interest was the discovery along the southern walls of rooms whose function was certainly religious. Thus, it was not really until the 1960s that we began to understand more about the sacred life of the Mycenaeans.

The Landscape and Citadel Hill

The site of the ancient citadel of Mycenae is approached either from the north, through the mountain pass from Corinth, or from the south from the modern city of Nauplia. Mycenae sits proudly at the northern end of the Argive Plain,

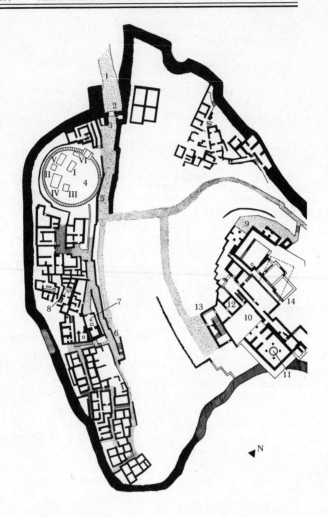

Fig. 16. Mycenae
1. *Outer Court*
2. *Lion Gate*
3. *Inner Court*
4. *Grave Circle A*
5. *The Great Ramp*
6. *Entrance to Cult Area*
7. *Shrine*
8. *Temple*
9. *Palace Propylon*

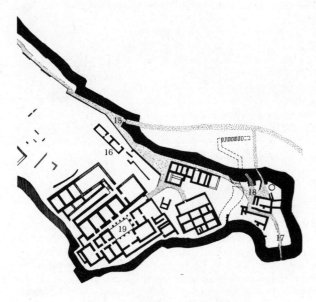

0   50   100   150 feet
├───┬───┬───┬───┬───┬───┬───┬──
0   10   20   30   40   50 meters

10. Great Court
11. Palace Megaron
12. Guest Chamber
13. Grand Staircase
14. Archaic Temple to Athena
15. North Gate
16. Storage Areas
17. North Sally Port
18. Underground Cistern
19. House of Columns

Approach to the Lion Gate, Mycenae, showing remains of cyclopean wall.

facing the citadel of Argos across the Inachos River and within sight of the Gulf of Argolis to the south.

At its back, rising 2,600 feet (800 m) on either side, are the mountains Marta and Zara. As Scully has argued so forcefully, this site embodies the ancient vision of the Earth Mother and affirms devotion to her power by the founders of Mycenae. Terra-cotta figurines of the Mycenaean goddess are commonly shown with upraised arms. That figure is represented in this landscape by the two mountains within whose protective shadow the fortress sits. The image of being protected within the conical mountain shapes is seen throughout Mycenaean sites, particularly in the *tholos* tombs, whose architecture embodies the form of the goddess in her function as underworld guide to the dead.

As the visitor approaches the Lion Gate, the conical Mount Zara is perfectly framed behind it. The triangle above the massive lintel appears as an image of the mountain. As articulated by the Minoans, whose influence is felt here, the column which appears in the sculpture is always associated with the goddess and is her symbol.

The Outer Court and Lion Gate

We know when we approach the citadel of Mycenae that we are in the presence of a fortress. We know about the structure of this bastion, but very little about its success in withstanding assaults. The assumption is that this fortress was never breached from without. The destruction which occurred in the twelfth century B.C. might well have been the result of betrayal from within. Certainly there was no breach in the outer walls that history or archaeology has

Detail of the Lion Gate, Mycenae, showing sacred column similar to Minoan architecture.

recorded. The famous walls of Troy were of similar construction and extent, and Homer recorded the ten-year attempt of the Achaeans to breach them. Finally, it was the ruse of the Trojan Horse that won entrance to the city. The walls held firm.

The fortification walls of Mycenae are thick and were much higher than they are today. In thickness the circuit walls averaged 20 feet (6 m). In height the walls probably averaged 40 feet (12 m), but nowhere is that height preserved in the present remains. Prior to the thirteenth century B.C. the walls were made of limestone. The present conglomerate walls were built over the limestone blocks around 1250 B.C. At this time the walls were extended to bring Grave Circle A within the walls of the fortress. The decision to bring the grave circle inside the fortress speaks to the sacred importance of the graveyard and to its valuable contents.

The Lion Gate presents the visitor with an awesome point of entrance. From a technical point of view, the Mycenaean engineers learned that the huge lintel would not break if the space above it was in some way relieved of the weight of the wall. The resulting sculpture is, then, both functional and emblematic. The triangle relieves the weight on the lintel, and it also represents a sacred emblem of power. The Minoan column, an image of the goddess, stands upon an altar. The two lions, front paws on the altar, frame the column. The missing heads were not carved from the same stone as the rest of the piece, but were most likely carved of steatite. They were fastened to the bodies by dowels, the holes for which are visible. It is most likely that the heads were lion heads rather than griffin heads, as some have speculated, in that the powerful modeling of the shoulders suggests a naturalistic carving of lions. The heads faced outward, looking right at the visitor approaching the gate.

The lintel itself, supporting this emblem, is a huge piece of conglomerate weighing 18 tons. It measures nearly 15 feet in length (4.5 m) and is 6½ feet thick (1.98 m). The supporting doorjambs are 10 feet high (3.1 m), making the doorway nearly square. Thick double doors, covered in glistening bronze, gave access through the gate. Pivot holes in the lintel show that the doors were mounted on beams fitted to the doorjambs. Also, holes in the jambs show that a large bar was used to lock the doors. This system of pivots and supports would have provided security against any attempt to use a battering ram to break the door.

Entrance and Grave Circle A

Inside the main gate, an area about 13 feet square (4 m) is marked out as an inner court. To the left is a small room whose position suggests a guardhouse, although the remains to the right form a more extensive set of rooms for that purpose, including stairs which gave access to the top of the walls. The room on the left may have been a shrine where persons entering or leaving the citadel marked the transition with prayer or offerings. However, Schliemann's excavations cleared these areas before more detailed studies could be done.

Grave Circle A was uncovered by Schliemann in 1876. Here, in several of the five shaft graves uncovered in that initial dig, Schliemann discovered the richest treasure in all of the history of Greek archaeological exploration. Among the gold cups, gold crowns, inlaid swords, and libation vessels were four gold burial masks, one of which Schliemann claimed as the death mask of Agamemnon (found in grave V). Only later was it learned that the masks had been placed on the bodies of more ancient kings or nobles of Mycenaean history. Grave Circle A dates from the sixteenth century B.C., with the last interment taking place in about 1500 B.C. Agamemnon would have ruled in the twelfth century.

Grave Circle A is part of a large cemetery which extends past Grave Circle B, well outside the walls to the south, but Circle A must have been regarded as very sacred to have been separated from the rest of the cemetery and enclosed within the new fortification walls. Such veneration makes it clear that the memory of former kings and great heroes gave strength to the present dynasty and to their belief in divine support.

Nearly 92 feet in diameter (28 m), the grave circle was a consciously designed enclosure intending to relate the geometric form of the circle to a sacred function, namely burial and ancestor worship. The graves were simple rectangular shafts sunk in the earth to various depths and not cut to any specific standards. In Circle A, six shaft graves have been

Exposed stonework of Grave Circle A, Mycenae, with shaft graves at various levels.

excavated, the sixth having been more recently discovered just to the right of the entrance. The circle was marked out by a low wall made of slabs, fitted vertically and horizontally. One horizontal slab to the left of the entrance shows the construction. Within the circle, a rubble wall snaked around the six shafts to mark the extent of the group in the circle and then was later covered over. Reconstruction of the circle also suggests that vertical slabs like modern tombstones were erected within the circle, possibly marking significant graves.

In all, the grave circles represent an important focus of Mycenaean life. The similarities to the Egyptian burial cults have not escaped scholars. In these graves, as in the *tholos* tombs much later, the soul is given food, weapons, wealth, and magic totems to overcome the terrors of the unknown. Although no sense of any heavenly destination is known in the Mycenaean religion, some belief in the soul's immortality is represented by this elaborate burial cult. The open nature of the grave circles and their prominent position within the fortress also suggest some ceremonial cult activity.

The Great Ramp

From the Lion Gate and running along beside the grave circle is the Processional Way of the citadel. The route of this major road within the fortress connects the Lion Gate to the North Gate and to the two gates of the most important areas in the citadel: the hilltop palace and the lower cult area containing temple and shrine activity. Fifteen steps take the visitor up to the cobbled ramp and to the top of the first slope. Continuing to the east, straight ahead, the ramp descends to the cult center.

To the left the ramp climbs the slope and divides, the left

Newly discovered cult area along fortress wall, Mycenae.

branch going down and around to the north gate and the right branch continuing the ascent to the palace. From the location of the supposed propylon of the palace, it would appear that the official entrance was on the north side. Residents would most likely have turned right here and entered the palace from the south, bypassing the propylon.

The Cult Center

Recent excavation by Mylonas and his associates, including Lord William Taylour, have revealed a whole new world within the citadel of Mycenae. The area to the south of the palace, served by the processional way and by a series of formal ramps and entrances, is now understood to have been a cult center. This designation describes an area uncovered in 1968 and 1969 which strongly suggests the existence of a temple and shrine rooms where religious activity took place. Such a discovery is important because it is the first major evidence of Minoan-Mycenaean religious practice outside of the royal palace quarters. No doubt shrines existed on the hilltop in Mycenae as well, but here, below the palace, we find a separate area served by priests and designed for ritual and sacrifice.

The cult center is reached by following the ramp until it encounters scattered rubble which finally gives way to grass and becomes a worn trail snaking down to the retaining walls of the first buildings. The original ramp has been discovered and cleared away. It was reached by a set of stairs and a door, the threshold of which still exists. The ramp turned sharply back to the west and then turned once again to the southeast. At this point the visitor may be stopped from further investigation, unless the Greek Archaeological Society has recently opened the site. But the nature of the area can be determined from this vantage point.

If the area is now open, access to the so-called temple is provided by a recently installed set of stairs. The rooms involved are quite complex in design, with several levels and small alcoves where many unique figurines were discovered. The most interesting of these was a tall (2 foot) clay goddess with raised arms and ugly demeanor, perhaps chthonic in character. She is hollow at the base, and it has been suggested that these idols might have been designed to be fitted on poles to be carried during ceremonies, but no evidence has yet appeared to show such usage.

In the original finds of this area were also many clay snakes, quite realistically modeled, which supports the view that Mycenaean religious practice included the worship of household snakes, a common Greek practice in Archaic and Classical times. Snakes were associated with healing and with the mysteries of immortality. Thus, here in the cult center, where libation tables, idols, and other common cult features were found, scholars are finding the connections between Mycenaean and later Greek culture. It is quite likely that this cult center was related to burial and that the character and position of the temples and shrines were meant to suggest earlier Minoan cave sanctuaries.

The Palace

Back on the processional way, the visitor may approach the palace from the traditional entrance at the northern propylon. Here the ancient visitor to the palace was directed into a narrow set of entrances and rooms which only after many turns and corridors lead to the King's Megaron. Adjacent areas, no longer visible, were also accessible from this entrance. The porch of the propylon was supported by a single column, and we are reminded of the west porch entrance at Knossos and of the goddess whose image the column represented.

The Court

After the propylon, a stairway to the left, now gone, gave access to a corridor and rooms adjacent to the megaron. Another corridor went straight ahead, turned left, and led to the courtyard, the true beginning of the royal quarters. The open courtyard resembles a tower in that it sits above the slope of the hill and commands a magnificent view of the valley to the west. To stand here and survey the Argive Plain is to feel the power possessed by the occupants of this citadel.

The conical hill across the valley is the cone of Argos. To the right, due west, is Mount Artemision, nearly 6,000 feet high (1,770 m). The rugged land to the west is Arcadia, sacred to Artemis, whose anger at the House of Atreus caused its eventual destruction. The image of the reclining goddess, outlined by the receding hills, haunts the western horizon.

The Megaron

East of the court, entered through two porticoes, is the Megaron, the central room of the palace. The stone bases of two wooden columns remain to show the construction of the portico entrance to the Megaron. This main room measured 42 feet (13 m) long and 37 feet (11.5 m) wide. Typical of Mycenaean palaces, the center of the Megaron is taken up by a wide (11 feet, 3.3 m) circular hearth, above which would have been a chimney or roof opening to allow smoke to escape. Evidence of the hearth is presently marked by a partial ring of stones in the floor. Note, too, the bases of four columns which supported the roof of the Megaron.

What remained of the Megaron has allowed some reconstruction of the appearance of the room. Fragments of frescoes depicting scenes of war were discovered covering the northern wall. The king's throne stood at the center of the south wall. Custom suggests that similar thrones were provided for distinguished guests. Tables for food and stands for wine and other vessels for libation were carried in according to the need. The floor was decorated with stucco, no doubt brightly colored. We have the oral tradition of Homer to tell us something of the interior of these resplendent megarons. In Book Four of the *Odyssey,* Telemakhos and Peisistratos are prepared for their welcome to the court of Menelaus at Sparta:

> What a brilliant place
> that mansion of the great prince seemed to them!
> A-glitter everywhere, as though with fiery
> points of sunlight, lusters of the moon.
> The young men gazed in joy before they entered
> into a room of polished tubs to bathe.
> Maidservants gave them baths, anointed them,
> held out fresh tunics, cloaked them warm; and soon
> they took tall thrones beside the son of Atreus.
> Here a maid tipped out water for their hands
> from a golden pitcher into a silver bowl,
> and set a polished table near at hand;
> the larder mistress with her tray of loaves
> and savories came, dispensing all her best,
> and then a carver heaped their platters high
> with various meats, and put down cups of gold.

Such was the splendor of life in the Megaron. Indeed, when the feasting was finished and the hearth died down to glowing embers, guests went off to sleep in the *xenon* or guest room of the palace, which is preserved to the west of the Megaron on the other end of the open court. The king would have retired to his private quarters, which were above the Megaron to the north. Both of these quarters were furnished with a private bath and a private open court.

THE ARCHAIC TEMPLE

On the summit of the citadel are the foundations of the Archaic temple to Athena erected during the sixth century B.C. Doric in style, the temple was oriented to the northeast (more east than north) and probably was aimed at the rising of the Pleiades, the constellation in Taurus which rises in the east with the sun to mark Athena's feast day. The importance of this temple for Mycenae is that it was probably placed on the ruins of a hilltop shrine associated with the rites performed by the king in his official function as chief priest.

The North Section

Too many visitors to Mycenae reach the palace and end their explorations there. But much more remains to be examined, in particular the impressive North Gate, the adjacent storage areas, the north sally port, and the famous secret cistern, one of the most remarkable pieces of engineering of the Mycenaean era.

The North Gate and Magazines

A well-worn path across the top of the citadel leads down toward the North Gate. On the right, in the eastern section of the complex, lie the remains of houses which were occupied by artisans. The closest ruins were workshops. The farther foundations are of a more elegant dwelling, with a peristyle courtyard. The latest speculation is that these rooms were part of the palace and were connected to the hilltop rooms. The so-called House of Columns might have

The North Gate, without relieving triangle, Mycenae.

been part of the royal household, perhaps the queen's megaron.

Continuing down the slope to the northwest brings us to the North Gate. Here again is the same style of construction as the Lion Gate, with the exception that the huge lintel stone is not "relieved" by a triangle above it. Rather, two stones were placed so as to leave a space just above the lintel and force the rock-splitting weight onto the two supporting posts. The modern double doors give some sense of how the originals were placed. The gateway is designed in such a way as to prevent large numbers of invaders from converging on the wooden doors at the same time. Inside the gate is a similar square court as that at the main gate, and again a small room on the left, serving either as a guardhouse or a shrine.

Nearby, partially hidden by the remains of the cyclopean wall, are storage rooms, some still containing amphorae found during excavations. The area gives an indication of the relationship between the wall and storage rooms built into it all along the perimeter. These rooms would have been filled during time of siege and would also have contained the stored wealth of the citadel.

The Sally Ports and Cistern

At the eastern extreme of the citadel are two narrow doors cut into the wall. The arched design is called corbel vaulting. These doors were intended to be hidden from the outside and were evidently used to allow defenders to leave the citadel to confront attackers outside the walls.

When long sieges were perhaps more common and a regular water supply meant survival, the Mycenaeans dug beneath the wall and deep into the slope to the level of the groundwater, there building a secret cistern which served the citadel. The engineering of this cistern is remarkable. It is still possible to descend to the level of the cistern, but a flashlight and steady nerves are both necessary. When Henry Miller made his visit to Mycenae just before World War II, he declined to visit the cistern:

> We have just come up from the slippery staircase, Katsimbalis and I. We have not descended it, only peered down with lighted matches. The heavy roof is buckling with the weight of time. To breathe too heavily is enough to pull the world down over our ears. . . . I refuse to go back down into that slimy well of horrors. Not if there were a pot of gold to filch would I make the descent.

Miller expresses something of the foreboding felt in this descent into the underworld, still full of myth and power. But the actual fact of this tunnel and the wonder of its construction may overcome the natural fears. There are three turns in the descent. The first cut is through the wall, sixteen steps to a landing, then a left turn down twenty steps to another landing to a sharp right turn for the major descent of fifty-four steps to the cistern. The well is 16½ feet deep (5 m).

The Tholos Tombs

There are nine *tholos* tombs in the vicinity of Mycenae, four of which may be conveniently visited. In the immediate area of the main gate are two tombs, one called the Tomb of Aegisthus and the other the Tomb of Clytemnestra. To the north of the Tomb of Aegisthus and across the road is the Lion Tomb. The most important and impressive of all the tombs, the Treasury of Atreus, is located farther to the south, down the main road. It should be noted right away that these names have little to do with their actual history. These are local names, attached to the tombs by way of connecting the mythology of the citadel and the tales of Homer.

The *tholos* tombs are later in construction and use than the two grave circles in the ancient cemetery. In general the tombs date from 1550 B.C. to 1200 B.C. Since the tombs have long since been pillaged, it is not known what family might have laid claim to them. Burials did occur according to dynasty, and tombs were opened and closed several times in order to bury members of one family.

Tomb Construction

It is evident that these royal tombs were part of the sacred traditions of the Mycenaean peoples. Their roundness expressed the sacred nature of the passage to a higher life for privileged persons. The lesser chamber tombs which dot the countryside are rectangular or are simply shaped to fit the terrain and rock into which they were dug. The *tholos* tombs, however, were dug into the rock in perfect form, overcoming the geological challenges confronting the builders.

The first step in building a tomb was to select a proper place in terms of landscape features. The most important of the tombs, Atreus, faces Mount Zara and is itself a conical hill, creating its own sacred image. The builders fixed a point, a sacred act of locating the spiritual center of the tomb complex, and inscribed the circle which would be the diameter of the tomb. Then they dug down from the top of

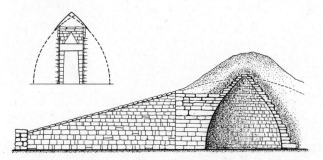

Fig. 17. *The precision of construction shown in* tholos *tombs, Mycenae. Evidence shows almost no shifting of stones over three thousand years.*

the hill, carrying the dirt and rock away until the level of the surrounding terrain was reached. This gave a cleared area, perfectly round, with the entranceway or *dromos* serving as the access for the sledging of the stones which would form the beehive shape.

In geometric terms, the shape of the beehive tomb was determined by placing a stake at the edge of the tomb circle, extending a cord through the center to the opposite edge, and inscribing an arc upward to the top or a point above the center. This arc dictates the incline of the tomb as it rises, but only to a point several feet from the very top, where the peak is formed. At this point the arc is surrendered in order to accommodate the needs of holding up the completed arch. The proper distribution of the weight required that a perfect triangle complete the roof.

This method of construction meant that the tomb had to be constructed within a cleared space and that scaffolding be used to raise each level. In the Atreus tomb, the huge lintel stone over the door weighs at least 120 tons. The logical answer to the perennial question of how that stone was placed is to see it moving slowly into position up a ramp built into the side of the hill. In this sacred undertaking the stones were moved in the fullness of time and without strain.

The Tombs of Aegisthus and Clytemnestra

Aside from the specific measurements of these tombs, which differ slightly, the major differences between the two are age and condition. The Aegisthus tomb is the oldest of the group, and its collapsed condition reflects, perhaps, a less advanced knowledge of construction. The tomb can be examined from the top since its vault has collapsed. The process of final vaulting must have been a matter of experimentation over many years, perhaps centuries, until the correct balance between weight distribution and ceiling angle was reached.

The Clytemnestra tomb is the newest or most recent in this immediate area, having been completed around 1250 B.C., the same time as the Lion Gate and expanded fortifications. Some restoration work has repaired the vaulting in this tomb, above the height of 28 feet (8.5 m). One notable feature of this tomb's construction is the band of wider blocks at the level of the lintel, so constructed as to provide a firmer base for the rest of the vaulting.

During the third century B.C., the Hellenistic occupants of the area constructed a theatre nearby, one row of which can be detected above the *dromos* of the tomb. The placement of the theatre suggests that the existence of this tomb remained unsuspected until the nineteenth century when it was discovered by the Turkish landlords then in power.

The Treasury of Atreus

Here we have the finest expression of the *tholos* tomb, the apex as well of Mycenaean sacred architecture. The con-

Monumental stone set as foundation for the dromos *of the tomb of Atreus, Mycenae.*

struction of this tomb was so precise and exact in its detail that in the three thousand years of its existence, the tomb has not settled an inch, so firm are its foundations and fixed its vaulting. Also, like the fabled acoustics of the theatre at Epidauros, so too the sound quality of this tomb seems quite magical.

If the visitor is fortunate enough to be alone in the tomb or a group can focus its attention on the quality of the sound, then someone whispering along the wall can be heard throughout the tomb because the structure functions like an amplifier. A foot simply turning in the dirt of the floor sounds like the grinding of huge stones. Whether or not this quality of sound had any significance or purpose is unknown. But one can imagine that chanting of funeral hymns in this space would have been imposing and very powerful.

The Dromos *and Doorway*

The entrance to the tomb, cut into the natural side of the hill of Panayitsa, is nearly 120 feet (35 m) long and 20 feet (6 m) wide. As is evident some of the conglomerate blocks which line the walls are of monumental size. The stone on the right of the entrance, for example, is 20 feet long (6 m) and 4 feet high (1.25 m). The doorway, still in excellent condition, measures 17.7 feet high (5.4 m) and 8.8 feet wide (2.45 m) at the threshold and is slightly narrower at the top. The doorway was decorated with elaborate designs, fragments of which are in the National Archaeological Museum in Athens and the British Museum in London. As the column base on the left side of the door reveals, the door was framed by two half-columns, cut of green stone and elaborately carved. Above the door, where the relieving triangle is now revealed, two more half-columns and a decorated panel completed the facade.

Dromos *of the tomb of Atreus, with relieving triangle and trapezoidal doorway, Mycenae.*

The threshold to the tomb is an interesting construction. Two pieces of conglomerate were placed against the door-jambs and then wedged into place by pieces of limestone, driven into the space so as to press the conglomerate blocks out against the jambs. Also worth noting carefully is the subtle carving around the door, including the lintel stone, to fuse each individual block into the whole design.

The major circle of the tomb measures 48 feet in diameter (14.6 m) and the height at the center measures just over 44 feet (13.5 m). There are thirty-three rings of conglomerate blocks making up the corbel vaulting. Many of the blocks show holes and bronze nails used to mount the gold and bronze decorations—rosettes and spiral designs typical of Minoan and Mycenaean sacred architecture.

On the north side of the chamber is a side room, rectangular in shape, 20 feet square (6 m), a rare occurrence in such *tholos* tombs. Some speculate that in multiple burials, the bones of earlier occupants may have been moved to this chamber in order to clear the main chamber for the new ceremonies and bodies. It has been suggested, for example, that the Mycenaeans believed that as long as the flesh clung to the bones, the soul remained with the body, but when the bones were bare, the soul had fled and the bones could be moved with impunity.

The Funeral Cult

If we imagine the Atreus tomb, newly prepared and open to receive its first occupant, we can fit the details into a general picture. The following account is given in Lord William Taylour's *The Mycenaeans* and was compiled from several sources:

"The great bronze doors with their gilded bosses would be swung back to receive the cortege and in the dim light the vault with horizontal bands of bronze would gleam with a thousand gold rosettes. Spread out on the earthen floor was a carpet of gold to receive the body of the king, arrayed in his robes of state, crowned with his diadem, his seals of office attached to his wrist, and his favorite dagger at his side. Around him would be laid the vessels of food, the flagons of wine, jars of oil and unguent, and all the necessities for the sustenance and care of the body on his last journey. Weapons of war would be added too: swords, rapiers, daggers, and spears, the mighty figure-of-eight shield, the well-stocked quiver, and the bow.

"One rapier had a special task to perform. It is taken from the pile and to the words of a solemn incantation the blade is bent so that its spirit may be released and be swift to do battle for its master, should threatening demons bar his way. Then the signal is given for the slaughter of the horses that had drawn the chariot with the bier, and that have been fidgeting nervously in the *dromos,* apprehensive of the doom that awaits them. There follows the slaying of the rams and other sacrificial beasts within the vaulted tomb itself. The fires are lit, the sacrifices roasted, and all partake of the funeral banquet. In the still glowing embers the mourners cast their last tributes to the dead, and then withdraw."

After the ceremony, the great door was sealed, using smallish blocks, and then the entire *dromos* was filled in, making the hill look natural once again. For subsequent burials, the *dromos* would be cleared again and the door unsealed. Such labors occasioned the death of kings.

The Museum

The new museum at Mycenae opened in the summer of 1988. Mycenaean artifacts are being transferred there from the National Archaeological Museum in Athens and the museum in Nauplia.

3
THE TEMPLE
CULTURES

With the decline of the palace cultures of Crete and the mainland in 1100 B.C., the Minoan-Mycenaean world went into eclipse. A darkness spread over the Aegean world for a period of four hundred years, and the territory that was to become Greece transformed itself from a palace culture similar to other Mediterranean cultures to a wholly new world. During this dark age, migrations from the north and east continued. A brew of new ideas, new values, new gods, and new economic conditions spawned a new culture, but very little of the change was recorded and almost nothing of the transformation left its mark in the archaeological record.

The major development, the *polis,* or Greek city-state seemed to emerge as if from some obscure laboratory. Historians have been able to explain the development in general terms, but the mystery remains as to how the *polis* actually emerged as an idea and a fact of civilization. Some say that in the aftermath of chaos from the destruction of the palaces, aristocratic families joined in leagues for defense, establishing settlements surrounding the important sacred sites.

TEMPLES AND SANCTUARIES

The most evident changes during the Dark Age were the decline of the palaces as centers of religious power and the emergence of the temple sanctuaries in their place. The priest-king gave way to the unmanifested god, and the temple sanctuaries, which had been minor adjuncts to the palace, now emerged as the prominent feature of the acropolis, the sacred high ground of the city. The secular dwellings moved off the acropolis and became prosaic in design, although some country villas were impressive enough.

Since the temple was designed to house a god and not a priest-king and his retainers, the design features changed accordingly. The temple emerged as a holy sanctuary with areas of limited accessibility, all covered over with a wide roof supported by columns. The design and placement of the

Engraving of the western facade of the Parthenon, Acropolis, Athens.

temple in the landscape elevated the mind of the worshipper to the holy purpose and called upon the god to manifest himself or herself for the benefit of the pious in attendance. Architecture became the sculpted likeness of the god.

THE NEW REALITY

The culture which emerged after the Bronze Age was in many respects modern. Iron was in common use now to make weapons, household goods, and temple fittings. Cremation replaced elaborate burial of the dead, who vanished from memory into the void. The gods themselves became distant powers unrelated to daily life. Epic poetry was sung describing heroic deeds of the past, of a time not connected with present culture. Political power was held by aristocratic, landowning families who shared power and raised armies to protect their interests.

And yet there existed a minority view, a minor world in which the spiritual values and powers once so central to the culture now were kept alive by a new elite. This group of priests, poets, architects, and aristocrats came to prominence as the philosophers and statesmen of the Classical Period. It is their monuments of language and stone which remain for us to examine and cherish. The significance of their work was preserved after the decline of the Roman Empire by the scholars of Islam, who with patience and dedication cherished the essential truth of the ancient knowledge until Renaissance scholars discovered it once more.

ATHENS

Modern Athens is hard to love, especially in the heat of a summer day, in the haze of car and bus exhaust, when this city of over three million swells to six as it does in the height of the tourist season. Visitors in the hot months are advised to plan their tours of the many treasures to be found here in the early morning and late afternoon. Midday is for rest, trips to the close islands, or a visit to the National Archaeological Museum. But late at night in the twisting streets of the Plaka and in the restaurants set up in the small quiet squares, far away from the tourist cafés in Omonia Square, the city turns on its charm and becomes not only friendly but inviting.

Life has always been a struggle for the Greeks. The land yields its fruit sparingly, and each year the sprouting of new grain and fruit blossoms is greeted with religious celebration. To the devout, Easter affirms the hope of a new crop each spring. Because the countryside is grudging in its support, many Greeks have had to migrate to the city to earn a living, exchanging their attachment to the land for the demands of the service industries which support the tourist trade.

Without planning or restraint Athens has grown away from its acropolis to cover the surrounding hills and spill into the connecting valleys. Most of the construction consists of gray concrete with narrow balconies used on summer nights to catch a breath of breeze from the sea. Despite its sprawl and noise, Athens is still a Mediterranean city and has a slower pace hidden beneath its frantic need to compete in the Common Market. So on summer nights, when business ends, each neighborhood collects itself in its square, tablecloths are spread on folding tables, and space is created for a more leisurely way of life. Supper runs very late, often past midnight, and it is always surprising to see the snarls of traffic on the roads so early the next morning as Athenians race to work after only a few hours of sleep.

THE ANCIENT SITES

The ancient treasures of Athens center on its acropolis, where the Parthenon still sits gleaming, even though huge

The Acropolis, Athens, seen from below, with the Roman arches of the Odeion of Herodes Atticus in the foreground.

cranes shift rubble in the middle of its inner sanctum. But a complete experience of Archaic, Classical, and Hellenistic Athens includes much more than an admission ticket to the Acropolis, and visitors are urged to schedule enough time to see and absorb the full spectrum of this remarkable ancient culture.

Surrounding the Acropolis, which contains the Parthenon, Propylaia, Erechtheion, and Museum, are the ancient Theatre of Dionysos, the Asklepieion, the Odeion of Herod Atticus, the ancient Agora, the Areopagus, the Kerameikos or ancient cemetery, the Pnyx, where the debates of the Athenian democracy took place, and the Olympieion, sanctuary of the great temple of Zeus. To the north, outside the ancient Dipylon Gate, lie the remains of Plato's Academy, seldom visited and nearly lost in the winding commercial streets.

In addition to the Acropolis Museum, there are two other important museums containing ancient artifacts: the Agora Museum, beautifully situated in the renovated Stoa of Attalos, and the National Archaeological Museum, home of the major collection of ancient treasures in Greece.

HISTORY

The recorded history of Athens takes us back to Neolithic times, in the Third Millennium, before the Mycenaean kings and before any Minoan influence. Neolithic remains discovered on the slopes of the Acropolis point to continuous settlement of the hill from at least 2800 B.C. Clearly, the earliest settlers recognized the advantages of this site, protected as it is by the surrounding mountains, elevated off the plain for defense, and provided with ample water from springs within the hill.

In Mycenaean times, the palace stood on the hilltop, probably next to the site of the ancient Temple of Athena, the remains of which were discovered between the present Parthenon and the Erechtheion, which was named after Erechtheus, an early, legendary king of Athens. Evidence suggests that the early Temple of Athena was part of a sacred enclosure connected to the Mycenaean palace.

In the Dorian invasions, after the Trojan War in the twelfth century B.C., Athens withstood attacks on the Acropolis and managed to adjust to the effects of radical change which convulsed all of the Hellenic world. The last king of Athens, Kodros the Pylian, was killed defending the Acropolis against the Dorians, who never did win a complete victory over the Athenians. Indeed, the identity of the Athenian stock has always presented a mystery for historians and anthropologists. Those who claim kinship to the original clans and families who made up the earliest population seem to be indigenous, although very little evidence beyond certain linguistic clues provides more information.

RULE BY THE FEW AND THE MANY

The form of government which history records after the Bronze Age resembles an oligarchy in which authority rested with *archons*, officials who shared power and administered the business of the city. The *archons* were chosen by the leading families from their own number and served an indefinite time. In general, the *archons* divided their responsibilities into secular, religious, and military areas of rule. The effect of this form of divided authority was to remove leadership from sacred ground, hence the shift of power from the Acropolis to the Agora, which from the Archaic period onward became the center of all secular and some religious life.

Oligarchy as a form of government served Athens throughout most of its history. Rule by the few, the *aristoi*, varied in its details and flexibility, sometimes leaning heavily on the people, but more often tending to tyranny. Cycles of repression and freedom have characterized Athenian government from Mycenaean times to the present. Democratic impulses have always played an important part in Athens' struggles for independence.

INVASION AND DESTRUCTION

In the summer of 480 B.C., a date which marks the end of the Archaic Period, the Persians overran Athens and destroyed the sacred buildings on the Acropolis before they in turn were defeated by the Greeks at Salamis and Plataea. Although not the first time that the defenses on the Acropolis had been successfully breached, this defeat and subsequent destruction were deeply felt by those Athenians who had wisely fled the attack and then returned to view the desecration of their sacred shrines. They resolved to let the ruins stand as a reminder of this outrage, but they buried the beautiful sculptures which had adorned the sanctuaries. Many were subsequently discovered thousands of years later when excavation began, and they now reside in the Acropolis Museum.

PERICLEAN ATHENS

What took place under the leadership of Pericles in the fifth century B.C. in Athens has already been described in the Historical Overview. This period was the apex of Athenian history, and what we see today around the Acropolis dates mainly from this period of monumental construction, public debate, and artistic achievement. The Walls of Themistocles, for example, rose on the Acropolis to protect against further Persian attack. Portions of former temples were used, especially on the north side where column drums are fitted alongside regular blocks to form the wall. The Parthenon (447–438 B.C.), the Propylon, and the Temple of Athena Nike were completed during this time, with the Erechtheion finally finished at the close of the century.

FROM ROMAN TO TURKISH RULE

Athens declined in power and influence after the fifth century B.C., although it continued to host many of history's great minds, Plato and Aristotle being the most prominent. During the rule of Alexander, the Roman invasions and subsequent domination, the Acropolis and the city surrounding it rose and fell with the whims and curses of conquerors. In A.D. 429 the Acropolis ceased to be a place where the Olympian gods were worshipped. Christian basilicas replaced the temples and the architectural profile of the hill changed forever.

After the fall of Rome, Athens fell victim to invader after invader until Greek independence was finally achieved in 1833. First, the Crusades passed through in 1204, followed by the Franks, the Turks, and the Venetians, who in 1688 destroyed the Parthenon when a cannon shot ignited gunpowder being stored there by the Turks. Had not this explosion occurred, the Parthenon would be complete, or nearly so, today.

MYTHOLOGY

The mythology of Athens tells the moving story of a city and a people born to excel and fated to suffer and find redemption in tolerance and acceptance of that suffering. It is the story of glorious deeds, terrible defeats, and a unique spiritual destiny. The hero and king Theseus is the embodiment of this myth, and his story is the story of the city. It seems certain that a Theseus did rule as king in Athens during the Bronze Age and did consolidate the towns in Attica into an expanded and powerful *polis*.

THE HERO AND THE SPIRITUAL PATH

Theseus was the spiritual son of Poseidon, the god whose power ruled the sea and whose separation from Zeus the father parallels the human separation from the divine. Theseus was the earthly son of Aegeus, king of Athens, but he was born secretly in Corinth through the magic of the sorceress Medea. Theseus grew to manhood away from Athens and without knowledge of his patrimony. Against the day when Theseus might be strong enough to undertake the life of a hero, Aegeus had hidden a sword and a pair of sandals beneath a huge rock, there to be discovered and used if the young man was capable.

When Theseus visited Delphi as a youth, he demonstrated the necessary qualities to become a hero. Shown the rock which covered the spiritual symbols of his heroic quest, he moved it easily, took the tokens, and followed the road to Athens. On the way he met and destroyed various monsters, including Sciron, who bore a huge club used to kill wayfarers. Theseus seized the club, and after killing Sciron with it, used it to fight his way to Athens. The substitution of the club for the spiritual sword signifies a love for earthly power with its more sensual rewards and the hero's connection to the figure of Herakles.

As a guest at a banquet in Athens, Theseus drew his sword to slice a piece of beef and was recognized by Aegeus who proclaimed him son and heir to the Athenian throne. The rest of the now familiar tale forms an important part of the mythology of Crete, and the tale of Theseus and the Minotaur appears in the mythology of Knossos.

This myth, with its blend of success and failure, shows the typical path of the hero seeking earthly and spiritual glory. Theseus is tempted by earthly fame and turns his back on true wisdom. His betrayal of Ariadne, who showed him the secret of the labyrinth, demonstrates the blinding effects of earthly fame and the inability to recognize spiritual guidance.

THESEUS AND PERSEPHONE

The accounts of Theseus are extensive and powerful, full of his love affairs, military victories, and political triumphs. Another myth serves to show how his spiritual quest takes him, as it does all true heroes, to the underworld where he must encounter his own mortality. Since the abduction of prized possessions was a heroic pastime, guaranteed to incite warfare among neighboring city-states, Theseus and his companion-in-arms Peirithous set out to make new conquests. Their first adventure took them to Arcadia, where they insulted the Dioscuri, Castor and Polydeuces, who ruled Sparta, by carrying off the beautiful Helen, then just a child.

Some years later, seeking to know if he would ever marry Helen, whom he had hidden away, Theseus consulted an oracle of Zeus who trapped Theseus and his companion by suggesting that the adventurers seek instead to win the release of Persephone from Hades. Persephone's presence in Hades was a result of natural law, a union of chthonic and Olympian powers, resulting in her presence in Hades for four months of the year. Such an attempt by mortals would have been an outrage, and when Theseus appeared in Hades he was confined to a stone seat, fused to it so that movement was impossible. He was, in effect, bound to the earth. Confinement to this stone seat, the Chair of Forgetfulness, signified his complete loss of spiritual awareness.

Theseus gained his freedom from this mortal bondage through the heroic intervention of Herakles, who literally ripped him from the stone seat to set him free. This rescue was another example of the special bond between Herakles and Theseus, a binding friendship which overcame many difficult trials. This theme of the special bond which exists between those who have suffered is seen again in the story of Theseus and Oedipus, that suffering hero whose misery knew no bounds.

THESEUS AND OEDIPUS

When Oedipus was forced to leave Thebes after the revelations of his terrible deeds, he wandered homeless with his daughter Antigone for twenty years, until one day he came upon the sacred grove of the Eumenides at Colonus, a small town just one mile north of the Sacred Gate into Athens. Here Oedipus vowed to remain, knowing in his newfound wisdom that the gods had destined him to die in this place.

His terrible appearance frightened the local elders, who called King Theseus to come to their aid and to decide the terrible question of whether or not Athens should grant refuge to a man such as Oedipus. Theseus, in his wisdom, saw that this blind old man would bring a special gift, his unparalleled suffering, to the Athenian people, and he pledged to honor Oedipus as a citizen by granting him an honored burial and eternal rest for his bones. This insight was meant to demonstrate the special wisdom achieved by the Athenians as a result of their collective suffering and their protection by Athena, goddess of wisdom.

These myths describe the struggles and suffering of

Athens itself. The sense of adventure, the spiritual promise darkened by arrogance, the glorious victories tempered by the wisdom of moderation and justice, these all reflect the history of this great city.

THE SITES

THE ACROPOLIS

> *Not Magnitude, not lavishness*
> *But form, the site;*
> *Not innovating willfulness,*
> *But reverence for the archetype.*
> —HERMAN MELVILLE, 1857

One always has the sense in approaching the Acropolis of Athens of being in the company of all mankind. It is one of the universal places, where the collective mind and soul meet and gather to a point of perception. Even the most dull of heart have been transformed by this space. As a sacred place, divinity was attracted and made manifest here. Athena, in particular, was manifested in this site. She was goddess of the city, protectress, source of wisdom, nurturer of greatness, and dispenser of justice.

There are three ancient monuments left standing on the Acropolis: the Propylaia, including the Temple of Athena Nike; the Erechtheion, containing the famous Karyatides statues (these are all reproductions but four of the original statues are in the Acropolis Museum); and the Temple of Athena Parthenos, more commonly called the Parthenon. In addition, and sometimes neglected by hurried visitors, there is the modern Acropolis Museum, which houses friezes from the Parthenon and many fine archaic statues from the period before 480 B.C. One *kore,* or statue of a young girl, in particular, is a highlight of a visit to Greece. She is the famous Almond-Eyed *Kore,* sculpted in 500 B.C. The purity and grace of this statue demonstrate the highest standards in sacred Greek art.

EXCAVATION AND RESTORATION

Foundations of earlier temples, sections of wall and carefully marked rows of marble blocks attest to the years of excavation and research. After Greek independence from the Turks was achieved in 1833, restoration work on the Acropolis was begun. First, years of "foreign" construction had to be cleared away to expose the ancient ruins. The first major piece of work was the restoration of the Temple of Athena Nike, which had been torn down in 1687 in order to strengthen the fortification walls.

Beginning in 1885 archaeologists began clearing the hilltop down to bedrock. This standard technique of excavation sifts the various levels of construction in order to establish accurate dating of building foundations and artifacts discovered at each level. During this period of investigation the rich finds of sculpture buried after the destruction of 480 B.C. were discovered. Beginning in 1895 actual reconstruction began on several monuments, particularly the Parthenon, which had been damaged severely by an earthquake in 1894. Work on the site has been continuous ever since, except for the period of World War II.

Today a cooperative effort by many nations, institutions, and individuals continues the work of restoration and repair. The major concern on the Acropolis is the condition of the marble, which is deteriorating from the acid content of the air in Athens. Automotive exhaust, held over the city by the bowl of surrounding mountains, is eating away those monuments which remain outside and exposed. Some necessary precautions have been taken to minimize the damage. For example, visitors may no longer walk on or touch the Parthenon or the Erechtheion. The Karyatides have been removed from the Erechtheion, preserved in the Acropolis Museum, and replaced by reproductions.

THE SACRED WAY

Let us picture for a moment the Panathenaia, the celebration of the birth of the city, which took place every year in July, the beginning of the Athenian year. Every fourth year the Greater Panathenaia took place to signify a Panhellenic principle of the birth and death of kings. This festival formed in a great procession north of the Agora at the Dipylon Gate. It made its way through the Agora to the northwest corner of the Acropolis walls, past the Klepsydra Spring, and then up a winding path to the main entrance to the Acropolis.

The procession was rendered on the great frieze of the Parthenon and showed the extent of the participation from all elements in the city. Horsemen, elders, young boys, and especially the young girls of Athens processed, the latter carrying the new robe, the *peplos*, for the statue of Athena. The sacrifice of many sheep and bulls at the great altar provided an unaccustomed feast of meat for the populace of the city, which gathered for the collective banquet in the Agora. But the important moments of the celebration came with the approach of the procession up the Sacred Way to the Propylaia and then into the sanctuary of the Temple of Athena Parthenos.

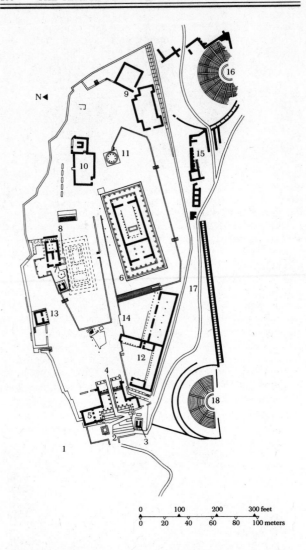

Fig. 18. *The Acropolis, Athens*

1. *Klepsydra Spring*
2. *Propylaia*
3. *Temple of Athena Nike*
4. *The Propylon*
5. *The Pinakotheke*
6. *The Parthenon*
7. *The Erechtheion*
8. *Karyatides*
9. *Acropolis Museum*
10. *Sanctuary of Zeus*
11. *Roman Temple*
12. *Sanctuary of Artemis*
13. *Cistern*
14. *Sacred Entrance*
15. *Asklepieion*
16. *Theatre of Dionysos*
17. *Peripitos*
18. *Odeion of Herodes Atticus*

THE PROPYLAIA

When the term "propylaia" is used, the reference is to the group of buildings that make up the entrance complex. The term "propylon" refers to the actual entranceway through which one passes to enter the sanctuary. The modern visitor can approach the Propylaia as the ancients did by walking up the slope from Dionyssiou Areopagitou—the broad avenue used to approach the site—and by continuing across the saddle connecting the hills of the Acropolis and the Areopagus. The paved walk goes down (to the north) beneath the Acropolis wall, through a gate to bring the visitor within sight of the fence surrounding the Agora excavations. To the right, along the Peripitos, the ancient road which runs around the Lower Acropolis, are the remains of the Klepsydra Spring, where the Panathenaic Procession stopped for the ritual of purification.

The visitor, now following the route of the procession, can return up the path, turn left, and approach the massive Propylaia. The Propylaia served as a transition to another world, a sacred world in which human beings and gods met in communion. The sacred purpose of the Propylaia was to still the mind, purify the thoughts, and prepare the body for the meeting with the goddess.

The sacred purpose was accomplished in several ways. First, the months of preparation for the festival, particularly the weaving of the *peplos,* prepared the mind by focusing attention on the devotions to the goddess. Second, the spectacle of the procession and the walk from the Dipylon Gate in the bright July sun brought an intense clarity to the mind. Third, the actual buildings of the Propylaia stirred feelings of awe and respect and actually created the proper

View of the remains of the Great South Propylon, Acropolis, Athens.

tone for worship. Pausanius described his first approach to the Acropolis in the second century A.D., when the Acropolis was still well preserved.

> The Acropolis has one way in; it offers no other; the whole hilltop is sheer and strong-walled. The formal entrance has a roof of white marble, which down to my own times is still incomparable for the size and beauty of the stone.

For a man familiar with the monumental splendors of Imperial Rome, this comment is noteworthy. What Pausanius encountered as he approached the Propylon were high monumental walls on either side of the temple facade of six Doric columns. The approach to this facade during the Classical Period would have been along a winding ramp, so constructed as to permit large numbers of animals to walk up the steep slope into the sanctuary. In Roman times stairs similar to the present ones gave access to the interior spaces. Some sense of the winding path presently exists on the approach below the stairs.

TEMPLE OF ATHENA NIKE

The ancient path was so situated as to provide at an eastern turning a dramatic view of a special temple of freedom. High on the right side of the Propylaia and separate from its monumental bulk is the small, exquisite Temple of Winged Victory, or Athena Nike. Designed and built by Kallikrates from 427 to 424 B.C., this expression of freedom and triumph over adversity sits lightly upon its platform as if ready to take flight. The temple is amphiprostyle, that is, having columns front and rear, in this case in the Ionic order. A small frieze surrounded the building, depicting battle scenes in which Athenians eternally defeat the Persians.

The Propylon

The six Doric columns supporting the entrance introduce a general theme of patterns of six in the Propylaia. Six is the sacred number of creation and is a feminine number of love and completion. Six anticipates the divine seven, which in turn suggests a desire to unite with the divine presence. Thus, the entrance sets the tone for the encounter within. The roof of the Propylon was also supported by two rows of three slimmer Ionic columns placed on either side of the central passage. The high roof elements, some of which remain in the northeast corner, drew the attention up and gave the worshipper a strong sense of stature, allowing the mind to expand into the space.

In other, less impressive places, the pilgrim entering a sanctuary passed through a much simpler propylon, pausing to prepare for the experience ahead. In Athens, the propylon was a temple, or was at least laid out like one, and the pilgrim had the sense of entering an inner sanctuary normally forbidden to anyone but the priests. Also, there was always

View of the remains of the North Propylon and Pinakotheke, Acropolis, Athens.

the sense of rising, being drawn upward to the sacred space beyond.

To the left, or the north side, of the Propylon was the Pinakotheke, or gallery of art, in which paintings done on wooden panels lined the walls. None of the paintings has survived, but Pausanius reported seeing Odysseus stealing the sacred bow from Philoctetes, Diomede carrying off Athena from Troy, and Orestes killing Aegisthus. Other heroic subjects carry out the theme of the journey of the hero in Homeric lore.

Once through the sacred gate of the Propylon, the visitor is greeted with the form of the Parthenon as the dominant image within the sanctuary. The procession bore to the right and passed along the northern colonnade of the temple and around to the eastern entrance, there to await entrance into the presence of the cult statue.

THE PARTHENON

The Temple of Athena Parthenos means Temple of the Virgin Athena, the maiden goddess of Athens, who sprang full grown from the head of Zeus the Father. As such, she was pure in mind, heart, and body, and was Wisdom Incarnate. The Parthenon, like all temples in Greece, was an image of the god housed within and was an icon of Athena's attributes. It was also designed and built to attract her spirit to the place, to embody her presence so that her worshippers might commune and feast in her presence and be united with her.

View most treasured by pilgrims of the Parthenon from the entrance to the Acropolis, Athens.

The Parthenon has attracted more attention from scholars, historians, archaeologists, architects, poets, and madmen than any other building in the world. It stimulates artistic and philosophical theories and expressions of adoration or loathing, even what seems like indifference. Pausanius, for example, who describes so many Greek monuments in admirable detail, wrote almost nothing of the Parthenon itself, attracted as he was by the sculpture on the pediments and the massive gold and ivory statue of Athena inside.

Siting of the Temple

From early Archaic times a temple dedicated to Athena had been located on the Acropolis, first on the northern side and later in approximately the position of the present temple. Generally, we can speak of three periods: the first, circa 530 B.C. when a temple stood to the north of the present site; the second, circa 480 B.C., when an unfinished temple was destroyed by the Persians; and the third, in 438 B.C., when the present Parthenon was completed. All three temples faced to the east, but the third temple was shifted several points on the compass to the north from east, possibly to adjust to the shift in stellar movements over the years.

It was Francis Cranmer Penrose, former director of the British School of Archaeology, who, while examining the site in 1891, first proposed that the Parthenon had been oriented to the rising of the Pleiades, the constellation also called the Seven Sisters, which is clustered near Taurus, and which rose in the east every spring. Jane Harrison, in her book *Epilegomena and Themis,* points out that when the Pleiades rose twenty-seven days after the vernal equinox (about April 16 on our calendar), the Athenians celebrated the festival of the first harvest. From Frazer's *Golden Bough* we also learn

that when the Pleiades set in the fall, it marked the time of
the fall planting.

Also, Scully points out that the Parthenon is oriented to
the horned Mount Hymettos, seen from the Acropolis to the
east as two gentle peaks rising at the end of the ring of
mountains which sweep around from the south. Since we
know that the Mycenaean palace was located on the Acropolis and that the earliest temple was adjacent to it, it is likely
that the orientation to Hymettos was always a part of temple
siting in Athens.

History of Construction

When the decision was finally made to rebuild the Acropolis
after the destruction of 480 B.C., it was Pericles as general
and leader of the Athenian people who led the way. Pericles
had been reared an aristocrat and tutored by Anaxagoras, the
Ionian philosopher known as *Nous,* or Mind. As Plutarch
tells us, Anaxagoras "was the first of the philosophers who
did not refer the first ordering of the world to fortune or
chance, nor to necessity or compulsion, but to a pure,
unadulterated intelligence, which in all other existing mixed
and compound things acts like a principle of discrimination,
and of combination of like with like."

Pericles was very much the student of Anaxagoras. His life
was a model of discrimination based on the principle of
mind, and although critics, including his enemy Thucydides, accused him of terrible excesses, particularly in the
cost of building the Parthenon, what they failed to understand themselves was the principle Pericles followed in
building the Acropolis, namely that the intense, focused
labor of thousands of people working together to one end
would produce a gathering of consciousness on that site
which would recapture what had been lost over many
hundreds of years and several disasters. Mind, as his tutor
had told him, was capable of creating a world, and Pericles
saw his role as creator of a conscious *polis* dedicated to
Athena.

In charge of the work was the sculptor Phidias, whose
command of sacred geometry and architecture established a
high level of work and resulted in a unity of construction
which we have come to call the triumph of Classical art and
"the glory that was Greece" (E. A. Poe, 1836). The architects
of the Parthenon were Iktinos and Kallikrates, and the
temple they began in 447 B.C. and crafted for nine years was
an expression of the Greek cosmos, a temple of the universe,
of God, and of man.

Sacred Number in the Parthenon

There were several aims held in common by the architects as
they envisioned this sacred temple. First they knew that the
new temple had to rise in approximately the same position
on the Acropolis as the old. The position was sacred. The
actual point on the ground from which the building would be

generated was already known. Second, they wanted a wider temple than was to be found in previous temples. The facade would present eight columns rather than six, meaning that the total number of columns in the outer colonnade would be forty-six. In the Pythagorean canon, integers of numbers larger than ten were added together to reflect sacred principle. Here, four and six yielded ten, the sacred number of divine revelation, the number of perfection.

As well, the number eight, seen in the facades of the temple, was the octave, the One sounded again, only now as a new note, reached through the manifest world of growth and seeking. Eight is the highest feminine number and is the mark of completion in the creation.

Principles of Construction

There is disagreement about which geometric principles served as the basis of designing and building the Parthenon, that is, among those who accept that geometric principle was indeed the starting point. The more prevalent view sees the principle of the Golden Proportion as the starting point (see pp. 76–8). Another view sees the basis of design in the principle of the circle and its square. Whichever view is favored, the fact remains that the Parthenon was designed according to geometric principle and number proportion (see Fig. 19).

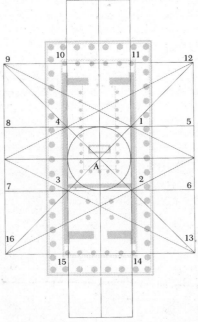

Fig. 19. Ground Plan of Parthenon, Athens, with circle and square geometry; system of Tons Brunés.

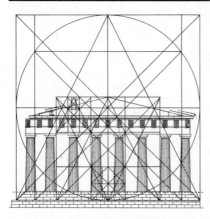

Fig. 20. *Front of Parthenon with circle and square geometry. Intersections dictate placement of key temple elements.*

According to the theory of the circle and square, the architects located the center or the point from which the form would generate. In this case, that point is located directly behind the platform of the cult statue, shown in the diagram as Point *A*. A circle is inscribed, the diameter of which will measure the width (60 Greek feet) between the inside of the *cella* walls. From that circle the exterior square is constructed (1, 2, 3, 4) and from that square ten more squares are added, making the larger square (9, 12, 13, 16). The base square (1, 2, 3, 4) gives the ruling dimensions of the building.

For the front or facade of the temple, the same basic square is stood on end and used to determine the height of the peak of the roof and the spacing and position of the columns across the front. Also, the doubled square gives the width of the stylobate and the center point of the pediment. This design principle explains why the space between the two outside columns is smaller than the other column spaces in the facade. On the ground plan the division of the base square into nine smaller squares requires that the final space between the last columns be narrower to account for that geometric pattern, which also gives the edge of the stylobate.

This geometric theory permits us to see how a temple design can be generated from a single sacred point on the ground, evolving from point to manifest form through the expansion of geometric relationships (see Fig. 20). In the case of the Parthenon, the controlling measure seems to have been the selection of the diameter of the initial circle. Since the stylobate is 100 Greek feet wide (the Greek foot measuring 12.16 inches relative to the modern foot of 12 inches), the diameter of the controlling circle was 60 feet. Sixty marks the width of the cella. Sixty also marks the height of the pediment from the bottom step. Thus, the initial diameter fixes the key measurement for the building.

The other theory of design uses the root five principle

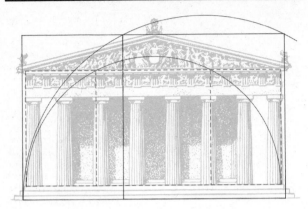

Fig. 21. Front of Parthenon with Golden Proportions.

called the Golden Proportion. In this design, the ground plan and facade design both conform to the laws of the Golden Rectangle (see p. 77). Here, a circle is inscribed from the same central point, just behind the cult statue. The diameter of this circle, however, is the distance between the center of each exterior column adjacent to the center point. This diameter (which measures about 94 Greek feet) then forms the basis of inscribing an arc based on root five (see Fig. 21). This arc fixes the center point for the four corner columns on the ground plan. This same circle (and its square) also fixes the dimensions of the facade of the temple as well.

Thus, we see that there are two design principles at work in the formation of this structure. In fact, the two working together, the generative and regenerative, determine all the important dimensions of the temple and determine its overall harmony and power. The principles of sacred geometry were designed to produce harmonies which would manifest the qualities of the Goddess Athena. This belief in the power of geometry meant that sacred knowledge could take form with the result of bringing the divine into communion with the human. The temple was the means of bridging the distance between the two worlds, and the bridge was designed using geometric shape, proportion, and number.

The confusion which might be produced in the mind by this geometry, whichever plan was used, dissolves in part when we simply appreciate that a building of this elegance and magnitude was designed using the simplest of tools: a compass, a straightedge, and a line. Of course nothing at all would have come from simply playing idly with these tools. There had to be present the laws of sacred science applied by individuals long exposed to those principles, which were passed down through the millennia from the temple priests of Egypt and before that from the dim recesses of the East.

In later years these same principles were followed by the architects of the Gothic cathedrals of Europe.

In addition to the geometric arguments, there are also elaborate theories about the Parthenon as an expression of astronomical principle. When Penrose measured the building in 1846, he determined that the two fronts of the building measured 100 Greek feet, which corresponds to many ancient descriptions of the building as being *hekatompedon,* or a hundred-foot temple. Penrose then went further, based on knowledge gathered from Egypt concerning the astronomical measurements of the Great Pyramid as a guide to dimensions of the earth. What he determined was that the width of the stylobate of the Parthenon was equal to one second of one degree of arc of the circumference of the earth. That this correlation is much debated and rejected by many scholars speaks to the extraordinary difficulty in duplicating these measurements and the disagreement about the degree of sophistication of the temple builders.

Materials and Decoration

The next step in making the bridge between the divine and the human was through the use of appropriate materials and the arts of decoration. The Parthenon was made of the purest white marble, quarried ten miles away on Mount Pentelicus. The marble was checked three times on delivery from the quarry: for color, for damage in transit, and for grain, or natural flaws in the stone. The estimate is that over twenty-two thousand tons of marble were quarried for the Parthenon.

The decoration of the Parthenon was the most ambitious of any temple in the world, before its time or afterward. Although the design was essentially Doric, which called for

Engraving of frieze section from the Parthenon showing Panathenaic procession.

simpler decoration, the architects designed the entablature of the interior colonnade to include a frieze, a feature normally belonging to the Ionic order. The frieze ran around the entire building, forty feet above the floor, and was in relative darkness all of the time. Many observers have questioned the common sense of placing a frieze 40 feet (12 m) high on an interior entablature where its details could barely be seen. This analysis from the human perspective fails to appreciate the sacred intent. The frieze contributes to the whole, to a divine purpose. The temple was Athena's home.

The frieze was an ideal expression of the Sacred Procession in honor of Athena. The subject matter was essentially the same on both long sides and included relief sculptures of horsemen, chariots, elders marching on foot, musicians, tray bearers, and animals for sacrifice. At the west end, horsemen prepare to join the procession, and at the east end, over the entrance, the final presentation of the *peplos* was pictured, accompanied by gods, leading citizens, priests, and young maidens. Fragments of the frieze are in the Acropolis Museum, the National Archaeological Museum, and the British Museum.

The Parthenon had ninety-two metopes (pronounced met-o-peze), or sculpted panels, each measuring 4 feet by 4 feet (1.2 m x 1.2 m). The technical problems of placing the metopes were great because they had to be raised and fixed in place before the roof elements were set. This arrangement meant that they had to be completed quickly in order to be ready at the right moment, so as not to slow the rest of the work. The estimate is that they were carved between 447 and 442 B.C. and raised in the latter year. If the work was not completed, a blank marble block was raised and the sculpting was done in situ. Such a volume of work meant that quite a large group of artists was involved in doing the sculpting. The metopes were more than reliefs, most being full sculptures of striking detail. A few of the pieces, such as Number 32 on the north corner, remain in place. The others were removed, some by Lord Elgin while Turkey ruled Greece, and others to preserve them from damage. The Acropolis Museum has one metope (Room VII, #705).

Although very few metopes have survived, we know that the subject matter for most of them had to do with the Battle of the Centaurs. This piece of Athenian legend pitted Theseus and Peirithous the Lapith against the drunken Centaurs whose coarse actions disrupted a wedding feast. The subsequent defeat of the Centaurs represented a victory of human aspiration over its lower nature, a victory for the spirit in the fight to control human desire, in this case with help from the gods.

The Pediments

In all probability the last task in completing the temple was the carving and placement of the pediment figures. The

The Parthenon seen from the east, its sacred entrance, Acropolis, Athens.

record of payments to artists suggests late completion compared to the other work (perhaps not beginning until 438 B.C.), and since these colossal statues were placed individually, there need not have been any schedule pressure for their completion.

There were about fifty individual sculptures done for the pediments, an equal number for each end. The western pediment presented the struggle, won by Athena, between the goddess and Poseidon for possession of Athens. The other figures are legendary Athenians, such as Erechtheus and his ancestors. The eastern pediment illustrates the birth of Athena, with Zeus and Athena sharing the central positions and the other Olympians arrayed in harmony on either side.

The artistic achievement of the pediment sculptures is seen partially in the remaining figures of the eastern pediment. Still clinging to their narrow perch are horses and Helios the sun god. The figures rest easily and yet spill out of their confined space as if they were not to be restricted to the architectural limitation of a narrow triangular shelf. The effect was to lift the building up and away from its own weight by the creation of so much movement and harmony. Other examples of pediment sculpture may be found in the Acropolis Museum and the National Museum.

Details of Design

As the visitor to the Acropolis moves around the Parthenon, absorbing the life of this bridge between two worlds, there are subtle details that help the attentive observer appreciate the overall effect of grace and harmony. One such detail is *entasis,* the slight bulge in the circumference of the columns (a third of the way up) as they rise toward the entablature. This bulge, hardly visible to the eye, compensates for an optical illusion of concavity present in columns without *entasis* (see page 89).

*Detail of Parthenon roof construction, showing interlocking tiles,
Acropolis, Athens.*

Also, the columns lean inward slightly, just as the roof
elements overhang so as to compensate for the illusion of
outward leaning if columns were to stand exactly vertical.
This slight inward tilt all around means that the blocks
which make up the interior walls are ever so slightly
trapezoidal, shorter at the top than at the bottom. Thus, the
building is not "square" in our mechanistic sense of that
term.

Separating the metopes are triglyphs, marble carvings
which suggest patterns of three columns cut in relief. The
triglyphs appear to relieve the weight of the frieze as it sits
above the architrave. The triglyphs give the illusion of
vertical support in a horizontal element. On the top and
bottom of the triglyphs are the *guttae,* or "drops," which
suggest pegs or nails. These relieve the harshness of an
otherwise uninterrupted horizontal line at the top of the
architrave and along the bottom of the geison. Finally, along
the southern flank of the temple, where the current restorers
have set up shop, visitors may examine a display of roof tiles
set in position as they were in ancient times.

The archaeological evidence tells us that although the
Parthenon was essentially white, or left the natural color of
the marble, the decorative elements were painted in vivid,
primary colors. The pediment background was red as was
the trim above the architrave and under the frieze. The
triglyphs and *guttae* were deep blue. It is important to realize
that our conceptions of so-called "Classical" art should not
remain fixed on the faded ivory tones of weather-beaten
marble. These temples spoke clearly and vividly of their
sacred intent.

The Cult Statue of Athena

When the participants of the Sacred Procession of the
Panathenaia reached the eastern entrance to the Parthenon

and entered the huge doors of the *cella,* they were greeted by the colossal cult statue of Athena, sculpted by Phidias and dedicated in 438 B.C. The statue was surrounded by colonnades of twenty-three Doric columns, one set on top of the other, making a total once again of forty-six columns.

Set on a platform 26 feet wide (8 m) and 13 deep (4 m), the gold-and-ivory statue was over 39 feet high (12 m). The figure was supported by a huge wooden armature set through the platform into the temple floor. Athena was pictured in her long *peplos,* helmeted, holding in her left hand the huge shield and sacred snake. In her right, supported by a single column, was a small statue of Winged Victory. Her face and arms were done in ivory, imported from Africa and carefully molded in strips to cover the wooden base. The gold, which was closely guarded and accounted for, was beaten to thin millimeter sheets and inlaid. The gold remained on the statue until 296 B.C. when it was removed by the tyrant Lachares to pay his army.

THE ERECHTHEION

An important element in the sacred life of the Greeks was the existence and care of the *xoanon,* the ancient cult statue of a patron god. In the case of the Athenians the *xoanon,* or cult statue of Athena Polias—or the Patron Goddess of the City—was not the great statue in the Parthenon, but was, most likely, a small Archaic figure carved from stone of a sitting goddess. The *xoanon* was housed in a place regarded as highly sacred, an ancient sanctuary on the Acropolis now occupied by the Erechtheion.

In the myths of Athens both Athena and Poseidon vied for patronage of the city. One myth tells that Poseidon offered the horse as his gift, and Athena offered her sacred olive tree.

Engraving of the Erechtheion, showing multilevel design and use of Ionic columns, Acropolis, Athens.

The horse reflected the god's power, grace, and swift victory in battle. The olive reflected growth, renewal, and immortality. The olive tree was sacred because it was self-sown and because after the great conflagration of the Persian invasion, the olive sprouted leaves and fruit again after fire had destroyed the Acropolis. Thus, in the courtyard of the Erechtheion, Athena's tree stood, walled about in sacred ground.

When Pericles and Phidias planned the new Acropolis, they were greeted with a genuine problem on the site of the Erechtheion. Because of its ancient sacred history, the site had to serve at least four major functions: as the sanctuary of the *xoanon* of Athena, as a temple of Poseidon, as a tomb for Erechtheus, and altars for Zeus Hypatos (a local cult) and Hermes. In addition there were also minor functions. Room had to be made for the olive tree and altars to Hephaistos and to various heroes.

Principles of Construction

Ralph Waldo Emerson once said, "The pleasure a palace or a temple gives the eye is that an order and a method have been communicated to stones, so that they speak and geometrize, become tender or sublime with expression." The architect of the Erechtheion, perhaps Mnesikles, who designed the Propylaia, solved the problem of the sloping northern site and the multiple use of the sanctuary by working in several levels and by keeping the structure very "light." That is, he chose the Ionic order with its slim, graceful columns and the unique use of statues as columns, also slim and graceful in their supportive function.

The entire building, giving access from four levels and four directions, is held together in geometric pattern by the use of the equilateral triangle. Also, the number of columns throughout the building creates symmetry in an otherwise unbalanced configuration. For example, looking from the west (or from the Propylon) the viewer sees two tall, slender columns supporting the north extension, the four columns of the main temple and two Karyatides or *kore* columns supporting the south porch and balancing the entire side view.

The Karyatides

The six statue-columns which make up the south porch of the Erechtheion represent a brilliant fusion of the arts of architecture and sculpture. Here is an example of the vision of sacred intent worked out in innovative design and individual genius. Because the statues have suffered damage from modern pollution, they were removed in the 1970s and placed in the Acropolis Museum, where they may be admired at close range. The present copies on the building allow the visitor to see just how these graceful figures were integrated into the design of the building.

*Karyatides columns on the south porch of the Erechtheion, giving an
illusion of effortless support of the porch.*

The different levels of the foundation from east to west
made it unsuitable to run a colonnade down the southern
side of the main temple. The solution of the south porch
permitted a softening of the harsh lines of unrelieved *cella*
wall and also invoked an image of the young girls of Athens
who passed by during the Panathenaic Festival carrying the
peplos for the goddess. It appears quite impossible that these
slight figures should be able to support the porch roof. Theirs
is a graceful power in the service of Athena.

THE ACROPOLIS MUSEUM

Remarkably, the museum sits almost invisible in its hollow
at the southeast corner of the Acropolis and does not draw
attention from the Parthenon or obstruct the view of the
surrounding landscape. So hidden is it, in fact, that visitors
often miss its numerous treasures. In particular, the museum houses some of the finest examples of Archaic sculpture in the world, plus several pieces from the Parthenon
friezes, metopes, and pediments.

In general, the museum permits the observant visitor to
gain a considerable appreciation for the differences between
the Archaic and Classical Periods in sculpture. The pieces
from the Archaic Period, particularly the sixth century B.C.
and the early fifth century B.C. portray the ideal of spiritual attainment and reality in the human form. As the
work moves into the Classical Period, there is a change in
this expression of the ideal. The figures become more
naturalistic as aspects of individual personality emerge.
These changes reflect a shift in the ideas of soul, mind, and
consciousness held in the culture during the Classical
Period.

Archaic Displays

The first four rooms (marked I-IV) of the museum display remains of Archaic temples and early votive sculpture. The Archaic pediments in Rooms I and II give a vivid picture of the importance of the serpent in Greek religious belief. The dragon was a favorite image of the early Archaic period. It appears again and again in myth and sculpture. The early pediment in Room I, for example, pictures Herakles battling the Lernaean Hydra, a mythical serpent of great power and importance. The Hydra seemed to refer to the demonic fertility rites which were brought under control by the labors of Herakles and the worship of Athena. In more general terms, however, the dragon stands as a symbol of the passion that unmastered will destroy, but mastered serves the hero on his journey.

#624, in Room II, the Calf-Bearer, is dated 570 B.C. and illustrates a sacrifice to Athena. The large figure stands in an attitude of worship, holding the calf and expressing in his whole being a devotion to the goddess. The Archaic smile, so typical of the period, indicates a beatific state. The other Archaic votive sculptures, particularly the *korai* in Room IV, exhibit the same beatific attitude. They are exemplars of devotion and served to lead worshippers by their example to the desired state.

The famous Almond-Eyed *Kore* (#674) in Room IV stands as a remarkable fusion of Archaic and Classical genius. Her expression, the gentle draping of her garments, the patina of the marble, all indicate most loving attention from the artist as well as expressing a special moment in the history of sculpture. She is dated 500 B.C., and she stands at a critical point in the sacred life of the Athenians. In the aftermath of the Persian invasion of 480 B.C., this and other statues were buried, literally given funeral rites, as a recognition of the

Detail of the marble statue of the Almond-Eyed Kore, *500 B.C., Acropolis Museum, Athens.*

sacrilege committed by the invaders. This *kore* lay in the earth for thousands of years before being discovered, with others, in 1885.

More than any other sculpture in Greece, this *kore* represents the embodiment of spirit in matter. She is both a specific woman and an abstraction. She is the expression of consciousness in a human being, caught by the sculptor's art in a moment of grace.

The Classical Displays

The break from the so-called idealized strong style of the Archaic Period and shift to the "severe" style of the early Classical is nowhere more dramatically displayed than in Room VI and the Kritios Boy, #698. So named as being most likely a statue by the sculptor Kritios, this figure begins a new vision of being in the spiritual life of the Greeks. The slight break in the right knee drops the right hip and introduces naturalism. The facial expression of this transitional figure (dated at 485 B.C.) still holds something of the Archaic idealism, but there begins to emerge a separation and an individuality that betrays a loss of contact with the spiritual vision of the Archaic Period.

While the new Classical style seems to reflect a loss in spiritual presence, it marks an interesting shift in consciousness. The new philosophy placed the emphasis on the development of the human soul and a more interior journey to divinity. A fresh emphasis on public debate and intellectual discussion focused more attention on the powers of the human mind (*nous*) and the structure of the human soul (*psyche*). As has been noted elsewhere, the works of Plato mark the culmination of this new definition of consciousness. The new sculpture began to emphasize the human form as the temple within which God would be found.

A vivid example of the new style is found in Room VIII of

Poseidon, Apollo, and Artemis from the east frieze of the Parthenon, Acropolis Museum, Athens.

*One of the original
Karyatides, showing
sculpting of hair and
clothing elements to
accommodate weight-
bearing requirements,
Acropolis Museum,
Athens.*

the museum. A panel from the east frieze of the Parthenon shows three gods sitting in human poses. Poseidon speaks to Apollo, who turns to hear what he is saying. Artemis holds her robe over her breasts in maidenly modesty. The naturalism of these figures brings god and human being together. This scene could easily be an aristocratic gathering or a symposium of philosophers.

Also in Room VIII is a lovely, flowing sculpture from the parapet of the Temple of Athena Nike. The graceful, winged figure is pictured untying her sandal, a very human but also devotional act. She is fully draped but still exposed through the transparency of her garment. As a servant to Zeus and to Athena, with whom she is always found, Nike was a transitional divinity, that is, immortal but in service to the gods. She was, even through Roman times, a beloved figure, perhaps because she seemed to be at a midpoint between the divine and human condition.

The Karyatides

The last display in the museum is the new, specially created home for the Karyatides, which were removed from the Erechtheion south porch to preserve them from the ravages of polluted air and vibrations from passing aircraft. These column-statues were carefully designed in order to meet contrary needs: to reflect feminine grace and to support tons of entablature. One solution to that problem was to increase the bulk at the neck by the addition of thick plaits of hair, which despite their bulk still fall gracefully down the back. From the front, however, the statues appear to support the weight without effort, an effect which is enhanced by the falling of the chiton in front to expose the neck.

Nike untying her sandal, from the Temple of Athena Nike, Acropolis Museum, Athens.

THE THEATRE OF DIONYSOS

Beneath the wall of the Acropolis, carved into the southeast hill, lie the remains of the world's most famous theatre. Here, during the fifth century B.C., the plays of Aeschylus, Sophocles, Euripides, and Aristophanes were performed (see Historical Overview). Visitors to the Acropolis cannot gain entry to the theatre site without leaving the hill and returning to the main avenue, off of which is the gate. After paying the small fee, visitors will appreciate the relative peace and quiet to be found among the trees and ancient stones of this sanctuary, called the Precinct of Dionysos Eleuthereus.

The present remains of the Theatre of Dionysos are mostly Roman. But careful attention to the earlier remains will gradually expose the Classical theatre and before that the sixth century B.C. remains of temple and dancing ground. When drama was first performed, the only stage was a cart which was rolled into place in the Agora, where small audiences could watch the new art form. It is most likely that the first primitive plays, developed as is now believed by Thespis in 534 B.C., were performed in the marketplace and were not associated with the worship of Dionysos, at least not with his cult located at the present site.

What took place in the Precinct of Dionysos Eleuthereus in the sixth century was probably related to the Dithyramb, hymns of praise and invocation devoted to Dionysos and

Theatre of Dionysos, as seen from the wall of the Acropolis, Athens.

performed during his festivals. In particular, the Greater Dionysia was held each year during the month of Elaphebolion (March–April) to celebrate the release from the bondage of winter and the gifts and powers of new life. Groups of young men sang and danced in honor of the god on the dancing floor, which was a large circle 66 feet in diameter (20 m) in its earliest form. It had an altar at its center. The smooth dirt floor was carved from the hillside and supported by a terrace.

Behind this dancing floor there was also a small temple of Dionysos. A few poros stones from that temple form part of the later Periclean hall. This small temple, built *in antis,* faced to the east and measured 44 feet long (13.4 m) and 26 feet wide (8 m), with two columns at the entrance.

Beginning with the plays of Aeschylus in the 470s B.C., theatre as we know it truly began. The early "cart dramas" and the sacred Dithyramb were combined to create a new, powerful art form. To accommodate this new form there must have been just behind the circular dancing floor, now called an orchestra, a modest scene building (or *skene*) which provided the actors with a place to change costumes and masks and to provide a place to portray interior scenes.

In this early theatre the audience sat on the terraced hillside on wooden benches or wooden planks set into the hillside. The orchestra, with its central altar, was simply packed dirt, and the modest wooden scene building provided the necessary backdrop to the action. Behind the *skene* could be seen the small temple of Dionysos, also modest in its appearance.

During the time of Pericles, when the Acropolis was being renovated, the theatre also received attention. In order to provide for a larger scene building, the orchestra had to be moved north, toward the Acropolis walls. The new scene building was deeper and wider and may have had three doors and a larger raised stage supported on a stone foundation. The *skene* was provided with a device called an *ekkyklema,* a platform which could be rolled out of the central doors to reveal an interior scene, usually bodies of those who died offstage. The *skene* also had a roof which supported the *mechane* or sort of a crane which revealed and sometimes lowered gods to the stage from above. The use of this crane created the term *deus ex machina* to refer to godlike solutions to insoluble problems.

Thus, at the height of Classical tragedy, the theatre had a wooden scene building with raised stage, three sets of double doors, a round orchestra with central altar, and an auditorium of wooden seats rising up the hillside toward the Acropolis wall. It was in this theatre that the great tragic poets developed their craft and the comic poets hurled insults at all the noted figures of the time, including the great lover of wisdom himself, Socrates.

In addition to these developments, undertaken in support of the high regard in which drama was held, Pericles also built the Odeion, the remains of which can still be located to the east of the theatre above the auditorium. The huge square building was modeled after the famous tent of the Persian king Xerxes, who was defeated by the Greeks and whose opulent shelter was a prize of war. The Odeion measured over 200 feet by 225 feet (62 m by 68 m), and the centrally peaked roof was supported by an inner colonnade. During the Greater Dionysia, the Odeion was used for musical contests in honor of the god.

It was during the time of Lycurgus (338 to 326 B.C.) that major work was done on the theatre. The stone auditorium was constructed at this time, essentially as we see it today except for the Roman additions in the front rows of seats. The retaining walls on either side were constructed and the seating area extended up the slope to accommodate audiences of over fourteen thousand.

In the late Hellenistic period (the late second century B.C.), a permanent stone *skene* was constructed. This most likely had two stories, the second set back so as to provide a wide stage for the actors. On the ground level three doors opened onto the orchestra. There is a good deal of earnest debate on the subject of raised stages in the Greek theatre. The physical evidence for them is scarce because the wooden elements would not survive anyway, but the plays argue well for their use from the fifth century B.C. onward.

The many changes during the Roman period have been difficult to trace. During the Imperial era the orchestra was paved and cut off to accommodate an expanded scene building. One inscription dates this work at A.D. 61. The new *skene* and *proskenion* (proscenium) construction presented a high, elaborate facade, now partially echoed in the backdrop of the Odeion of Herod Atticus nearby. Also, many of the marble carvings scattered about the site belong to the Roman period.

An indication of the desecration of the theatre and the abandonment of its sacred and religious function is the evidence of stone and cementing work ringing the orchestra which made the area watertight in order to accommodate sea battles and other spectacles popular during the Imperial period.

THE SACRED LIFE OF DRAMA

The importance of the Theatre of Dionysos lies in the genius of its first poets, those who understood that this new form called tragedy could serve a spiritual purpose. The myths employed by Aeschylus, Sophocles, and Euripides were transformed into experiences designed to move people and to lift them away from the deadly habits of daily life. The plays spoke the truth of human life and sang of the cost in suffering for those who sought wisdom and justice.

The plays written during this period were more or less fifteen hundred lines long, lasted under two hours, and were composed in verse of varying meters and lengths. With a few exceptions the thirty-three complete tragedies we have left of the thousands which were performed all have certain fundamental unities. The action took place in one day, in fact close to the actual running time of the play. They took place in one setting, usually before the king's palace but sometimes on an island or on the beach at Troy. The plays were structured in patterns of dialogue and choral odes to lead the attentive listener through an emotional, intellectual, and spiritual *agon* or conflict, resulting in catharsis.

This purging of the emotions, accomplished by watching a tragic figure struggle with his or her growing understanding of the world and the ways of the gods, was religious in the very best sense. To accomplish these ends, actors were trained in music and movement. They played several characters during the course of the play, now a king and now a prophet, spinning out the beautiful rhythms of Greek speech and sounding the cries of agonized self-knowledge. To magnify their work, the actors stood on high boots and wore vivid masks which had built into them a sort of megaphone to project the voice to the ten thousand or more spectators in attendance.

The tragic plays were performed over three days during the Greater Dionysia, from sunrise to sunset, a genuine marathon of drama. Three tragic poets were chosen each year to produce three plays each and were assigned actors and chorus by the *archon* for the year. The chorus members rehearsed for months and were supported financially by wealthy citizens of the city. Judges awarded first, second, and third prizes based on the overall quality of the three plays presented. On the fourth day the comic poets had their turn, releasing the tensions of the previous three days with bawdy, raucous plays which celebrated freedom from the necessities of a difficult life and which often satirized the absurdities of politics.

THE CLASSICAL SITE

The visitor to the site of the theatre and sanctuary of Dionysos will be aware immediately that the remains of the classical theatre are difficult to find. But they are there. Just within the gate, for example, on the right is the foundation of the altar at which offerings were made to the god. On the left are the foundations of the later Temple of Dionysos built in the Classical Period. Behind it, along the walls of the early Classical hall are a dozen or so stones from the Early Archaic temple, including a cornerstone at the northwest corner.

Around in front of the foundations of the Roman scene building, on the right side of the orchestra near the water channel which drained the theatre, is an arc of six stones of the wall which supported the terrace of the earliest dancing floor. From this point the observer is able to sense how far back from the present one the original orchestra must have been. On either side of the present orchestra are the retaining walls from the Periclean construction. These walls indicate where the entranceways called *paradoi* were located.

Since the orchestra is now roped off to protect the marble from further damage, visitors must circle around to either side to climb up into the auditorium. The thronelike chairs are from the Roman period but are most likely accurate copies of similar chairs of honor from the fourth century B.C. There were originally sixty-seven such thrones in place. The center throne was for the priest of Dionysos and was elaborately carved. We are able to make out two satyrs, two griffins, and several human figures. The other thrones were for various dignitaries whose names were inscribed on the backs.

LATER MONUMENTS

High up in the orchestra, carved into the Acropolis rock, is the choregic pillar monument of Thrasyllos, erected in 319 B.C. to celebrate the victories in the Dithyramb won by the poet. The placement of this monument marks the extent of the stone auditorium of the Late Classical Period. To sit for a few moments at this height gives a sense of the size of the theatre and of the task undertaken by the actors to communicate by voice and movement the content of the plays. In 270 B.C. the son of Thrasyllos, named Thrasykles, celebrated

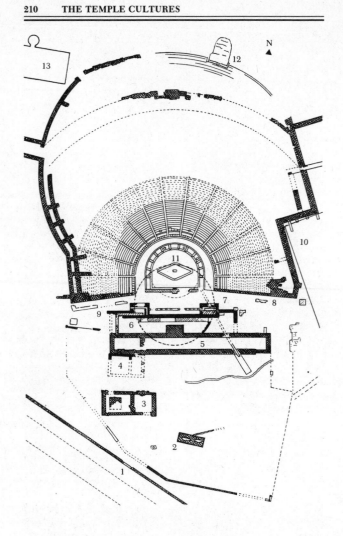

Fig. 22. *Theatre of Dionysos, Athens*
1. *Entrance to Site*
2. *Altar*
3. *Older Temple*
4. *Earlier Temple*
5. *Hall*
6. *Skene*
7. *Circle of Classical Orchestra*
8. *East Parados*
9. *West Parados*
10. *Odeion of Pericles*
11. *Roman Remains*
12. *Monument of Thrasyllos*
13. *Asklepieion*

his own victories by building bases for victory tripods, and later still, during Roman times, the two tall columns were erected for the same purpose.

Cutting through the upper rows of the auditorium is the main path or road which circles the Acropolis. Called the *peripatos*, this road passed through the upper retaining wall and down a fairly steep ramp to the Asklepieion. The modern visitor must scramble around the ruins of the wall and climb up the slope to reach the road.

THE ASKLEPIEION

In 419 B.C. a private citizen named Telemachos gave the funds for the purchase of the land and the construction of a modest Asklepieion, or healing sanctuary, near the sacred spring which for years had provided fresh water to this site. Telemachos must have been a friend of the poet Sophocles, whose interest in healing and willingness to house the sacred snake of Asklepios have been documented. Sophocles knew that there was a close relationship between drama and healing. The intent of drama was to heal, to bring the individual to a unity of body, mind, and spirit through the movements, speech, and rhythms of the play.

At the same time, the cult of Asklepios had been firmly established in hundreds of centers throughout Greece and the Aegean. Here in Athens, the establishment of a minor Asklepieion near the theatre was a natural enough culmination of the ancient connection between the healing arts of drama and the cult of Asklepios.

The original fifth century B.C. Asklepieion was made from wood and probably included only the bare minimum necessary to provide for the rituals of purification, sacrifice, and

The Asklepieion as seen from the Acropolis wall, Athens.

The Temple of Asklepios within the sanctuary of the Asklepieion, Athens.

healing. Later, in the fourth century B.C., more substantial stone buildings were erected. These included temples to Asklepios, to Hygieia (goddess of health), an altar, the Propylon, and the important *abaton,* where patients slept to induce healing dreams. The *abaton* was a two-storied Doric stoa and was an ambitious structure for this site, enclosing as it did the ancient spring and a sacred offering pit, which suggests something of the chthonic qualities of this cult.

The sacred spring is now enclosed behind a wall which probably dates from the sixth century A.D. when a Christian basilica was constructed right over the former temple and *abaton.* The Christian Church continued the tradition of healing, however, being dedicated to the *Aghioi Anargyroi,* or doctor saints.

The visitor to the present site will have little difficulty finding the various remains. They are indicated clearly by stone markers. The only obscure site may be the Propylon, which is along the road to the west. Today, during quiet times, usually early or late in the day, it is not surprising to find Greek pilgrims beneath the sheltering trees, close to the sacred spring, sitting in meditation. This area still has aspects of holiness, and visitors are urged to approach "in a sacred manner."

OTHER MINOR SITES

THE ODEION OF HEROD ATTICUS

Brief mention here should be made of the amphitheatre which dominates the southwestern slope of the Acropolis. As the *peripatos* winds around the rock from the east, it passes through a huge stoa, the remains of which extend almost to the Theatre of Dionysos. This is the Stoa of Eumenes II of Pergamon, who built it in the second century B.C. Connected to it is the Odeion, built by Tiberius Claudius Herodes Atticus much later, in the second century A.D. Atticus was a Greek orator, amateur philosopher, and possessor of great wealth. In his admiration for Athens he gave some of his wealth for the construction of the Odeion, which still serves the public as a theatre and concert hall.

THE AREOPAGUS

To the west of the Acropolis across the saddle that now is crisscrossed with paved walks and refreshment stands is the Areopagus, the small hill where the ancient Council of Areopagus met to rule on matters of justice. It was here in legend that Orestes pleaded his case before the council and won acquittal by the tie-breaking vote of Athena. It was also here in A.D. 51 that Saint Paul preached the new gospel to the Athenians.

In Archaic and early Classical times the Council of Areopagus was very powerful. Its life members, the Areopagites, were chosen for their good character and judgment. To the Greeks of this time the issue of justice, or *dike,* was all-important. The question of justice stood before all other questions in the life of the *polis*. The word encompassed a broad spectrum of concerns, including the nature of divine justice as well as issues of social behavior. In the concept of *dike* was contained the meaning of human action, divine retribution, and immortality.

A walk around the hill today is like a stroll in the country. Paths wind through the trees. Caves invite curious investigation, and the hilltop rock yields a fine view of the Acropolis and Agora. Little remains of any construction, and archaeologists still debate the locations of key buildings. We do know that during the Bronze Age the Areopagus was a burial ground. Several Mycenaean chamber tombs have been discovered, the contents of which are now displayed in the Agora Museum. The tombs were refilled after excavation because of the instability of the rock and surrounding slope.

THE PNYX

A ten-minute walk from Areopagus to the next hill to the southwest is the Pnyx, the hill where the Athenian Assembly met to debate questions of public policy. Only the stone steps of the place of assembly still remain, but the hill affords a view of the Acropolis. It is from this site in the summer that the Light and Sound Show is performed. This tourist attraction yields little but dramatic lighting effects and explains why visitors to the Acropolis encounter junction boxes, cables, and instruments in awkward places.

Funeral stele *from Athens, called the* Ilissos. *These* stele *are similar to tombstones and were either inscribed or sculpted.*

THE KERAMEIKOS

To the north of the Pnyx and the Agora lies the Kerameikos, the ancient cemetery of Athens. This site is especially interesting on two counts. First, it is the location of the important Dipylon (or double) Gate, the Sacred Gate, and the Sacred Way to Eleusis and second, it is the main evidence known to us of ancient burial practice after the Bronze Age.

With the decline of the Mycenaean palaces, the practice of building and maintaining family tombs also declined, to be replaced after the Dark Age by single burials and cremation. The Kerameikos preserves the record of burials after the Bronze Age. We have learned from excavation that about two-thirds of the burials involved cremation urns. The pattern, especially in Classical and Hellenistic times, was for the family to place a *stele*, or decorated marble plaque, over the burial mound, which was usually a simple pit lined with stone. The cremation urns were also buried in like fashion. Some of the *stele* are fine examples of relief sculpture and are on display in the small museum on the site.

Although the family tombs were no longer in use after the Bronze Age, there remained in the culture the strong emphasis upon family mourning and expensive funerals and other honors for the dead. So excessive were these funerals on occasion that laws were passed regulating expenditure, number of mourners, and lavishness of monuments. Such laws indicate the excesses to which some families extended themselves to promote the family name and position in Athenian society.

Visitors to the Kerameikos pay a small fee at the entrance, which gives access to the grounds and to the museum. The grounds to the south or toward the remains of the Dipylon Gate reveal as in no other place the magnificence of the main entrance to the city. Next to the Dipylon Gate is the Sacred Gate, used only for formal processions and particularly for the mass march to Eleusis for the Mysteries. For those interested in the details of the Kerameikos area, a detailed map is available at the ticket booth.

THE TEMPLE OF OLYMPIAN ZEUS

The area known as the Olympieion is an enclosure which includes the Arch of Hadrian, the Temple of Olympian Zeus, and the remains of many ancient buildings which once lined the famous Ilissos River, which now runs underground through the modern city. The Temple of Zeus was the largest temple built on mainland Greece. Measuring 362 feet (101.4 m) by 143 feet (43.5 m), the temple had 104 Corinthian columns, 13 of which remain standing. The great temple was begun by the Peisistratid tyrants in 515 B.C., although nothing of their effort now remains.

In 174 B.C., King Antiochus IV of Syria sought to complete the temple, changing the design to include the Corinthian order. After ten years, work ceased, not to begin again for several hundred years. Completed in A.D. 131 by Hadrian, the temple finally achieved its purpose, although late and without strong association with Greek culture.

Engraving of Temple of Zeus, with the Parthenon in the background, Athens.

THE AGORA

> *Look upon the dance, Olympians,*
> *Send us the grace of Victory, ye gods,*
> *Who come to the heart of our city*
> *Where many feet are treading and incense steams;*
> *In sacred Athens come to the Market-place,*
> *By every art enriched and of blessed name.*
> —PINDAR, *SPRING DITHYRAMB*

Although the Acropolis has always represented the spiritual soul of Athenian life, the Agora, or ancient marketplace, represents her mind and body. After the Bronze Age, as Athens emerged from the Dark Age, the Agora gradually became the center of daily life. Here the laws were written and displayed, the food and crafts bought and sold, and the democratic spirit born and nurtured. In the poem above we sense something of the special spirit of the Agora which lived in the hearts of the Athenians.

A visit to the Agora captures more of the life of ancient Athens than can be found anywhere else. The site may be reached from three different directions: the west from Plateia Theseiou, the north from Hadrian Street, and from the southeast. We will begin from the southeast entrance, just below the Acropolis wall and an easy walk down the path from the Propylaia. The American School of Classical Studies at Athens runs this excavation and has prepared excellent guides to the area. Our purpose will be to focus on the Archaic and Classical Agora and to indicate something of its sacred life.

HISTORY

The history of this small area has produced a rich source of archaeological records. As is the case in most excavations in Greece, the record begins in the Neolithic Period, in about 3000 B.C. when chamber tombs were discovered in the Areopagus slope. Further digging in this area revealed Mycenaean grave sites plus graves from the later Geometric Period (900–700 B.C.).

In the Archaic Period the area just below the future site of the Temple of Hephaistos developed as the center of Athenian civic and economic life. Ground plans for the Agora in 500 B.C. show the area beneath the small hill called Kolonos Agoraios to be devoted to civic and religious buildings. In addition to a large square building called the Bouleuterion, or Council House, there were small temples to Meter (another name for the Earth Mother) and to Apollo, a shrine to Zeus, and farther north the Altar of the Twelve Gods and the

Royal Stoa. Also were to be found the first Heliaia, or law court, and the ancient fountain house.

In the fifth century B.C., growth in the Agora was rapid, with many additional buildings rising to meet the needs of the growing city. The Temple of Hephaistos was begun in 444 B.C. and completed around 415 B.C. The *Tholos* was constructed as was a new council house. New and commodious stoas and a circular orchestra appeared in the center of the grounds in a space later to be occupied by a Temple of Ares.

During the Roman era the appearance of the Agora began to reflect the control and values of an alien presence. Buildings were erected to glorify various emperors or Roman governors, as well as new deities. General crowding shifted construction to the east where the Roman Agora has now been excavated. Beginning in A.D. 267 a series of destructive attacks leveled most of the buildings, with the exception of the Temple of Hephaistos, which fortunately for us has managed to survive almost intact. From the Byzantine era and beyond, the Agora slowly became residential until serious excavation began in 1931 when over three hundred private houses were torn down to permit work to begin on the site.

ARCHAIC AND CLASSICAL REMAINS

Beginning at the southeast entrance to the site, the visitor is greeted with the long stretch of the Street of the Panathenaia, the route of the procession of the major religious festival in the Athenian year. The road enters the Agora from the north at the Dipylon Gate, where the procession formed.

Remains of the Eleusinion sanctuary in the Agora, Athens.

The Street of the Panathenaia is not the same as the Sacred Way to Eleusis. The two roads more or less converge at the northern boundary of the Agora, where the Panathenaic Way becomes the main road through the ancient city. Ancient records indicate that the Athenians may well have used this road for horse racing during the festival games.

The Eleusinion

A most sacred structure in the Agora was the Eleusinion, the sanctuary devoted to the Eleusinian Mysteries in Athens (see Fig. 21). Here, each year, sacrifices were made to Demeter and Kore (Persephone), and sacred objects were stored for a time before the procession to Eleusis began on the nineteenth day of Boedromion (September 27 or 28). Also, records indicate that the Council of 500 met at the Eleusinion on the day following the Mysteries when the initiates had returned to Athens.

The sanctuary is on the east or right as the visitor looks down the road into the Agora site. A break in the wall with a stone threshold marks the position of the ancient Propylon. Since very little work has been done on this site recently (as of the winter of 1987), the foundations of the temple are obscured by deep grass. Evidence points to the early fifth century B.C. as the likely date of construction of this small temple. Siting of the temple indicates that, although quite small, it was well placed and could be seen easily as a dominant feature even though it sat in the shadow of the

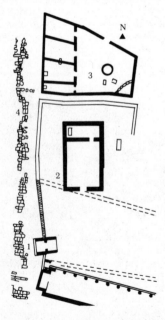

Fig. 23. *Eleusinion, Athens*
1. *Propylon of Sanctuary*
2. *Temple of Demeter*
3. *Priests' Quarters*
4. *Panathenaic Way*

Acropolis. As the plan indicates, there was below the temple a lower sanctuary containing a building with four rooms and a round pit or altar. The lower building may well have been designed for the storage of objects sacred to the Mysteries and for the use of the priests.

Some of the mystery surrounding this sanctuary is reflected in the reference to it from Pausanius. As he passed through the Agora toward the Eleusinion, Pausanius began a story of Eleusis, in particular the lineage of Triptolemos, but he stops his account in deference to the sacredness of the Mysteries. "I wanted to go on with this story and describe the contents of the Athenian sanctuary called the Eleusinion, but I was stopped by something I saw in a dream. I must turn to the things it is not irreligious to write for general readers. In front of this shrine, where also is the image of Triptolemos, you see a bronze steer being led to sacrifice. Epimenides of Knossos is there too, sitting down. They say he was out in the country one day and went into a cave to sleep, and sleep kept him there until he had slumbered away for forty years, and afterwards he wrote poems and purified cities, Athens with the others."

In the Agora Museum visitors will find remnants of a *stele* discovered here in the Eleusinion on which are inscribed the details of the sale of property belonging to Alkibiades, the infamous youth of Athenian society who was exiled in 415 B.C. for sacrilege to the Eleusinian Mysteries. The confiscation of his property and subsequent vilification were indicative of the sacredness of these ceremonies and the beliefs which lay behind them. That a number of *stele* were erected in the Eleusinion in silent witness to this event indicates the concern of those in power that no further mockery of the Mysteries take place.

The Southeast Fountain House

Visiting the Agora (see Fig. 24) is much like walking around inside a puzzle, particularly if the task is to find those pieces which are the most ancient. The archaeological method is to work down through the layers imposed by years of shifting debris, of disasters, of deliberate rearranging of elements, of collapse from one level to another, recording all the time what each inch reveals. After that process is complete down to bedrock the guesswork begins. What was found? What should be left in place? What are the dates? Is the information reliable? What corollary evidence is there to support identification of the find?

In the case of the fountain houses in the Agora, there have been many arguments. The literary record indicates that a fountain house of sacred importance was situated in Athens, and archaeologists have supposed that it was located in the Agora. In the 1930s the square fountain house in the southwest corner of the Agora was identified as the one in question. Twenty years later, however, the Southeast Fountain House was uncovered and subsequently has been

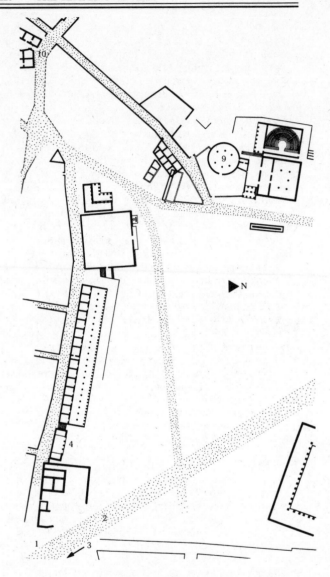

Fig. 24. *The Agora, Athens, fourth century* B.C.
1. *Southeast Entrance*
2. *Panathenaic Way*
3. *The Eleusinion*
4. *Southeast Fountain House*
5. *Altar of the Twelve Gods*

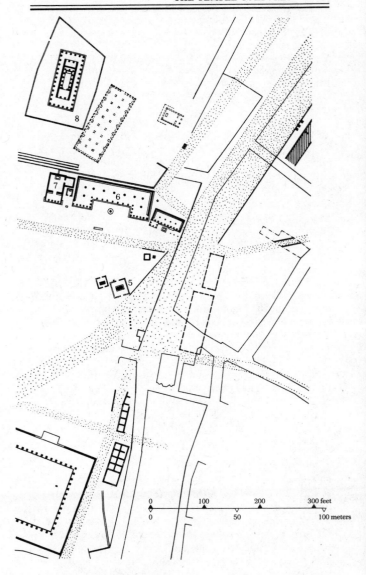

6. Stoa of Zeus Eleutherios
7. Temple of Apollo Patroos
8. Temple of Hephaistos
9. Tholos
10. State Prison

identified as the original. Thus, it is with some hesitancy that we say that what Pausanius calls Nine-Springs is located just behind the Church of the Holy Apostles on the left down the road. The Southeast Fountain House was in use from Archaic times as a source of water for daily use and a place where those who wished for special blessing went to bathe.

The foundations of the Southeast Fountain House are difficult to distinguish, but they show it to have been a long, rectangular building 60 feet (18 m) long and 23 feet (7 m) wide. Its northern entrance was framed by three columns. Although in early times the fountain was no doubt fed by a natural spring, later, when the demand for water was greater, a pipeline ran to it from a more plentiful source. A large earthen pipeline, still visible, ran beneath the Panathenaic Way, by the Eleusinion, and fed the nine spouts, which, if urn drawings are accurate, were in the shape of animal heads.

Altar of the Twelve Gods

At the end of the Street of Panathenaia is the northern entrance to the Agora and where one of the plans of the Agora is located for the convenience of visitors. The plan of the northern section reveals that from Archaic times an Altar to the Twelve Gods and the Eschara, or ground altar, were located here. The famous Altar of the Twelve Gods will be hard to locate since its foundations now rest mostly within the railroad right-of-way, but a corner of it may be found near the retaining wall. This altar was important in ancient times not only for its dedication to the Olympians but also because from this spot all distances to other cities and important sites were measured.

Temple of Hephaistos

Hephaistos was the crippled god, cast by Hera from the beauty and perfection of heaven to dwell in the caverns of the sea, where he transformed the substance of the earth into that selfsame beauty and perfection. He was the god of the artisan, a role he shared with Athena as patron of artists. For their worship, the Athenians erected this temple (444–416 B.C.), known also as the Theseion for Theseus, legendary king of Athens. The Temple of Hephaistos has survived for over two thousand years because it, like the god it represented, continued to serve the masters who possessed the Agora from age to age until, ironically, it survives as the least crippled temple in Greece.

Approximately half the size of the Parthenon, the Temple of Hephaistos is of the Doric order, with six columns on the short sides and thirteen on the long, as usual following the formula for the long side of twice the columns of the short side plus one. The total number of columns is thirty-four, which in the Greek manner of numerology equals seven, the sacred number of Divine Completion. The placement of the

Temple of Hephaistos, seen from the point of approach, the Agora, Athens.

temple makes it clear that it was designed to be approached from below, in front of the eastern facade. Excavation has not revealed the approaches except that remnants of sanctuary wall strongly suggest that no other approach was possible. Thus, the temple shows to best advantage from a point directly below its entrance. After its completion in the late fifth century B.C., the Agora was clear to the east in front of the temple in line with the circular orchestra.

When completed the Temple of Hephaistos contained cult statues of Athena and Hephaistos made by Alkamenes. Unlike the Parthenon, the metopes in the smaller temple

Side view of Temple of Hephaistos, showing excellent state of preservation, the Agora, Athens.

were more modest in scope and were done only for the eastern facade and the near panels on the north and south, again a confirmation of the limited perspective planned for the building. The carvings were of the nine labors of Herakles plus four attributed to Theseus. Inside the peristyle above the *pronaos*, the frieze also featured the labors of Theseus, the dramatic nature of which resulted in the temple becoming known in its time as the Theseion.

As visitors descend by the southern path from the Theseion, they may wish to stop at the Agora Plan which has been thoughtfully provided at this slightly raised site. It affords an opportunity to locate prominent features and possibly to imagine what the site might have looked like in the Classical Period.

The Tholos

It is not surprising that the Classical Greeks would establish their seat of government in a round building. As mysterious as these round buildings are to us—here, in Delphi, and at Epidauros—it seems clear that they were always regarded as sacred. The associations which are connected to them include sacrificial pits and cult centers for local heroes and gods. It was in this *tholos* that the ruling council met to eat, to be paid, and to sleep so that someone of the ruling council would always be available.

Attentive searchers will find several foundation stones of the *tholos* plus three column bases of the six interior columns which held up the peaked roof. In addition, there are the remains of an Archaic *tholos* to the south of the Classical site, which also included several other important buildings, all devoted to the administration of the city.

The State Prison

Of particular interest to lovers of Socrates and Plato is the site of the State Prison in the Agora where Socrates was confined for a month between his conviction by the Athenian Assembly and his death in 399 B.C. Tentative identification of this site was made recently, using as evidence the age, size, and structure of the building, the supporting literary evidence from Plato's dialogue *Phaedo,* and the discovery in one of the rooms of thirteen small vials typical of those used to contain poison.

The supposed prison site is located in the southwestern corner of the Agora. The ruins are now merely foundation stones just above the ground, and the building is located just below and to the west of some prominent Roman ruins. In the northernmost room there is visible the rim of a large amphora which might have been used as a bathing tub by prisoners, as we note in the *Phaedo:* "When he had spoken these words, he arose and went into the bath-chamber with Crito . . ." After his bath, late in the afternoon, as the sun touched the western hills, Socrates drank the portion of hemlock and soon died, saying as he did, "Crito, I owe a cock to Asklepios; will you remember to pay the debt?" It was the custom for those cured of an illness to pay the priests of the healing god Asklepios a cock. Having been cured of the disease of life, Socrates clears his debts and departs for the next world.

The Agora Museum

The Stoa of Attalos was an important addition to the Agora in the second century B.C., a gift of King Attalos II of Pergamon. Restored completely by the American School of Classical Studies, it now houses many valuable finds from the Agora excavations and serves as well as the center of archaeological activities within the site. Visitors are welcome to visit the main exhibit area on the ground floor and the colonnade of the upper floor, where models are exhibited of the Acropolis and Pnyx. The second floor also affords a comprehensive view of the site and is a pleasing vantage point from which to conclude a visit to the Agora.

The obvious delight of a visit to the Stoa of Attalos is simply the reward of being in a completely restored ancient building—to sense its comfortable size, to feel the expansive luxury of its openness, and to experience the movement of light and air through its colonnades. Here is a building designed for human use which gives its inhabitants the stature idealized in sculpture and immortalized in images of the gods.

The museum contains a chronological ordering of artifacts from Neolithic to Turkish times, a span of nearly four thousand years. There are sixty-three exhibits in the main gallery, plus the sculptures in the ground floor colonnade and the terrace.

One of the notable finds in the Agora (unearthed in 1907) was the monumental marble Apollo Patroos, the cult statue from the small temple located below the Theseion. The Apollo is one of the few "larger-than-life" sculptures extant in Greece and, despite its fragmentary condition, still communicates a sense of power. Also in the colonnade is the lovely marble Nereid which may well have come from the Temple of Hephaistos. This graceful female figure shows the movement possible in sculpture, in particular for those pieces which were placed high on temple pediments where their garments were ruffled by the breeze.

In the main gallery attention is drawn to the various burial displays from the Mycenaean Period and the transitions shown in cults of the dead through the Archaic Period. Also of great interest is the mold for a bronze statue in Case #23. This exhibit was carefully reassembled from a molding pit found at the western edge of the Agora, and it shows the various stages and difficulties encountered by those artisans who worked with metals. Case #36 contains a particularly beautiful bronze of Nike dated between 420 and 415 B.C. as an example of the art of molding. Far from being lapses in technique, the various channels visible in the bronze work were provided as anchors for gold and silver sheets which covered the head in its original state.

THE NATIONAL ARCHAEOLOGICAL MUSEUM

A visit to this impressive collection of treasures demands both time and focused attention, the latter in particular because the exhibits are packed together and can be lost simply in the profusion of riches. As is true of all the references to museums in this guide, the purpose here is to mention just some of the high points of the collection. The museum has a number of impressive full-color guides to the full collection, all reasonably priced.

The museum is laid out in wonderful symmetry. The central hall, Room #4, contains the impressive Mycenaean collection, including the famous Schliemann gold masks, cups, and jewelry. On the left is Room #5, the Neolithic collection, and to the right is Room #6, which contains the Cycladic collection. Then, beginning in Room #21 and moving in both directions (Rooms #7–31 and 34) is the Archaic, Classical, and Hellenistic collection of sculpture. Rooms #36–40 house the bronzes and Rooms #41–43, the Roman sculpture.

ROOM #4, THE MYCENAEAN COLLECTION

In Case #1 are collected many important items of gold and silver found in Mycenaean tombs. Of special interest are the gold seal-rings which give us glimpses of religious and secular life. Item 992, the Minoan Pantheon, shows four female figures, one either a goddess or priestess, surrounded with Minoan religious symbols, including the double ax, the sun and moon, and the figure-eight shield and poppies. It is from small but vivid portraits such as this one that we have gained our very limited knowledge of Minoan religious belief.

The gold bull with disks and the bull rhyton illustrate the practices of sacrifice in Mycenaean and Minoan culture. The sacrificial animals were elaborately decorated in gold. In particular, the horns were often gilded. Also in this case is a grave *stele* from Mycenae inscribed with the typical and important spiral designs so often seen in decoration. The spirals evoke images of the labyrinth and the initiatory rituals of Minoan religious practice.

In Case #3 are five gold death masks found by Schliemann at Mycenae. These masks reflect the wealth of the palace cultures and the importance of the cult of the dead in Mycenaean religious ritual. Number 624 is the mask wrongly identified by Schliemann as Agamemnon's. Subsequent study has placed this mask nearer 1550 B.C., a date much earlier than the period when Agamemnon would have occupied the throne of Mycenae.

*The gold death mask
attributed by
Schliemann to the
body of Agamemnon.
This mask, however,
belongs to an
earlier period.*

The fresco fragment in Case #14 is an outstanding example of Mycenaean artistry. Close examination of the black lines which outline the figure show that the artist worked the wall with great control. The line of the upper arm, for example, moves in one perfect curve from elbow to the tip of the index finger. Such control is extremely difficult, particularly in fresco painting. The attention to the task here demonstrates a high degree of sophistication which is sometimes lost in our fixation with the representational in art.

In general the quality and delicacy of the work in this room support the assessments made of the advanced state of Mycenaean culture. One can see in these artifacts the great care and precision which resulted in the beehive tombs and the other monumental architecture left to us at Mycenae. Here was a culture of sensitivity and depth as well as aggression and grandeur.

ROOM #6, THE CYCLADIC COLLECTION

The Cyclades refer to those islands in the Aegean Sea which form a rough circle around the sacred island of Delos, traditional birthplace of Apollo. Cycladic culture refers to the period between 3200 and 1100 B.C. when most of the artifacts in this collection were produced. Much disagreement centers on the nature and significance of the female figurines in this room. The controversy involves possible identification with the Earth Mother cults which probably existed in the Neolithic Period and the function and use of the figurines involving those cults.

Those who argue that these figures represent divinities or sacred subject matter point out the emphasis upon geometric principles in the design: the triangular heads, torso, and genitalia and the circular patterns in breasts and hips. Since greater realism was certainly possible, the abstract qualities of the design suggest divine qualities rather than human features. Such qualities as fertility, elevated stature, and perfection of form come to mind.

A middle position suggests that these figures represent human beings in various postures of worship. The folded arms remind us of the frescoes from Knossos showing worshippers during religious rituals. And since many of these figurines were found in graves, there is the logical conclusion that they were placed as tokens of respect for the gods of life and death to guide the deceased on to the next world.

In any case, these early examples of sculpture point out once again the extraordinary skill and power of so-called primitive work. Time spent in this room softens a little of our modern arrogance. The clear superiority of this work over most modern art suggests that mankind has lost touch with certain principles and forgotten the power of early inspirations.

ROOMS #7–13, ARCHAIC SCULPTURE

A short detour back through the lobby (keep your ticket stub handy) will bring you to the Archaic collection, a jump of five hundred years but only a step in conception and brilliant articulation. Special attention should be given to the various *kouroi*, certainly one of the finest collections in the world of these idealized male youths.

One is able to see the powerful symmetry in these visionary expressions of humanity. Our eye lingers on these figures because they so clearly express the laws of balance and symmetry in the one form we know so well: our own. The finest example of geometric and sacred principle applied to the *kouros* is in Room #13, the *Kouros* of Croesus (#3851). It dates from 520 B.C.. We see here balance, power, serenity, unity, and wholeness. The figure does not represent a particular individual, even though it was dedicated to a real youth named Croesus who died in battle. The figure transcends personality while typifying the ideals of human achievement.

ROOMS #14–21, CLASSICAL SCULPTURES

Room 15 contains two of the great treasures of the Classical Period, the bronze Poseidon (#15161) and the relief of the Eleusinian Mysteries (#126). Comparison of the Poseidon, an idealized portrait of a god, with the Croesus *Kouros* shows the development of sculpture from the Late Archaic to the Early Classical Period. The Poseidon bronze is dated 460 B.C. and was recovered in 1928 from the sea off the coast of Euboea. The god is pictured in action, throwing his trident, whereas the *Kouros* stands in perfect stillness. Poseidon has individuality and is recognizable as the god.

The famous Eleusinian relief showing Demeter on the right and Persephone (Kore) on the left giving an ear of corn to Triptolemos, is a brilliant example of relief sculpture. The figures appear quite full despite only a slight protrusion from the background. Also, the two goddesses look with such affection at the boy who will bring the mysteries of agriculture to mankind. Demeter's motherly gesture in touching Triptolemos, probably in benediction, brings a focus to the work that tells us that this is a Classical work. Artists of this period concentrated their attention on the balance and structure of the whole work and not merely on a single figure.

Of note in Rooms #19–20 is the Roman copy of the famous statue of Athena housed in the Parthenon and sculpted by Phidias. Called the Athena of Varvakion (#129), this copy gives us information about the monumental original without, certainly, competing with it artistically. We are able to see the *peplos*, the small statue of Winged Victory in Athena's right hand, and the helmet adorned with a sphinx and two griffins. Also evident is the great serpent coiled behind the shield. Similar copies of the monumental statue must have been fairly common throughout the ancient world.

Famous Kouros *of Croesus—520 B.C. Excellent example of idealized Archaic man, National Archaeological Museum, Athens.*

Marble relief of Demeter, Kore, and Triptolemos, found at Eleusis and emblematic of Eleusinian Mysteries, National Archaeological Museum, Athens.

ELEUSIS

Queen of fragrant Eleusis,
Giver of Earth's good gifts,
Give me your grace, O Demeter.
You, too, Persephone, fairest,
Maiden all lovely, I offer
Song for your favor.

—HOMER

The Mysteries celebrated at Eleusis from Mycenaean to Late Roman times were part of a long tradition of initiatory rituals among the Greek-speaking peoples. Some of these rituals and their elements must have been inherited from Near Eastern sources going back another four or five thousand years and transmitted through Crete and the Minoans in the Bronze Age. Other elements arrived from the north from as early as Paleolithic times in the rituals of the nomadic hunting tribes. Purification, procession through a labyrinth, sacrifice, isolation in the darkness, and final epiphany in the light are all characteristic of initiatory rites.

The Mysteries were rituals of death and rebirth, both seasonal and personal. The *mystai* (or initiates) "died" to the old self just as seeds "die" awaiting germination in the earth, and then, like the sprouting grain, the new souls were reborn into the company of those who have gone before (*epoptai*). In the rebirth was an implicit affirmation of immortality, a hope closer in concept to the Christian belief than to the traditional Olympian system. In fact, in the Mysteries, the Virgin Mother bears the Savior for mankind. Also, the Mysteries were bound up with the cycles of lunar and solar movements, with the dying of the sun in winter, and the rebirth of the light in the birth of the son.

Another major difference between the Eleusinian Mysteries and traditional beliefs was the focus at Eleusis upon the worshipper rather than upon the god who is worshipped. The *mystai* were the center of attention, and the great Telesterion where the final secret was unveiled was designed for human *and* divine habitation. The purpose of the ceremony, then, was not so much to invoke an epiphany of the goddess within the ceremonial space, but rather to induce an internal epiphany in the participant, to re-create the myth of Demeter-Kore for the individual. Therefore, in its internal sense the great secret of Eleusis was, as Kerenyi has said, ineffable (*arrheton*), which means unknowable as well as "under the law of silence." Ineffable though it may have been, however, the experience was very real, and its reality has made the ceremony an event of considerable interest and importance throughout subsequent history.

HISTORY

In the ancient world, Eleusis was the site of the Mysteries, that secret ritual of initiation which for nearly two thousand years was so central to Greek life. So important was it that in A.D. 364 when the Emperor Valentinian ended all nocturnal rites, he was persuaded to lift his ban on the Eleusinian Mysteries on the grounds that life would end for the Greeks without them. The Greeks believed, in fact, that the Mysteries held the universe together, that without them the cycle of birth, growth, decay, death, and rebirth would cease. If the Olympian gods were remote, even indifferent to human suffering, the Mysteries revealed a compassionate and immediate Mother who promised eternal life to the initiate.

The origins of the Mysteries at Eleusis are obscure. This much is known: settlement on the slopes of the hill of Eleusis has been traced back to the eighteenth century B.C., or the Middle Helladic Period, prior to domination of the Mycenaean culture. The early structures appear to have been simple houses, and no temple or sanctuary has been located. Later, during the Mycenaean Period, about 1500 B.C., a simple megaron was built on the spot where much later the famed Telesterion, or ceremonial chamber, appeared. The megaron seems to have been designed and built for ritual purposes and may mark the beginnings of the annual rites.

Tracing sources and influences during this period is difficult, but the sense seems to be that the Mysteries were inaugurated during the fourteenth century B.C. and took shape from Minoan, Mycenaean, and Thracian influences. Early myths tell of the warfare between the Athenians and the Thracians for the control of Eleusis, control of both the rites and the trade routes from the north, west, and south which converged at the Eleusian marketplace. From the Late Mycenaean times Eleusis seems to have been under the control of the Athenians, who incorporated the initiatory rites into their own festivals.

ARCHAIC AND CLASSICAL TIMES

Gradually, from at least Homeric times onward to its end, the Eleusinian Mysteries developed into a Panhellenic rite celebrating the divinity of Demeter and her daughter Kore, or Persephone, a name associated with Kore as queen of the Underworld. In the seventh century B.C., during the period when Solon the lawgiver was influential in Athens, the sanctuary at Eleusis was greatly expanded, indicating the growing number of those who annually took part in the rites. From this period up to the Persian invasions the sanctuary continued to grow.

In the Historical Overview there appears a full description of the episode in 480 B.C. involving Eleusis as contained in Herodotos' *Persian Wars*. Although not regarded as history by most realists, this description captures the central importance of the Mysteries to the Greeks and their acceptance of the historical fact that the defeat of the Persian fleet occurred at least in part because Xerxes made the mistake of engaging the Greeks in battle during this sacred time, thus preventing the initiates from their annual pilgrimage. This Persian sacrilege was punished by the gods, whose divine appearance or epiphany on the road to Eleusis inspired the Greeks to victory.

During the great period of building and expansion under the leadership of Pericles in mid-fifth century B.C., the sanctuary of Eleusis was further expanded, repaired, and transformed into an international center for the worship of Demeter-Kore and the transmission of the Mysteries to a much broader range of participants. After the fall of Athens, Eleusis fell from its position of splendor for a time but maintained its rites and physical integrity. No power would commit the sacrilege of harming the inner sanctum, regardless of the animosities aroused or the allegiances involved. Thus, through the Macedonian period and the chaos of the Late Hellenistic times the sanctuary remained relatively unharmed.

RISE AND FALL UNDER ROME

The Romans showed a great interest in Eleusis, mostly because its rites were so universal and the secret of its initiation so appealing. The early emperors were lavish in their support of the sanctuary and made many changes in the design of the site. Many of the remains we visit now are Roman, but despite a general tendency to overwrought design on the part of Roman architects and builders, the remains at Eleusis retain a Classical flavor. No doubt the priests of the sanctuary held their sacred ground when it came to extensive changes in the character of the site.

The later Roman period, when the first Christian emperors took control of the empire, saw the first signs of the end of the sanctuary. The beginning of the end came in A.D. 364 when the Emperor Valentinian put an end to all nocturnal rituals as being anti-Christian, presumably because they were seen as being of the Devil. Such a conclusion was natural enough since for years the Mysteries had been associated with the worship of Dionysos and were chthonic in nature. But Valentinian amended his edict when it became apparent that Greek spiritual belief was so bound up with the rites at Eleusis that an end of the Mysteries would mean an end to the Greek people. Initiation meant life itself.

Only thirty-two years later, however, in A.D. 396, Alaric the Goth swept down upon Eleusis from the north and destroyed the sanctuary. The Mysteries might have survived even this physical destruction had it not been for the internal subversion by Greek factions within the priesthood who permitted and perhaps even encouraged the destruction, so perverted had the rites become by that time. As with many of the ancient sites in Greece, the modern period saw general desecration and neglect until the nineteenth century A.D. when excavation began and a great world treasure was once again revealed.

MYTHOLOGY

Although there is evidence of a pre-Homeric myth of Demeter from Crete, most of the mythology upon which the Eleusinian Mysteries are founded has come down to us from one source, the Homeric *Hymn to Demeter,* which was written in the eighth century B.C. The elements of the Homeric myth were woven into the general patterns of initiatory ritual to form the unique character of the Mysteries.

The myth is based on the story of the two goddesses, Demeter, or Mother Earth, and Kore, the Maiden, also known as Persephone, goddess of the underworld and wife to Hades. The name Persephone was seldom used, because it was perceived as being part of the secret of the Mysteries and was not to be uttered lightly. The pattern is similar to writing G-d in the Jewish faith to keep the name of the Lord sacred and pure.

THE MYTH OF TWO GODDESSES

Demeter was the daughter of Cronus and Rhea and sister of Zeus. She was worshipped as Mother Earth, provider of grain and the other fruits gathered from cultivation. Demeter had one daughter, the *Kore,* or Maiden, by Zeus, her brother. One day Kore gathered flowers with her companions. It was a day of great beauty, full of sun, welcome breezes, and new flowers. She wandered from her friends, attracted by the beauty of the narcissus . . .

"It was a thing of awe whether for the deathless gods or mortal men to see; from its root grew a hundred blooms and it smelled so sweetly, so that all wide heaven above and the whole earth and the sea's salt swell laughed for joy. And the girl was amazed and reached out with both hands to take the lovely toy; but the wide-pathed earth yawned . . ."

And Hades, god of the underworld, emerged in his chariot and seized Kore and bore her to his home below. There he made her queen of the dead, confined to rule forever in the darkness. In the depths, Kore refused to eat, to accept any advances from the lord of the dead. Meanwhile, Demeter

*Detail of the Well of
Demeter, preserved
through the ages as a
sacred place, Eleusis.*

mourned the loss of her daughter and roamed the heavens
for nine days searching for her. Finally, she learned from the
all-seeing sun what had transpired, and in a rage she left the
company of the deathless gods and came to the earth, to
Eleusis, where she appeared as a crone, or old woman, alone
and mourning.

She sat in sadness beside a well and was approached by
the four daughters of King Celeus of Eleusis. She was
invited to the palace, there to be accepted by Queen Metaneira in the great hall. The grace and bearing of the old
woman was such that Metaneira urged her to stay and to
become nurse to her newborn son Demophoon. Demeter,
still mourning the loss of her daughter, agreed to nurse the
boy Demophoon, who under her care grew strong and noble.

Indeed, Demeter's care of the young prince included the
slow process of making the boy immortal by placing him at
night in the burning coals of the hearth. The queen, curious
as to how her son was growing into such a godlike figure,
stole one night into the nursery, only to see the boy being
placed onto the coals. She screamed, whereupon Demeter
revealed herself in all her immortal splendor and said, "You
mortals are thoughtless and unknowing; you cannot distinguish between evil and good." The goddess then left the
palace and demanded that a great temple be built for her
nearby. There she would be worshipped.

Because Kore remained with Hades, Demeter caused the
earth to dry up and freeze and remain barren throughout the
year. No grain grew, no olive or fig trees bloomed, and no
animals could feed or reproduce their kind. The gods were

without sacrifices from mankind. All was dead. Knowing this could not be, Zeus dispatched Hermes to demand of Hades that he release Kòre and thus restore the fruitfulness of the earth. Hades appeared to agree and relinquished his bride, even returning her in his chariot. But before she left the underworld, Kore ate one seed from a pomegranate, an act which sealed her union with Hades.

In the power struggles among the gods, rights and privileges must be maintained. Laws must be honored. All-powerful Zeus is all-powerful only to a point. Demeter demands the return of her daughter. Hades demands his prize. Because Kore ate the seed, sealing her union with Hades, she had to serve her husband as queen of the dead for one-third of the year. For the other two-thirds she returned to her mother.

Thus, the earth remains barren for four months and is fertile for eight. Demeter restored the fertility of the earth for those eight months of the year. She also celebrated her partial victory by teaching her rites to mankind, initiating all who desired to know her mysteries. As a final gift, she selected one of the noble youths of Eleusis, Triptolemos, and instructed him in the arts of cultivation, so that mankind could settle in one place and enjoy the fruits of agriculture.

The Meanings of the Myth

Modern interpreters of the myth of Demeter-Persephone fall into three categories: those who see the myth in terms of nature and an explanation of seasonal cycles of growth and decay; those who see the myth primarily in human terms, both of human cycles of birth, death, and resurrection and of psychological cycles of separation, initiation, and return; and finally, those who see the myth in spiritual terms as a description of the triumph of consciousness over repressive subconsciousness, or the triumph of the sublimation of the soul's struggle with earthly desire.

The Classical understanding of the existence of the human soul (or *psyche*) as a unique and structured entity within each individual was developed by Socrates (as related to us by Plato). He taught that the soul, or *psyche*, was the center of life, the reason for being, and the object of philosophical and spiritual attention. The soul had a structure, just as an individual did. It had a body, a mind, and a spirit, just as an individual did. And as this soul was both present and vital to existence, it became important to discover the nature of the soul and the laws by which it operated.

The myth of Demeter-Persephone is related to these new Classical ideas about the soul in that the Mysteries, which grew out of the myth, were intended to be the initiation of the individual soul into the brotherhood of the saved. The soul struggled just as the individual did to deal with its earthly and divine situation. It sought release through the perfection of its divine attributes, striving for rhythm (*eurhythmia*) and harmony (*eurharmostia*) with the gods.

Although the myth has agricultural connections and can be read at this simple level and also has psychological connections which can be applied to physical and mental existence, the most important interpretations have to do with spiritual transformation. There are certain themes which have become associated with the Eleusinian Mysteries and its Homeric myth which appear again and again in the history and conduct of the rites. The first is the marriage of the Olympian sky gods to the chthonic gods of the underworld, or the marriage of conscious and subconscious forces and the resulting containment and transformation of the latter. Demeter is the Olympian spirit of the earth, a force of conscious spiritual power. Hades is an underworld god, king of the dead, keeper of souls, a symbol of subconscious power, but still a spiritual force as brother to Zeus. Persephone is the innocent maiden abducted to the underworld against her will. She is a savior for mankind, queen with Hades and yet virgin (pure spirit) on Olympus where she lives eight months of the year with her mother. Her return is the affirmation of immortality possible in the purified soul of man.

The second theme of importance in the Mysteries is the initiation ceremony and its spiritual significance. Here the themes of spirit (consciousness), earthly desire (subconsciousness), repression (separation and denial), and sublimation (transforming subconscious desire into consciousness) are played out in the myth. Persephone is the innocent earthly desire attracted to the sensuous narcissus and swept underground to marry Hades (repression). If she eats of the food of death (the pomegranate provided by Hades), she will forever repress her desires and become a captive to them, unable to transform them to conscious spirit. Because she represents the human condition in this myth, Persephone eats a seed from the pomegranate taken from Hades' orchards and appears condemned. Thus, she has that within her which must be sublimated and transformed. Demeter represents that spirit which exists unblemished by earthly desire and which has the power of transformation.

As the result of intervention by Zeus (pure Consciousness), Persephone is permitted, despite having eaten of the fruit of death, to return for most of the year. She is thus able to transform her state through grace and her mother's power over nature. To sublimate rather than repress desire means to keep a pure spirit and heart in spite of contrary desires and to be obedient to the spiritual powers who are working on behalf of salvation. Thus, the key to this mystery is the difference between unhealthy, destructive repression, and healthy, life-enhancing sublimation.

Repression means to cover, to separate, to deny, to hide. It means to internalize to the point of spiritual stagnation. It is the route of cynicism, the path of darkness, and it produces destructive guilt. Sublimation, on the other hand, means to transform, to uncover, to join, to affirm, to open. It involves trust and conviction, and it is the path of light. To know the difference when faced with earthly desire is to know the proper path to enlightenment. To be able to exercise the will to follow that path is to know enlightenment. To accept help from spiritual guides and gods is to understand the nature of human limitation and is the key to successful sublimation.

The Rites

The old Archaic myth of the two goddesses became ritual in the two major celebrations associated with the Mysteries: the Lesser Mysteries in Athens and the Greater Mysteries in Eleusis. There appeared in the rites an additional element from the Orphic tradition in which Persephone gives birth to a male child, the result of her abduction by Hades. The child is identified frequently with Dionysos, particularly in Classical times. The cry "Iakche" (ee-ak-ay) which is associated with the Mysteries and with other celebrations of Dionysiac revels refers to Iakchos, a demigod often identified with Dionysos himself.

Candidates for initiation into the Mysteries had to be adults, slave or free, citizens of Athens or aliens, who presented themselves as pure of hands (no murderers, for example) and able to speak Greek. The language requirement seems to have been based on the need to understand the instructions and the ability to sing the various hymns and call out the sacred words which were so important a part of the ritual. Although only adults were initiated, one boy, especially chosen, took part each year, presumably to represent the figure of Iakchos or Dionysos in the ceremony. The boy and his family were much honored that year.

The Lesser Mysteries took place in Athens, in a sanctuary called Agra near the Ilissos River. This sanctuary dedicated to Artemis should not be confused with the Eleusinian in the Agora. The Agra site is located on the Arditos Hill near the present site of the modern Olympic Stadium. The date for the Lesser Mysteries was the twentieth of Anthesterion (mid-February), and the candidates for initiation, the *mystai*, gathered at a small temple of Meter, mother of the gods, for purification and sacrifice. This ceremony was a necessary part of the initiation and could not be missed if the initiate wished to participate in the Greater Mysteries seven months later.

Little is known of the details of the Lesser Mysteries, except that the candidates were "consecrated" at this time through purification rites as proper *mystai* in the *myesis* or beginning of the ritual of initiation. According to the late poet and scholar Robert Graves, the Lesser Mysteries enacted a marriage between Dionysos and a minor goddess, Thyone (or Semele). Many commentators suggest the working out of sexual themes as central to these rites.

THE GREATER MYSTERIES

The Greater Mysteries began on the fourteenth of Boedromion, which we generally associate with September 22, and lasted for nine days, corresponding to the wanderings of Demeter in search of Kore. On this day the officials from Eleusis, including the high priestess, the Hierophant (high priest), the Dadouchus (torchbearer), left from the sanctuary at Eleusis and marched along the Sacred Way to Athens, a distance of just over 12 miles (20 km). The procession was met by youths from Athens assigned to conduct the official party to the Eleusinion in the Agora, where the cult objects (*heira*) were deposited temporarily.

The next day, the fifteenth of Boedromion (September 23), was regarded as the first official day of the Mysteries. On this day the officials of the Athenian *polis,* including the Archon Basileus, whose task it was to maintain the Athenian religious calendar, met with the Eleusinian party to inaugurate the Mysteries. Sacrifices were made on the Acropolis to ask Athena for her blessing, and a ceremony took place in the Agora giving a blessing to the *mystai.*

The Pig Sacrifice

On the sixteenth of Boedromion (September 24), early in the day, throughout Athens the cry was heard, "*Mystai* to the sea." A procession formed in which each initiate took a sacrificial pig to the sea, washed it and himself, sacrificed the pig, and then buried the body in a deep pit. This sacrifice was intended to enact a symbolic death for each initiate, a letting of blood, and a burial in which the personal self or ego died so that the new greater self could be born at Eleusis during the secret nocturnal ceremony.

The sacrifice of the pig, one for each participant, is a significant act. The death of the animal, especially on such a personal, individual basis, created a genuine psychological space within the initiate, an emptiness which had to be filled or replaced with something else. The intention was that the space would be filled with light and would signal the birth of a new life for the soul. In this way the death and burial of the pig as a substitution forced the initiate to strip away the old, material view of existence and to live with the resulting emptiness until such time as it was filled, more than a week later, with a new spiritual realization.

Preparation and Procession

The next two days, the seventeenth and eighteenth of Boedromion were spent in preparation for the procession to Eleusis. Additional sacrifices were made, and the participants from the different cities were gathered together. A special celebration for Asklepios was held, honoring the god of healing and affirming the ancient practice of allowing special dignitaries to enter late into the ritual as, legend had it, Asklepios himself had done. It is also worth noting that Asklepios, in his capacity as a healer, was associated with Hades, god of the dead. Having power over life and death, but also being the compassionate god, made Asklepios an integral part of the ritual.

On the nineteenth of Boedromion (September 27) all the participants gathered for the procession to Eleusis. The day was known as *agyrmos,* the gathering. This day marked the beginning of the rule of secrecy. As a result, the details from this point on are both sketchy and intriguing, since we realize that the rule of secrecy meant that what was regarded as *arrheton,* or ineffable, contained within its awesome aspect the power to create a mystical experience among the *mystai.*

The procession formed at the Eleusinion in the Agora. The officials from Eleusis, including the priestesses carrying the sacred objects in baskets on their heads, led the *mystai* and a whole crowd of celebrants through the Agora, through the Kerameikos and out the Sacred Gate. At the head of the procession a priest carried a wooden statue of Iakchos, the boy god whose birth would be a culminating event in the secret ritual.

Myrtle leaves were woven into the hair of the marchers and each initiate carried a myrtle bough, sacred to Dionysos and symbolic of the death of the old life and the birth of the new. The myrtle, for example, was carried by Greek colonists when they left their homeland to start a new home in a distant land. The participants also sang hymns along the way and chanted sacred words and phrases, all designed to keep the mind focused on the object of devotion, in this case the statue of Iakchos.

One of the familiar aspects of any initiation is the so-called hazing or mockery which greets the candidate who desires inclusion into a secret society. This mockery is usually intensely personal and is meant to humiliate and to reveal for the initiate the folly of his or her gross existence. The procession to Eleusis included such mockery as the line of initiates crossing the Kephisos River in Athens. On the bridge spanning the river, groups of mockers, probably Eleusinians, greeted each initiate with insults. Thus exposed, the old self literally died for shame.

After the *gephyrismoi,* or "bridge jests" as they were called, the procession began the long climb up to the pass at Daphni, where ritual stops were made at temples sacred to Apollo and Aphrodite. In Euripides' *Helen* we learn that it was Aphrodite who managed with beautiful music to relieve Demeter's mourning during Kore's confinement with Hades. Such gifts and power to relieve sadness were celebrated during this solemn procession. At this point, too, the procession came in sight of the twin peaks of the island of Salamis,

which to *mystai* of the Classical Period would have suggested the great victory over the Persians and the miraculous
advent of the mystical *mystai* on that occasion.

It should also be mentioned here that some archaeologists
put the bridge-jesting ceremony closer to Eleusis at the
crossing of the Eleusinian Kephisos River, where now a
Roman road and bridge have been uncovered on the left side
of the National Highway leading into Eleusis. The weight of
evidence seems to place the bridge in question closer to
Athens.

As night fell on the procession, the torches were lit and the
throng came down the pass and approached the sanctuary of
Eleusis. The darkness must have matched the mood of the
participants, who by this time were tired, thirsty, and
hungry. During the Archaic Period, a large dancing ground
outlined the famous Well of the Beautiful Dances, where
initiates or specially chosen dancers enacted in ritual movements the arrival of Demeter in Eleusis after her nine days
of fruitless searching.

THE NIGHTS OF THE MYSTERIES

As the initiates arrived in Eleusis and entered the sanctuary,
they came, as had Demeter, searching for Kore, which in
their case meant searching for the return of an innocent
"soul" from the ravages of the underworld. The actual events
of the next two nights are obscured by the rule of secrecy.
What is available to us now are unconnected details: descriptions from literary accounts, illustrations from pottery and
sculpture, and interpretations based on archaeology and
anthropology.

In the abstract, the initiates were now exposed to the
horrors of the underworld, to its darkness, uncertainty, fear,
and loneliness. Even in a crowd, this experience must have
left each participant feeling isolated, filled with an emptiness
which resulted from this temporary but vivid separation from
all that was ordinary and familiar. For the next two days the
individual was exposed to the drama of the Demeter-Kore
myth.

First, the *mystai* had been prepared for this moment by
days of fasting (to what degree is uncertain) and the
day-long march. Before the candidates entered the Telesterion, they took part in further sacrifices and rites of purification, both at or near the ancient well and at the Cave of
Hades, or as it was known then, the Precinct of Plouton, god
of the underworld. At the entrance to this cave was an
omphalos, the world navel which marked the transition from
the world of light to the world of darkness. This moment and
this place marked the symbolic descent by Kore into the
underworld, the place of death from which only the purified
may return to "live again."

Within the Telesterion, the huge building specifically
designed for this ceremony, the participants moved among a

Sacred Precinct of Plouton, a natural cave with an altar. Often seen as entrance to the underworld, Eleusis.

grove of columns in dim light provided by torches and then stood, perhaps for hours, on rows of narrow steps which line the sanctuary. In the middle of the Telesterion was another small building, the *anaktoron,* entrance to which was re- served for the high priests and priestesses and from which a great fire would burst at the crucial moment of the ritual. Outside of this building, among the columns, was performed the drama of Demeter's wrath and Kore's return.

A Christian writer, Hippolytos, wrote that at a crucial moment in the ceremony the high priest shouted out, "The Mistress has given birth to a holy boy; Brimo has given birth to Brimos; that is, the Strong One to the Strong One." Piecing together the evidence has led to the conclusion that it was here that the young boy, representing both Demo- phoon in the Homeric myth and Iakchos in the Orphic tradition, played his part in the ceremony. Ringed by torches, the boy emerged in a fiery birth from the womb of the returned goddess. The transformation sought by the *mystai* is here represented by the birth of the new soul in fire, a burning away of the old self and the birth of the new out of the ashes. There is evidence of cremation near the Teleste- rion which would connect the sacred fire with ceremonies of death and rebirth.

During this drama, which may well have involved sym- bolic or actual intercourse between the high priest and priestess, the participants enacted ritual movements and actions with the sacred objects kept in the baskets which had been carried to and from Athens the week before. The baskets contained sacrificial cakes, sheaves of grain, and, perhaps, phallic objects which were used during the cere- mony by each initiate to mimic the implanting of the seed of life into the fertile goddess of the earth.

Evidence also suggests the sacrifice of a ram by the high

priest during the ceremony as a means of communicating with the underworld. According to Clement of Alexandria, who wrote a tract condemning the Mysteries, the actions involving the ram were undertaken as expiation by Zeus for the rape of Demeter which produced Persephone. Clement writes: "Zeus tore off a ram's testicles. He brought them to Demeter and threw them in the folds of her dress, thus doing false penance for his rape, as if he had castrated himself."

If this action was a part of the ceremony, it would have been undertaken as part of the drama of sacrifice and atonement in which the participants enact the abduction and rape of Kore, and celebrate the birth of a savior who will reestablish a new divine and human order. In this sequence the return of Persephone as arranged by Zeus is an atonement for his original rape of Demeter, the establishment of a higher order of divine justice, and the gift of immortality in which human beings now have their portion.

Finally, to the awesome sounds of a huge gong or drum which must have filled the Telesterion and the surrounding countryside with thunder, a great light burst forth from the *anaktoron* and in it appeared the *kore* in an epiphany. The appearance of the *kore* at the crucial moment of the ritual affirmed all of the content of the myth and the hope of the *mystai* for a renewed life. How this epiphany was accomplished is, of course, the central question of the Mysteries and is its great secret.

After the rites in the Telesterion, the newly initiated poured out of the great hall into the darkness, led by torchlight, and gathered in the nearby meadow. Chanting, dancing, and feasting released the tensions of many days of intense anticipation. The release was also an affirmation of

Remains of the Telesterion, with Mycenaean remains in the foreground, Eleusis.

life and must have also brought with it a sense of renewal. Seeing daily existence in a different light was quite literally an aim of the ritual, and this different "seeing" began as the moon rose over the celebrants as they experienced the release from what may have seemed a lifetime of darkness.

THE SECRET OF THE MYSTERIES

The secret of the Eleusinian Mysteries lies in the connection between the ritual itself and the dim historical record of the shift from the hunting cultures of the Late Glacial Period (8000 B.C.) to the beginning of the agricultural societies of the Near East (approximately 6000 B.C.)—although there is evidence that uncultivated grain gathering took place as early as 15,000 B.C. and probably earlier. The shift to agriculture was marked by the gathering of cereal grains (mostly barley) and the slow development of cultivation of these grains by conscious seasonal sowing of seeds and harvesting. With this gathering came settlement and thus "civilization" as we have come to use the term. The profound change in society which resulted marks a critical point in religious history as well.

The settling process broke a pattern of intimate communion with divine presence and shifted the relationship with that presence to one of sacrificial appeasement and distance. The historical patterns (after 6000 B.C.) of ritual all reflect a longing to be reunited with lost gods, with the apprehension that such loss was caused by the very process of human settlement. When human beings ceased to wander, they ceased to trust in the magical powers of the earth and sky to meet their needs. Settlement brought trust in human skills instead. Civilization meant that existence itself was now in the hands of human power. Offended, the gods withdrew, only to be invoked to come to the aid of men by sacrifice, first human and then animal.

In the myths of the Greek peoples, Demeter (as Mother Earth) gave the secret of agriculture to mankind. This myth established the gift of divine aid and suggested tangible presence. It is through this myth that a connection to divinity is maintained, and the hope remains that man may yet become reunited with all of his gods. There is in the myth reference to the barren conditions that wiped out the natural fruits of the earth upon which life depended. Certainly the last glacial period and numerous droughts remained in human memory to fuel such myths.

The Demeter myth describes these events quite accurately. After Demeter successfully wins the return of her daughter from Hades and settles for keeping her for eight months out of twelve as a lawful expression of Nature, mankind is able to see the connection between the natural law and the divine presence for which it longs. Therefore, the Eleusinian Mysteries were established to provide a ritual through which men could reenact the shift from nomadic to agricultural life, to include the real loss of their gods in a period of glacial darkness, and to be reunited (or forgiven) once again. This ritual pattern is the source of all initiation mysteries.

The secret of the Mysteries is the moment of the reunion, the appearance of Persephone as she emerges from the underworld. At this moment the initiate feels the emotional release from the dark night of the soul and is reborn to the light. The journey of the maiden is the human journey from its grain-gathering nomadic ways to the paralyzing darkness and cold of the underworld only to return again into the light and fecundity of his earthly paradise, a Garden of Eden still occupied by God. Man needs to know that he has not sacrificed union with the gods for the seeming comforts of civilization. Demeter is the forgiving mother, nurturing her children and providing for them the means to return to her bosom after life is over.

These facts help to explain why, in A.D. 364, when the Roman Emperor Valentinian ordered the Mysteries stopped, he was persuaded to allow them to continue on the grounds that life would cease for the Greeks without them. To fail to reenact the ritual would be to bring the darkness back to the earth once more. The guilt for having created civilization (a state of being known only to the gods before Prometheus stole fire for men) could only be assuaged by this ritual. To offend Athena might result in the destruction of Athens, but to offend Demeter would destroy life itself . . . forever.

The Nature of the Secret

In the ninth discourse of the *Bhagavad-Gita,* it is said that the Great Secret of the universe, of life itself, had several characteristics which marked it as a true secret. First, the secret had to be intuitional, that is, capable of being known by anyone wishing to know it and not dependent upon outside teaching or being revealed by an adept. Second, it had to be righteous, that is, lawful, within the bounds of the cosmos, according to universal principles. And third, it had to be pleasant beyond measure, that is, the secret had to be life-enhancing and exceed the pleasures of earthly existence.

These principles suggest that any great cosmic secret, such as that of the Eleusinian Mysteries, has to be available to all, full of light (thus goodness), and must exceed all the pleasures of the earth in its greatness. After all, if the Great Secret of the universe did not exceed the greatest pleasures of the earth, seekers would not care very much what it was, but would strive for the ultimate earthly delights as being the true aim of life.

It is evident that from the history and legends of the Mysteries a tradition has grown that a momentous event occurred that was in some measure miraculous. Such speculation is fueled by the modern sense that ancient peoples had access to levels of perception unknown to later mortals blinded by the excesses of civilization. By the time of the

Eleusinian Mysteries, however, certainly from the Archaic Period onward, there is little evidence that a tangible manifestation could have occurred on an annual basis and not have been reported by someone.

The secret of Eleusis was the miraculous experience of the event, an experience which would remain valid only if the secret was kept. The labyrinthine journey from Athens, the fasting and sacrifices, the terrors of the darkness, the drama of the birth from fire, and the return of the beloved goddess from the underworld, worked together to do in ritual what for many could not be done by philosophical inquiry and devotion. The initiates were given a metaphor for eternal life, worked out in images that reflected their daily lives.

At the final moment of the ritual the initiates must have been filled by the light that burst forth from the inner chamber. The void that many had felt for most of their lives and which had been ritually revealed in the pig ceremony a week earlier had now been filled, not by an idea or by esoteric knowledge but rather by the power of an ancient myth reenacted in their presence and felt at the core of their being.

THE SITE

The journey today from Athens to the site at Eleusis has some of the aspects of the ancient rite: the taunting jests, the dusty trek, the sense of labyrinth in which the spirit shrinks from its lofty intention and fears for its very existence. All these sensations may be experienced as the modern pilgrim tries to follow the Sacred Way and to appreciate the vitality and importance of this annual rite to the ancient Greek peoples.

The National Highway heading north out of Athens passes through urban sprawl typical of twentieth-century industrial expansion. Except for the relief felt at the pass at Daphni, where the natural beauty of the landscape and respect for its heritage have been preserved as a public park and campgrounds, the twelve-mile route demonstrates the denial of spirit so notable in modern life throughout the world today.

The site of the Eleusinian sanctuary itself has been cramped and nearly obliterated by the steady encroachment of a cement factory and the inexorable growth of the local port facility. The smokestacks of the factory seem for just a moment like columns against the dusty sky, and it takes a determined eye to see beyond them to pick out the ancient landscape features which directed the original founders of the sanctuary to establish the Mysteries on this particular acropolis.

What *is*, however, pleasant and a relief after the journey out of Athens or from the highway coming in from Corinth, is the relative peace and quiet of the site itself. Seldom do crowds arrive in tour buses or large numbers of tourists descend on the site all at once. One usually has an opportunity to gather oneself for a focused tour of a place which spans two thousand years of continuous occupation for a single sacred purpose, a purpose quickly felt as familiar features like the ancient well, the Cave of Hades, and the remains of the great Telesterion itself greet the attentive eye.

It is possible to enjoy a relaxed lunch or afternoon coffee in the small town which serves the sanctuary, and the modest museum at the site offers several important artifacts for inspection, including several marbles showing early representations of Demeter and Kore.

ORIENTATION

There are two ways of approaching a visit to Eleusis. One is to approach as an initiate might have, by locating the ruins of the Sacred Way to the left of the modern entrance and proceeding past the sacred well, through the Roman propylaia, past the Precinct of Plouton, up the Sacred Way, and into the Telesterion. The other is to seek a higher vantage point initially in order to grasp the general pattern of structural elements before attempting a closer examination.

Because the site is such a maze of ruins from Mycenaean to Late Roman times, it may be more useful to survey the site from an elevated vantage point and to sacrifice the pilgrim's approach. Such a point is available on the top of the ancient acropolis where now the Church of Panayia dominates the scene.

The Sacred Way, from the entrance to the Lesser Propylon, Eleusis.

From here, with the remains of the Telesterion down to the right, the visitor is able to grasp the sense of the development of the site over the years. The center of the sacred site, the Telesterion, was created by cutting into the rock of the acropolis to the southeast to level the ground for the massive foundations of the great hall. It was in this space that the first Mycenaean cult center was built. For the most part the natural features of the eastern slope were left alone in order to frame the cave where tradition has placed the descent to the underworld.

To the left, or north, where the entrances were built, the level ground accommodated several temples and in Roman times the massive propylaia and stone terraces which now dominate much of that area. To the east are ruins which are primarily Roman, including a triumphal arch, baths, and a retaining wall. Beyond the Telesterion to the east and south are the remains of the massive walls built during the Classical Period under the direction of Pericles. These walls guaranteed that no unwelcome visitor would invade the ceremonies and no invading army overrun the sanctuary.

OUTSIDE THE SANCTUARY

The visitor may now begin where the ancient *mystai* made their entrance to the site, at the point where the Sacred Way enters the sanctuary. The area has some modern facilities, mostly work areas and bathrooms for visitors, but here is where the ancient road from Athens ended. The first feature of interest is the Archaic well, still preserved, where tradition has it that Demeter sat when she arrived after her nine-day journey. Over the years the well has been preserved by walls and was included in the general terracing done by the Romans.

To the right, or north, are the ruins of a temple of Artemis, built by the Romans, now evident only as a dim foundation. Next to it are the remains of an *eschara,* or underground altar, at which offerings were made to the gods of the underworld. The outer court, which earlier would have been the dancing ground, focuses the attention upon the Great Propylaia, of Roman construction, where the *mystai* made their formal entrance to the sanctuary.

The Greater and Lesser Propylaia

The Hellenistic remains of the Greater Propylaia are sufficient to give a clear impression of the magnitude of this entrance way. Six marble steps approached a portico supported by six columns leading to three doors giving way to a rear portico supported by six more columns. The propylaia directed the initiate toward the Lesser Propylaia and the Precinct of Plouton, before which sacrifices were made.

The Lesser Propylaia also had three doors, but the center door was larger and framed by two Corinthian columns. The

The Greater Propylon, showing in the background a square floor with the bases of four rows of three columns each. The porch is the light area in a rectangular shape. The procession angled to the left after passing through this gate, Eleusis.

interior of the Lesser Propylaia featured another large door-way framed by two Karyatides, named Kistophoros by the Greeks because they carried on their heads the baskets containing the sacred elements of the Mysteries. One of these priestesses of the *mystica* may be seen in the Eleusis Museum (#5104 in the collection).

The Precinct of Plouton

Certainly one reason for the location of the Mysteries on this site was the existence of this cave. The associations with the Demeter-Kore myth are rich in detail, and tradition has it that it was here that Persephone was seized by Hades and taken to the underworld. The cave, then, was the point of transition. The *mystai* must have prayed that they would return from their dark journey into the light once more and that Persephone would be permitted to return to the living. Thus, the faithful prayed here and invoked the dark god who dwelled below.

In addition, there is archaeological evidence of the foundation of a platform which some observers suppose to have supported an *omphalos*. Sometimes described as a world navel, the image is, by Western standards, not wholly accurate. The *omphalos* was also an image of a pile of ash which covered and protected the coals of the hearth so that the fires could be lighted once more.

The Telesterion

In Mycenaean times a cult building was located on this site, not at the center of the present remains but to the east of the center. Remains can be distinguished to the left of the center line of stones. In the time of Pericles, the Telesterion was

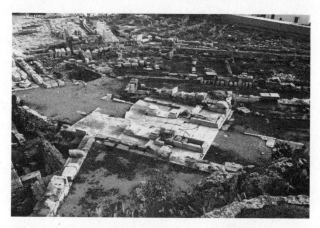

The Lesser Propylon, a much smaller entrance. The remains show door grooves in the marble floor. The file of initiates narrowed at this point before entering the Sacred Way, Eleusis.

rebuilt under the direction of Iktinos, builder of the Parthenon. The new building measured 170 feet by 174 feet (51.8 m by 53 m) and had a peaked roof which was supported by forty-two columns, six rows of seven columns each. Surrounding the central cult building and the columns were rows of eight steps on all sides. The initiates no doubt stood on these steps during the ceremony. Their vision of the ritual would have been blocked somewhat by the columns, but the effect must have been intended, or at least compensated for

The eight stone steps of the Telesterion, carved out of the natural hillside, Eleusis.

in some way, perhaps by the constant movement of the celebrants through the space.

In terms of sacred numerology we can see that the patterns of six and seven columns reflect both the creative principles of the ritual and the divine number of completion. The eight steps remind us of the eight steps of baptismal fonts, reflecting the idea of a new birth or new state of being for the initiates. The nearly square shape of the building suggests the manifest world out of which will arise, in fire rising from the center, a spiritual unity at the climax of the ritual. Such a conception lay behind the construction of all square-based pyramids in Egypt and Central America.

The Telesterion in the Classical Period would have held over three thousand initiates for the ceremony. Access to the huge building was gained from two side entrances opening directly onto the Sacred Way. There were entrances also on the eastern and southern sides. On the eastern side of the square a stoa was constructed of white marble in the fourth century B.C. It had twelve columns across the front and three on the sides. This Stoa of Philon, as it was called, seems to have been added during a period of aesthetic decoration of the sanctuary.

Outside the Telesterion

Since the sanctuary of Eleusis functioned throughout the year and was maintained by a council and a priesthood, there was need of support buildings, both within and outside the enclosure. To the south, built into the Classical fortification wall, was a Bouleuterion, or Council House, where the ruling council met to administer the affairs of the sanctuary. Its remains are indicated by the half circle of stones near the south gate. In front of the Bouleuterion are the remains of the wall erected in the fifth century B.C. when Iktinos was architect of the sanctuary. The massive wall behind the Bouleuterion was built by Lycurgus a hundred years later.

The ruins outside the sanctuary to the south include a gymnasium of Hellenistic construction and a Roman building devoted to the cult of Mithra, the Middle Eastern religion associated with Zoroaster. This cult was popular with the Roman troops who garrisoned the outposts of the empire. Mithraism had its roots in bull sacrifices which were associated with pledges of immortality for the initiates. It was one of the important mystery religions, which made it natural that its cult would appear at Eleusis during the Roman Period.

THE MUSEUM

The Museum of Eleusis offers several important artifacts excavated at the site. In Room #1, for example, a fine amphora of the Archaic Period (650 B.C.) illustrates on the neck of the vase the binding of Cyclops by Odysseus and on the body the myth of Medusa. #5235 is the Fleeing *Kore*, a marble pedimental sculpture depicting one of the friends of Persephone fleeing the scene of the abduction. #5053 is a marble piglet, emblematic of the sacrificial pigs which formed a part of the Greater Mysteries.

In Room #2 is a copy of the Eleusinian Relief of Demeter, Kore, and Triptolemos, the original of which resides in the National Archaeological Museum in Athens (see p. 229). #5076 is a marble Demeter from 420 B.C., typical of the Late Classical Period. The piece illustrates the conception of Demeter as Mother Earth in her capacity as nurturer.

Room #3 has a fine example of the attributes of Dionysos done in white marble (#5091). This Roman copy of a Classical piece shows the god as mortal, languid, amoral, almost careless in aspect. There is a sexuality here that is both masculine and feminine, but there is also a distance that does not encourage intimacy. He has long hair entwined with ivy and leans on a vine-covered support, his hand gently touching the grapes.

#5140 in Room #3 is a basin bearer, a statue of a girl holding a marble basin for water. Two of these sculptures stood at the entrances to the Telesterion and were used by the initiates to wash their hands just before entering the hall. The large hole in the center held the support for the large basin. Also worth noting in Room #3 is the headless sculpture of Asklepios, god of healing, which was found to the north of the sanctuary with other artifacts, suggesting the existence of an Asklepeion associated with Eleusis (#5100).

Room #4 contains two models of the sanctuary executed by Travlos. The first pictures the site as it might have looked in the sixth century B.C. when the Telesterion was much smaller. The second model represents the site during the Roman Imperial Period. Of particular interest here is the emphasis in that time on the outer court and the formality of the formal entrances to the sanctuary.

Room #5 holds the Karyatid (#5104) referred to earlier as one of two such columns framing the central door of the Lesser Propylaia. Tradition has it that this figure was half buried through much of modern times and was revered by the local people who associated it with Demeter and offered prayers to it for good harvests. Notable in this sculpture are the Gorgon head on the breast after the manner of Athena and the basket or *kiste* on the head, decorated with sacred rosettes.

Finally, in Room #6 or the Vase Room, there is a fine collection of pottery from all periods of Eleusinian history. The earliest pieces are Neolithic (in Case #1) and date from 2500 B.C. and earlier. Of importance in Case #5 is a stirrup jar dated from the Mycenaean Period containing an inscription in Linear B script. In Case #21 are two *kernoi,* or headpieces, used to carry offerings to the goddess. Cuplike receptacles held grains or oils. The *kernoi* are pictured in vase paintings depicting the procession to Eleusis.

EPIDAUROS

Epidauros is a sanctuary of Asklepios, a man, a myth, and a tradition worshipped throughout Greece as the god of healing. Epidauros is one of the important cult sites. The cult of Asklepios was involved more with individual worship and healing than with collective worship at the level of the *polis,* although it was renowned throughout Greece and was the site of major Panhellenic festivals in honor of the god.

Of the hundreds of local cults associated with Asklepios, the sanctuary at Epidauros was the largest and most important. A smaller sanctuary is nestled in the hillside just above the Theatre of Dionysos in Athens, and another sat just below the Temple of Apollo at Delphi. The connection of the cult to drama, in particular, was notable in the Greek culture. In the very best sense, drama was a healing art. It purged the viewer of unholy thoughts by the power of its subject matter and the patterns of the performance. At Epidauros, the magnificent fourth century B.C. theatre is almost powerful enough today to purge the viewer of the ills of civilization, even without benefit of a play.

HISTORY

The history of this site tells the story of the Greek concept of health, the idea of which was originally connected to worship, to "right thinking" from which came physical well-being. When the Olympians came upon the scene, Apollo became the god of the soul and its health within the body. In the worship of Apollo, the Greeks understood the need for moderation in all aspects of life. The balanced life was conducive to the health of the soul, and part of that balance was the proper and measured worship of Apollo and his son Asklepios, whose compassion for mankind made him a major cult figure.

Asklepios was worshipped as a god and was also thought of as an historical figure. His approach to medicine had the same duality. The cause of illness lay in the psyche, and the manifestations were both physical and spiritual. If a man

Theatre at Epidauros, showing near perfect condition and circular orchestra.

was not "thinking straight," he was not capable of relieving the physical symptoms of illness. First, the mind had to be aligned to the mind of Apollo, then the body might recover its balance and health.

HIPPOKRATES

In the history of Greek medicine the figure of Hippokrates is central. It is not a coincidence that this famous physician was born on the island of Cos, which was an ancient site in the worship of Asklepios. Hippokrates was born somewhere around 460 B.C. and was thus a Classical figure. He was present in Athens during the crisis of the Peloponnesian War, where he was an important figure both in philosophy and medicine. He died in Thessaly in 377 B.C. Aside from his famous oath, his greatest contribution came as a result of his theory of "humors." This theory relates to the laws of internal secretions, or hormonal controls operating in the system and affecting almost every aspect of physical and mental functioning.

It is now generally believed that the flow of hormones is responsible for the state we might refer to as "right thinking," that is, the balance of secretions within the body that controls mental as well physical health. It is in this area of medical research that we are coming closer and closer to understanding the relationship of physical, mental, and spiritual well-being in the human organism. Drastic fluctuations in human behavior caused by uncontrolled desires or the excessive gratification of basic needs can so disrupt the system that illness results. For the ancient Greek, the worship of Apollo was the first step in establishing a proper sense of life so that desires and needs were kept in balance. The active worship of Asklepios was usually prompted by signs of physical or mental illness, the symptoms of which were treated first. But there was always the principle and purity of Apollonian worship in the background or in the foreground if the patient was truly aligned with the laws.

THE HISTORICAL RECORD

Pausanius tells us that the recorded history of this site begins with the worship of Apollo of Malea, a name which means that the god is associated with a local cult and locale. Apollo's sanctuary is on top of Mount Kynortion, which rises just behind the theatre. This site dates at least from Mycenaean times and was certainly in continuous use from that period. Pilgrims to the Asklepieion frequently made the ascent to Apollo's sanctuary to make a preliminary sacrifice before entering the main sanctuary.

The Asklepieion itself dates from the sixth century B.C. and was in use well into the fifth century of the Christian era. Even a thorough sacking by the Roman Sulla in 86 B.C. failed to end its useful life. In its prime, however, in the fifth and fourth centuries B.C., the sanctuary was a brilliant example of the Greek vision of human health and spiritual well-being. Pilgrims arrived continuously for specific cures at the hands of the temple priests, but there were also festivals, the principle one being the Great Asklepeia, which took place every four years in the spring. The festival lasted for nine days, and over the years the activities displayed the full range of human expression. There were "gymnic" games of athletic skill in the stadium in which participants showed their prowess in sprints, boxing, wrestling, broad jumping and discus throwing. Added in later years were both musical and dramatic competitions.

True to the spirit of all festivals in Greece, there was a sacred intent. In the very best sense, the purpose was to reestablish for the pilgrim the proper hierarchy with nature, which, of course, included the gods as well. This intent was both abstract and practical. It showed once again that the great contribution of the ancient Greeks to Western culture was to articulate at the very limits of human understanding and knowledge what it meant to be a part of the cosmos.

MYTHOLOGY

The myth of Asklepios originates deep in the Greek past with the Earth Goddess. Both share the symbol of the snake as a sign of rebirth and eternal life, and it is this connection to the more ancient beliefs of the Earth Mother cults that gives Asklepios his closeness to the common people, that makes him a nurturing, sympathetic god. There is even evidence now that early images of Jesus closely resemble Asklepios, thus connecting him in the Greek mind with the transition to Christianity. Asklepios is also associated firmly with the

Olympian sky gods, giving him even greater importance in formal rituals and festivals.

As told to us by Pindar, Asklepios was the son of Apollo and a beautiful young virgin named Coronis, daughter of King Phlegyas of Thessaly. The unfortunate Coronis, already bearing the "fruit of the love of the bright god," made the fatal mistake of falling in love with a mortal. At Apollo's jealous urging, Coronis was killed by Artemis, but not before the baby was saved and sent off to be raised by the wise and gifted centaur Chiron, who, among other things, taught the young Asklepios the art of healing. When he reached manhood, Asklepios began his work. He was known for his great skill as well as his compassion.

The centaur Chiron is a symbol of bestiality, of physical man without a spiritual center. In many ways Chiron represented the secularization of medicine in Greece, that is, the change of medicine from a sacred science to medicine in the hands of professional practitioners. And since Asklepios is taught medicine by Chiron, Asklepios in turn becomes a symbol of a blend of sacred and secular medicine. Another way of thinking about the same idea is to see Epidauros as a center for the simultaneous practice of spiritual and physical medicine.

Central to the popularity of Asklepios among the people is the account of his death. In his compassion, he brought a human being back to life. Zeus struck and killed him with his lightning bolt because to bring a mortal back to life transgresses divine law and is punishable by death. Zeus reminds us that the proper end of man is spiritual life and not the eternal life of the body. The myth of Asklepios establishes the proper balance between the roles of Zeus, Apollo, Chiron, and Asklepios in the arts of medicine.

THE LOCAL GOD

Pausanius, our other valuable source of background, repeats another tale from his travels through Epidauros. The warlike Phlegyas, bent on conquering the whole Peloponnese, brought his retinue, including the pregnant Coronis, to Epidauros and was occupied in counting the population when his daughter gave birth to the young Asklepios. She took the child to the top of what may now be called Mount Titthion, or "the teat," where the child was suckled by a goat and protected by the goatherd's dog. This "natural" start in the god's life indicates his affinity with the earth and with the healing arts.

The mythology of Asklepios, then, emphasizes his position relative to the gods and mankind. On the one hand he is the son of Apollo, the bright but distant god of Olympus, and on the other he had a mortal mother. He was raised by Chiron, a centaur, whose associations with the earth and animal existence give him a common touch. He understood the suffering of human life in ways that Apollo could not.

THE SITE

> *At Epidauros, in the stillness, in the great peace that came over me, I heard the heart of the world beat. I know what the cure is: it is to give up, to relinquish, to surrender, so that our little hearts may beat in unison with the great heart of the world.*
>
> —HENRY MILLER

The natural environment of Epidauros is ample, gentle, and protective. From any point in the sanctuary the surrounding hills offer the viewer an undulating horizon line, a blending of earth and sky. It is peaceful here, and the feeling of peace is created by a unifying of natural elements. The architecture of the space exhibited similar principles of harmony through geometry and number for the purpose of stilling the mind, focusing the attention, and inspiring reverence and confidence to affect the desired cure. Each building within the sanctuary had its purpose and the appropriate design within the context. The key buildings were the Temple of Asklepios, the Tholos, the Abaton, and the Great Altar of Asklepios. Nearby were the ancient Abaton and the smaller Temple of Artemis (see Fig. 23).

But the sanctuary was only a part of the total effect of the

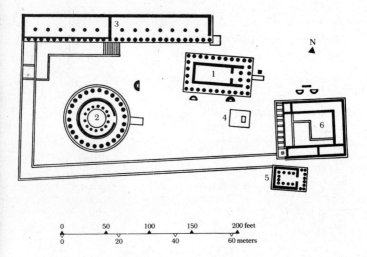

Fig. 25. *Sanctuary at Epidauros*
1. *Temple of Asklepios*   4. *Altar*
2. *Tholos Temple*   5. *Temple of Artemis*
3. *Abaton*   6. *Earlier Abaton*

complex of Epidauros. Included in the curative environment were also the stadium, where games of skill and athletic contests tested human endurance and strength, the gymnasium, where lectures and philosophical discussions enlivened the mind, and the theatre, where plays were performed as part of the cathartic process so vital to physical, mental, and spiritual health. These elements were added gradually to the site over a long span which really has its beginnings in the prehistoric period.

ARCHAEOLOGY AT EPIDAUROS

Archaeological work began on the site at Epidauros in 1881. At this time the theatre and several temples, the gymnasium, and connecting buildings were uncovered. This work, conducted primarily by Kavvadias, ended in 1927. After World War II work continued in the sanctuary and on Mount Kynortion, to the south, where a temple to Apollo was excavated. Most of these finds dated from the Archaic Period. The beautiful temples in the sanctuary date from the fourth century B.C. when the cult was enjoying a resurgence of devotion and support. Excavation below the fourth century B.C. level revealed prehistoric remains dating from the Early Helladic Period (c. 3000 B.C.). Also, human and animal figurines from the Late Helladic Period (c. 1400 B.C.) indicate cult activity during the Mycenaean era.

This early habitation shows that from the beginning there was a common theme in the veneration of the figure of Asklepios beyond the immediate concern for specific cures for specific illnesses. As we see the heart of the site, the sanctuary, we know that for the Greeks, even in the earliest eras, the world of spirit came first. Beginning with purification and followed by sacrifice and ending with thank offerings, the activity of the site centered on religious belief and practice. Attached to this central concern, however, were the games, the music, the orations, and the drama, all expressions of the very best of Greek culture. Seeing the theatre, the stadium, and the gymnasium, it is easy to conclude, as many have, that Epidauros was nothing but an elaborate spa for the wealthy of Greece, a place to dry out from the excesses of good living, where the guests were entertained and pampered by doctors, priests, actors, and athletes. Such is our history after all, our decline and fall.

But the evidence suggests otherwise. During the Archaic, Classical, and early Hellenistic Periods, the cult of Asklepios at Epidauros was a source of renewal and strength for the Greek culture. The games, music, and drama at Epidauros demonstrated the full range of the human instrument put to regenerative purpose. The speed, agility, strength, lyricism, eloquence, harmony, and passion, all elevated the spirits of the ill and weak, not to mention the depressed and cynical. In these contests and concerts the best were raised up as exemplars of achievement; they were honored above all others for having risen to such heights. In this honor was the aspiration of the whole race of men standing before their gods.

In the past several years, work at Epidauros has been renewed. The modern visitor will be interested to see fresh digs and new finds. There is some inconvenience in this activity in that areas will be roped off and access limited. But for the attentive visitor, this activity is an opportunity to see how archaeology is conducted, how areas are gridded and levels cataloged for later examination.

The Propylaia

Visitors to Epidauros will arrive at a parking area to the south of the sanctuary. The modern entrance to the site leads directly to the museum as a starting point. But the ancient pilgrim entered from the north. To follow this traditional approach means a walk across the site, away from the theatre to the northern boundary of the excavation. The ancient entrance, or *propylaia,* is at this northern extremity and was approached by crossing a small stream, now unfortunately quite dry and fenced off. The present ruins date from the fourth century B.C. and are located at a point where two major roads converged, one coming from the ancient village of Epidauros on the sea and the other from the direction of Argos.

Over 65 feet (20 m) in length the Propylaia was like a small temple, approached by a ramp (still in evidence). Across the front entrance six Ionic columns supported the entablature, on the architrave of which was inscribed the following verses:

> Pure must be he who enters the fragrant temple;
> Purity means to think nothing but holy thoughts.

The Greek inscription ends with the words *phronein hosia,* a phrase which carries more than the sense of the English translation "think holy thoughts." Included in that phrase is an idea of lawfulness, of turning one's attention away from the world and its temptations and toward the spiritual path, or to "straight thought." What made the pilgrim ill in the first place was bound up in the neglect of lawfulness. Too much of the world, of the pleasures and demands of daily life, usurped the proper place of the divine within the individual with the result that the body became ill, and the mind was clouded with scattered dreams and irrational fears. As a result, the emotional, or psychological, state was out of joint and needed correction.

In the more religious sense, purity also meant to be free of pollution. The admonition was made not to enter the sanctuary for ignoble purposes nor to ridicule the healing process nor to rob the sanctuary of its treasures. Obviously, the whole life of the sanctuary would be threatened by anyone entering without a proper respect for its holiness. Even today

Site of the North Propylon, original entrance to the sanctuary, Epidauros.

in Greece, the casual visitor is watched carefully to make sure that proper reverence in dress and behavior is observed in the sanctuary.

The modern pilgrim will not have much sense of the desired effect of entering the Propylaia and seeing the enclosure ahead. Today trees have replaced the six Corinthian columns which lined the inner passageway. Since columns take their history and meaning from trees, the substitution is not entirely inappropriate, but the sight lines are obscured by the present vegetation. Enough view remains, however, to suggest something of the intent in entering the sanctuary from the north. The sacred way lies ahead, up a gentle incline.

The Sanctuary

Our goal along the sacred way is the sanctuary proper or *heiron* of Asklepios, where the central activity of healing took place. To reach it, the modern pilgrim passes along the sacred way past Roman ruins on the left outside the once restricted portion of the sanctuary. There was, just outside, a small temple of Aphrodite, which offered a chance to pause to make a sacrifice and to pray for healing. As the detail map shows, the main buildings within the *heiron* were six, the most important being the Temple of Asklepios, a fourth century B.C. construction probably built on the remains of an older temple of Apollo. We know that from the late fifth century B.C. onward the site was devoted to Asklepios himself. This shift from Apollo to Asklepios illustrates the change in the perception of healing during the Classical Period. Later, as we shall see, the function of the *abaton* fell from favor and further secularized the practice of medicine at the site.

The Temple of Asklepios

The Temple of Asklepios was oriented to the east and Mount Titthion, the rounded hill sacred to the birth of Asklepios. We are reminded as we look on the sacred hill to the west that although Asklepios is the son of Apollo, from whom all healing arts arise, there is also the organic matter out of which the human substance is formed and which requires the healing arts.

As we learn from the archaeological record, the Temple of Asklepios was peripteral, in the Doric order, with six fluted columns at the ends and eleven columns on each side. The ground plan measured 76 feet (24.5 m) long and nearly 55 feet (13.2 m) wide. Its decoration was elaborate and brightly colored. In the *cella* (or *sekos*) the gold and ivory statue of Asklepios, carved by Thrasymedes of Paros, was of gigantic size and elaborate in design. The god was pictured holding the healing staff of life in his right hand and holding his left hand in firm control over the head of the serpent. The serpent represents a force to be conquered and controlled. In the brilliant structure of the *Tholos,* the art of Asklepios brought the power of the serpent under control for the benefit of mankind, just as Apollo mastered the python in the mythology of Delphi.

The decoration of the throne of Asklepios carried through this theme. The hero Bellerophon is pictured killing the monster Chimera, symbol of powerful and destructive imaginings. Perseus is also pictured with the head of the Medusa, whose demonic aspect turned men to stone. Paul Diel put it this way: "The ancient Greeks made use of an infallible

Bust of Asklepios, fourth century B.C. *This image was often used in statues of Jesus in Christian times, National Archaeological Museum, Athens.*

Foundation of Tholos *temple, showing recent excavations, Epidauros.*

talisman against all kinds of illness. This was the Gorgonian, a medal showing the severed head of Medusa. Thus, mythical inspiration deemed the condition of inner harmony, victory over guilty vanity, to be the supreme protection against illness not only of the soul but also of the body." Thus, the pilgrim gazes upon the symbolic figure of the god in his representation as the conqueror of human vanity and unchecked desires, two of the major causes of human illness. To worship this god was to sublimate (or make sublime) these desires, to give over control to a spiritual power.

The Tholos

At the western-most point of the inner sanctuary are the remains of the most impressive and beautiful buildings at Epidauros. The *Tholos,* or round building, was designed by Polykleitos in the fourth century B.C. and served a central purpose in the curative process of the sanctuary. Recent excavations have revealed much that has remained hidden for centuries. Pausanius offers important information about the *Tholos* when he reports that he saw in it many inscriptions, or *stele,* giving the names and particulars of men and women cured by the god. He also describes some of the decorative murals in the building. One was of Eros playing the lyre and another of Drunkenness holding a wine goblet.

As the remains reveal, the *Tholos* was built over a labyrinth of three concentric stone circles, with openings. This small labyrinth was accessible from a trapdoor in the *cella* floor, which had a black-and-white spiraled mosaic design. The exterior design of the temple must have been most impressive. A circle of twenty-six Doric columns supported an entablature sparsely decorated with rosettes sculpted in the center of the metopes. The inner structure was supported by fourteen beautifully fashioned Corinthian columns, one of

Detail of Tholos—*the labyrinth of three rings of stone, with narrow gates to center, Epidauros.*

which is to be seen in the museum. The sculpting of these columns reveals a control and a symmetry unmatched in ancient Greece. The design exhibits a startling control over natural growth, a perfecting of nature in grace and movement.

The purpose of the *Tholos* has been much debated. It is clear, however, that its symbolic purpose was to represent spiritual control over natural forces. The perfect circular shape is the circle of divinity, the unity of body, mind, and spirit. The exterior of the building is the perfection of Apollo, the form of the spirit embodied in geometric expression. It is also an expression of the imposition of spirit over the potentially destructive, repressed desires of human nature, represented symbolically by the labyrinth beneath the building. Indeed, the upper structure effectively caps and sublimates the lower forces of the labyrinth.

The Greeks expressed this relationship in the concept of *nomos* versus *physis,* or, roughly, law versus nature. The *nomoi* were those laws, both spiritual and secular, which controlled the forces of *physis,* or that part of human nature seen as something like a volcano ready to erupt. The *Tholos,* in its circular design and its natural imagery of plant life and its labyrinth of human passion, is a triumph of control, a resolution of conflict. The exterior of the temple is an expression of *nomos* on the labyrinth or *physis* of human nature, as if the volcano is being capped by spiritual law. The whole building, finally, serves to illustrate a picture of man properly aligned, with spirit over mind and mind over body. It is also a vision of perfect health, and the inscriptions within the temple serve to remind the pilgrim that those who have gone before have found health in this setting.

The ritual role of this building is unclear. Pilgrims might have been led into the labyrinth in a ceremony of the underworld, a passing through the dark night of the soul before emerging to the light and perfection of a new life. Another theory is that ceremonial snakes might have been kept in the labyrinth, again a symbolic statement of mastery over destructive forces. However, we do know that geometric form was for the Greeks a means of articulating forces and powers, and so there must have been a symbolic purpose for this beautiful building and a spiritual intent as a central part of the life of the sanctuary.

Recent excavations at Eutresis on the island of Euboea have revealed the presence of a round pit used for burnt sacrifices. The pit is 20 feet (6 m) in diameter and 10 feet (3 m) deep and gave evidence of ash, animal bones, and pottery. Imposed over this pit, which has been dated in the Early Helladic Period, was a later sanctuary containing a libation table and round hearth. It is certainly possible that these early round pits were the sacrificial precursors of the later *tholos* buildings.

The Abaton

North of the *Tholos* lie the remains of the *Abaton*. Shaped like two long stoa, or narrow colonnades, the Abaton was a place for sleeping and was reserved for the use of those whose cure called for this special ritual. The remains reveal two levels: the higher was approached up sixteen steps, the entire structure being 158 feet long (70 m) and 49 feet wide (9.5 m). During the extensive archaeological digs, many tablets describing miraculous cures were found in the *Abaton*. Now on display in the museum, some of the descriptions reveal clearly the role of the *Abaton*.

The sleep cure was called *enkoimisis* and was carefully prepared for in the process of cure. The patient went

Remains of the lower Abaton, where sleep cures were induced, Epidauros.

through rites of purification and sacrifice before entering the *Abaton* for *enkoimisis*. Certainly, there was some sense in which the god entered the patient in this sleeping state and affected a cure or through the medium of dream indicated what steps should be followed for a cure. Part of the myth of Asklepios includes accounts of snakes approaching the patient and actually licking or touching the affected area, thus accomplishing a cure. This myth once again expresses the idea of spiritual control of natural forces for the purpose of bringing the body back to its natural state of health.

The Cures

The *stele* found at the *Abaton* describe various cures involving *enkoimisis*. *Stele* I says, in part: "Cleo was with child for five years. After she had been pregnant for five years she came as a suppliant to the god and slept in the Abaton. As soon as she had left it and got outside the temple precincts, she bore a son who, immediately after birth, washed himself at the fountain and walked about with his mother. In return for this favor she inscribed her offering: 'Admirable is not the greatness of the tablet, but the divine power. Cleo carried the burden in her womb for five years, until she slept in the Abaton and the god healed her.' "

Another *stele* reads: "A woman from Athens called Ambrosia was blind in one eye. She came as a suppliant to the god. As she walked about in the temple, she laughed at some of the cures as incredible and impossible, [that] the lame and the blind should be healed by merely having a dream. In her sleep she had a vision. It seemed to her that the god stood by her and said that he would cure her, but that in payment he would ask her to dedicate to the temple a silver pig as a memorial of her foolishness. After saying this, he cut the diseased eyeball and poured in some drug. When day came, she walked out of the Abaton completely sound."

These two descriptions of cures can be treated quite literally and, at the same time, as symbolic. The silver pig, for example, would be a symbol of vanity and doubt, an expression of the refusal to acknowledge the spiritual element within. Also, being blind in one eye is an additional sign of denying the divine reality. Thus, sleeping in the *Abaton* can cure this spiritual blindness and can restore health or full sight. A five-year pregnancy can reflect a refusal to acknowledge the presence of the god within. Once recognized, the spirit, cleansed, can move about in the world and be venerated.

On the other hand, we may be witnessing here the literal description of miraculous cures. There are many descriptions of lesser cures which would clearly suggest actual physical illnesses being corrected through spiritual intervention.

As the visitor will see in the museum, the priests and physicians of the Asklepieion also employed surgical instruments and what we would call standard medical practice to effect cures. This evidence comes from a later period when Epidauros had lost much of its spiritual power. The whole archaeological record, however, is a history of the development of medicine and the story of the role of spirit in restoring health.

THE THEATRE

Nothing like the theatre at Epidauros remains in Greece. It is as if the perfection of its design and construction and its placement in the landscape have effectively shielded it from the ravages of men and time. Pausanius praises it in his own understated fashion: "The Epidaurians have a theatre in their sanctuary that seems to me particularly worth a visit. The Roman theatres have come far beyond all the others in the whole world: the theatre of Megalopolis in Arkadia is unique for magnitude: but who can begin to rival Polykleitos for the beauty and composition of his architecture?"

This great structure is not the theatre of Sophocles and Euripides, although their works played here in the fourth century B.C. as they do today in revivals. This theatre does not so much evoke memories of great drama as it does visions of great design. Nowhere is the power of sacred geometry made so accessible. In the fourth century B.C. the wealth and fame of the sanctuary of Asklepios attracted the best artists and builders in Greece to begin extensive renovation of the existing structures and to build new structures like the theatre. Among the most gifted of the builders was Polykleitos the Younger, whom we know already as the builder of the *Tholos*.

From the evidence we can be certain that Polykleitos was well versed in the principles of sacred geometry. At the time

Approach to the theatre, with monumental western parados, *Epidauros.*

that the theatre was being designed and constructed, Plato was teaching philosophy in his Academy in Athens. Over the entrance to the Academy was inscribed—in H.D.F. Kitto's translation—"A credit in geometry is required." Kitto also mentions in the same context that one of Plato's favorite sayings was "God is always doing geometry." What is meant by such a saying is seen in this theatre which embodies spiritual knowledge brought to light, made manifest. It is knowledge to be touched, walked on, sat in, enclosed by, to be experienced fully.

The acoustics are stunning. As the tour guides are delighted to demonstrate, a person standing in the center of the orchestra, at the site of the ancient altar, can tear a small piece of paper—such as an admission ticket—and the sound will carry to the last row of the upper cavea, 55 rows away. Why that is the case no one can articulate in terms of principles of sound, but since geometry made this theatre, we can suppose that geometry creates the acoustical effects.

Geometry and Number

The basic unit of measurement for the theatre—and indeed for many of the fourth century B.C. monuments—was the Pheidonian ell, which corresponded to 1½ Doric feet, or 19.3 inches. Taken flat, the radius of the outermost circle of the theatre is 120 ells. The radius to the inner circle or *diazoma* is 80 ells. It is this point which is probably the extent of the fourth century B.C. construction. Indications are that the upper cavea of 21 rows was added in the second century B.C., no doubt following through with the geometric implications of the original design. The final construction creates a seating arrangement in which the upper cavea has 21 rows

Central aisle of the theatre, showing size of actors from last rows, Epidauros.

and the lower 34. The ratio of 55 (the total number of rows) to 34 is 1.618, which is the ruling number of the Golden Proportion. The same is true of the ratio of 34 to 21. Sacred numerology also reveals several remarkable relations: 55 is the sum of the first ten digits added together, with 21 the sum of 1 through 6 and 34 the sum of 7 through 10.

As Doxiadis pointed out in his analysis of architectural space in Greece, planners used either a ten- or a twelve-part system in design and placing buildings on the site. At

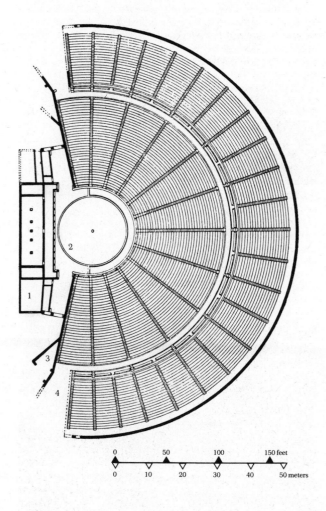

Fig. 26. The Theatre, Epidauros
1. Skene
2. Orchestra
3. Diazoma
4. Upper Cavea

Epidauros, the base was 10, and the aisles of the theatre radiate out at angles of 18 degrees, which is a multiple of ten dividing 360 degrees. This lawful design, so carefully executed, focuses our attention on the center of the orchestra very much the way a magnifying glass focuses the rays of the sun upon a burning point.

Here, in the dramatic competitions, the emotional and intellectual attention of the viewer is focused to create a unifying spiritual intent. It is still possible to experience something of this effect today, as dramatic performances of Greek plays are held during the summer months. It is worth the effort to arrange to stay in Epidauros for the evening, or to drive out from Athens for a production. Even if you do not understand Greek, the sounds of the language in the night air arrange themselves musically and reflect some of the ancient power. The movements of actor and chorus are also beautiful to see in this space. Sitting high up, perhaps near the seats of honor at the *diazoma,* the viewer watches as the action is shaped to a larger design than is usually experienced in secular theatre.

As a last note, during the day, when the theatre is open and is relatively quiet—since even schoolchildren remain in some control in this space—it is possible to sit still for a time. Meditation goes well in this space, and it is never surprising to see still, erect figures blending into the sacred geometry of Epidauros.

DELPHI

And they met together and dedicated
in the temple of Apollo at Delphi
as the first fruits of their wisdom
the far-famed inscriptions
which are in all men's mouths,
"Know Thyself" and "Nothing Too Much."

PLATO, *PROTAGORAS*, 343

Delphi was the spiritual center of the ancient Greek world, radiating out to include the civilizations which had formed around the Mediterranean Sea and the mountainous territories to the north. The natural setting of the sanctuary was in itself sacred, carved out of the southern approaches to Mount Parnassos by earthquake and rockfall and opening out onto the valley of the Pleistos River, which wound like a snake to the sea. As a cult center and sanctuary, Delphi established itself early as a place where revelation became manifest, and where the gods spoke to mankind.

Through most of its history, the god Apollo ruled in Delphi. Apollo represented the harmony of human desires, the Logos or Word of Zeus the Spirit, and the Logos was delivered from the mouths of specially chosen women who had demonstrated tendencies to oracular power. Their utterings were formed into hexameters by temple priests for communication to the faithful. Delphi was a matrix, that is, a place where spirit took form and was heard. In that sense Delphi is still a sacred place, revered by many Greeks and others in the world, although it is silent, no longer expressing the divine laws except as pilgrims are able to embody the sense of them in themselves from the power of the setting and the ruins so lovingly attended.

HISTORY

THE EARTH MOTHER CULTS

Thehistory of the sanctuary of Delphi tells the story of the development of Greek culture and religion. Prior to the

The Temple of Apollo with restored columns and monumental foundations, Delphi.

Archaic Period and the final sweep of the Dorian invasions, Delphi was the center of a cult which worshipped the Earth Mother deity, an underworld deity known as Ge, Gaea or simply the Earth. Bronze Age remains at Delphi have yielded limited but firm evidence of Mother Goddess shrines and figurines. Finds at the Korykeion Cave on Mount Parnassos have also confirmed Earth Mother worship and oracular activity.

The legends of the earlier period tell of the sibyls, the inspired prophetesses who gave oracle at the rock at Delphi and whose utterances were both wondrous and terrible. Oracles were also unpredictable, coming only during certain seasons and without warning. The sibyls were fairly common throughout the Mediterranean and were usually associated with sacred rocks and springs. This cult activity was the remnant of knowledge possessed by prehistoric peoples of the presence of spiritual activity at or near various features of landscape. Throughout the world, myths of the Earth Spirit express similar awareness of revelation occurring at sacred places which in later times became sites for cathedrals and temples. Such sites today include Delphi, Stonehenge, and Chartres.

From 1500 to 1100 B.C., Delphi was a Mycenaean village. The site of the present temple was probably the location of the megaron, within which the cult center for the worship of the Earth Mother Goddess was located. Sacrificial pits have been identified at the point where the inner sanctum or *adyton* of the temple was later placed and also within the sanctuary of Athena Pronaia. These common areas of worship suggest a continuous history of religious activity at very specific places.

THE WORSHIP OF APOLLO

The history of the site suggests that the worship of Apollo may have begun around 1000 B.C. when the god arrived from Dorian Crete or with the northern tribes of Thessaly. With the development of the *polis* and the arts of civilization, Apollo grew in stature and became the dominant god of prophecy. This shift in the image of prophetic power from the feminine to the masculine and from the nomadic to the settled was a function of two related developments.

First, the emphasis upon the *polis*, with its new laws and customs gave rise to a new attitude toward prophecy. The will of Zeus was sought out to affirm decisions made by rulers within the *polis*. Thus, prophecy and civilization were connected in Apollo. It is noteworthy in the history of Greek culture and religion that prophecy achieved such a high place in the official state religion. In many cases no important decision could be made without advice and consent from Delphi.

Second, and of greater spiritual importance, was the desire of civilized men to control and harmonize oracular activity. Such an emphasis was accomplished by the invention of the temple, the "machine" by which human vision and genius invoked the presence of the gods. In the case of Apollo, the temple was the sanctuary where oracular activity took place. The *adyton* held the sacred *omphalos* and the tripod upon which the priestess sat to receive her revelations. The temple controlled access to the place of prophecy, allowing the priests at a later time to give form to the proceedings, and, as it were, to make art out of the raw material of inspiration.

After the Mycenaean period, Apollo took the place of the Earth Mother and her sibyls at Delphi. Later, perhaps in the eighth century B.C., a modest temple of mud brick and wood was erected on the present site. The priests who assumed control of the sanctuary at that time retained the services of sibyl-like priestesses, usually peasant girls who had shown intuitive powers of utterance. The "divine madness" exhibited by these women was given form by the priests, thus providing measure and harmony to the utterances.

It was known and accepted among the Greek peoples that divine utterance was accompanied by fits of seeming madness, a frenzied behavior which marked the point where divine and human consciousness converged. The human instrument was taken over by the god. In such cases, the low-pitched voices of the women seemed to emanate from the abdomen (hence the ancient term "belly talkers"), and the utterances were always couched in the first person, so that it was clear that Apollo himself was the speaker. At such times the women were said to be *en theos* or "with the god," a phrase which gives to English the word "enthusiasm."

Early in the history of Delphi the worship of Dionysos was

introduced in conjunction with that of Apollo. This blend of the rational and irrational elements in religious belief and practice was probably a recognition of the natural forces present at Delphi and of the local beliefs which had accompanied the worship of the Earth Mother. Dionysos was the natural force of creative energy and enthusiasm recognized by the Greeks as an important part of the spiritual life of human beings. His presence at Delphi with the rational god Apollo expressed an awareness of these forces and a respect for them as both necessary and vital to self-knowledge.

POLITICAL HISTORY OF THE SHRINE

The political and economic history of the sanctuary was based partly on Delphi's strategic position on the mainland of Greece. The pass of Arachora led to the Plain of Boeotia from the important port on the Bay of Itea in the Gulf of Corinth. Those who controlled the port and the pass controlled trade and could exact tolls from those wishing to pass through, and such taxation is always a source of conflict.

After the seventh century B.C., Delphi acquired a reputation which reached beyond the Greek mainland to Asia Minor and Italy. Such fame made control of the shrine very attractive, and powerful city-states made attempts to achieve such control. The attempts earned the name Sacred Wars and there were three such wars of note from the Archaic to the Hellenistic Period.

The First Sacred War took place during the sixth century B.C. when the Thessalians headed a confederation of city-states in an attempt to break the tight control of the sanctuary by the local Phokians, whose tolls along the roads and at the port of Kirrha were correctly seen as an unwarranted imposition upon access to the oracle. Kirrha was destroyed in 590 B.C. after ten years of warfare.

THE RULING COUNCIL

At this point a new form of political and religious control evolved for the administration of the oracle. Twelve ancient families agreed upon the formation of a council with authority over the shrine. The administration included the temple hierarchy as well as secular leadership. The federation was named Amphiktyonia, and the ruling group was named the Amphiktyonic Council. The council met twice a year and established policy and a festival calendar for the shrine, including administration of the Pythian Games.

The Second Sacred War, in 448 B.C., in which the Spartans, Phokians, and Athenians sought to increase their power, finally resulted in an agreement of 421 B.C. in which Delphi emerged as an autonomous entity, uncontrolled by any *polis*, although influence was based on the political power of the moment. The Spartans achieved prominence in the councils of the Amphiktyonia, for example, after their victory in the Peloponnesian War. Their influence continued into the fourth century B.C. when the temple had to be rebuilt after earthquake damage to the sanctuary.

In 346 B.C. the Macedonians in their turn asserted control over the sanctuary. Philip II, father of Alexander the Great, became president of the Pythian Games and was the most powerful member of the council. During the next two hundred years the oracle declined in influence but remained active. Delphi dropped out of the historical record as being politically influential, but was transformed by the Neoplatonists who perceived of the oracle as a source of revelation and proof of man's immortal nature.

During the Roman era, Delphi enjoyed a renaissance of sorts, being favored by a series of emperors who built impressive monuments and stoas on the site. In 86 B.C., however, it was sacked by Sulla, who left it vulnerable to further attack. Indeed, the sanctuary was plundered on a regular basis after that, sometimes on a massive scale. Nero, for example, removed over five hundred statues during his reign. Many remained, though, as it was reported that during the time of Pliny the Elder over three thousand statues filled the sanctuary.

Legend has it that the Roman Julian the Apostate tried to revive the oracle (in A.D. 360) but received the following message from Delphi:

> Tell the king the fair-wrought hall has fallen to the ground. No longer has Phoebus a hut, nor a prophetic laurel, nor a spring that speaks. The water of speech even is quenched.

MYTHOLOGY

The myths of Delphi are twofold. They tell of Apollo's mastery of the oracular shrine, and they tell of the purification of the shrine from pollution. These two lines of myth parallel one another and describe the shifting beliefs and character of gods as oracles and of humans as the beneficiaries of those oracles. As has been the case in other sacred places, the ethos of Delphi has to do with the mysteries of divine epiphany. What is special about Delphi begins with its natural setting and its isolation from any major *polis* so that in the end the site had a unique and universal quality, quite unlike Eleusis, which had always been closely connected to Athens and her history and which was without a powerful natural setting to enhance its oracular power.

To the Greek mind Delphi was the center of the world. There were those who took that quite literally and were then ridiculed by the likes of Herodotos as being naive, but there were those who understood a different sense of this centrality. Delphi was the source of oracular wisdom, the center of revelation and therefore of divine knowledge. To acknowledge Delphi as the center was to accept faith in the gods as the source of life, fate, wisdom, and justice. Thus, Delphi was the point from which the circle of Greek culture, religion, and philosophy was inscribed.

THE MYTHS OF APOLLO AT DELPHI

Apollo was born of the goddess Leto, who was the daughter of Titans and rival to Hera. It was Hera who tormented Leto's pregnancy and pursued her throughout the world until, at last, she found peace on the lonely windswept island of Delos (center of the Cycladic world). There she gave birth to Apollo and his sister Artemis. While still a baby, Apollo demanded bow and arrows and with them sped to Mount Parnassos, where he sought out the great serpent Python, enemy of Leto. Overmatched, Python fled to Delphi, to the security of the shrine of the Earth Mother, but Apollo disregarded the sanctity of the shrine and slew Python, polluting the sanctuary.

Apollo then went either to the Vale of Tempe, which is another dramatic gorge and valley to the north beneath Mount Olympus, or to Crete where he was purified of the crime of murder and the pollution of holy ground. The divergence in the myths at this point reflect the various claims upon Greek origins for Apollo. In either case, after being purified, Apollo returned to Delphi where he persuaded Pan, the goat-god of wild places and evocative music, to reveal the art of prophecy. Inherent in this aspect of the myth is also the reconciliation between Apollo and Dionysos, that god and force of nature which makes itself felt in orgiastic music and dance.

The God of Music

Apollo's instrument is the seven-stringed lyre, a sacred instrument invented by Hermes and perfected by Apollo. As pictured often on pottery, the lyre was made from the large shell of a tortoise and the curved horns of a goat. Its rival instrument was the double-flute, played in particular by Pan and associated with Dionysos. The flute was a seductive instrument which produced passion, excess, and forgetfulness. The lyre soothed the passions and promoted peace, moderation, and spiritual awareness. In myth, Apollo defeats all rivals in the art of music, in particular those who play the flute.

What little we do know about ancient Greek music is supplemented by our knowledge of Pythagorean principles. The lyre must have been strung in such a way as to produce the mathematically graduated tones produced by precise stringing. The resulting harmonies must have contrasted dramatically with the sliding, imprecise tones of the double flute. The myths tell of contests in which Apollo wins the prize with his lyre in competition with flute players, such as Pan. These contests continued at Delphi in honor of Apollo, especially every four years during the Pythian games.

The God of Civilization

The musical victories also represent the conquest by the sophisticated city-states over the more primitive territories, like Phrygia and Arkadia, where the flute remained popular with the peasants. Apollo's defeat of the Python and his victories in musical contests signal the triumph of civilization over the nomadic habits of an earlier time. In spiritual terms the connection to music symbolizes the control of higher orders of the mind over the lower, or emotional, rule. As the consciousness of Zeus, Apollo is the hope of man that divine consciousness will rule. The connection to consciousness emerges not only in Apollo's function as the god of prophecy but also in his associations with light.

Although Helios is the sun god, Apollo was in a similar way associated with light. Apollo illuminates the arts of civilization and champions the victory of Reason. He is the builder of temples, the father of sacred geometry and architecture. He represents the belief that the divine may be understood through the study of philosophy as opposed to the revelations of divine frenzy. But Reason triumphs only in a state of purity, where no pollution exists.

Because he is the pure god, Apollo is also the god of healing, and in that capacity is the father of Asklepios, god of healing. But there is a double edge to this healing sword. Apollo is also the bringer of plagues, which are always regarded as signs of spiritual pollution. One of the curses of civilization is the presence of plague in the crowded, infested streets, and Apollo brings with him this curse.

Engraving of Pan with his pipes, and goat-footed satyr figure.

The Distant God

The myths of Apollo as they are told by Homer in the *Iliad* describe a god distanced from the Greeks and often using his powers to oppose their aims. He was on the side of Troy in the great war, bringing death to Greek heroes. His oracle was also vague on the subject of Greek success in the Persian Wars. This distance and ambiguity on the part of the god reflect his Asian roots and the elusiveness of his word. Apollo's weapons are the bow and arrow, shot from a distance and striking suddenly, without warning.

This aura of distance removed Apollo from the daily lives of the people, and he became an elite god, known well only by artists, poets, and intellectuals. The gods of the people, Pan and Dionysos, Aphrodite, and Artemis, continued to live in the wild places, clinging to the rocks and springs, murmuring their words of affection and devotion, meeting ordinary needs and soothing the troubled spirits of ordinary people. That is why Dionysos came to share the sanctuary of Delphi with Apollo, residing in the temple for the three winter months while Apollo went to the distant north to dwell.

The myths of Delphi serve to describe the natural surroundings and to set forth the story of civilization. Apollo is the imposition of order upon chaos. Even as the rocks of the Phaedriades break loose from the trembling earth to destroy the temple, the power of human consciousness gives form once again to the chaos and builds another geometric expression of devotion and sacrifice to such awesome power. Nowhere on earth is the tension between these two powers so dramatically displayed, even now.

THE SITE

Delphi is a spiritual statement. It sits precariously in the lap of a nurturing power which opens out beneath the twin peaks of Mount Parnassos. The sanctuary is an aspiration of a human desire to know and to become one with its ruling gods. The site for the sanctuary is imposing. The cliffs of the Phaedriades, or the Brilliant Ones, surround the small rock plateau out of which has been carved enough level space to establish a temple and its supporting buildings. The site opens out to the south and is crossed all day by the sun and swept by sea breezes. The valley of the Pleistos River below is fertile, planted with olive trees, and extends to the port town of Itea and the Gulf of Corinth.

The altitude of the site is deceptive, seeming higher than its 1,870 feet (570 m). The deception is caused by the steepness of the ascent from the valley and the frame of the hills across the way, sacred to Athena and her site at Marmaria. The site is also very small, only 6 acres (24,000 m^2), huddled against the cliffs near the Kastalian Spring which still rises with fresh water from the cleft formed by the Phaedriades.

WHAT TO SEE AT DELPHI

Delphi offers four distinct areas to the visitor. The first is the Sanctuary of Athena Pronaia at Marmaria. Pronaia means "Before the Shrine" or gate to the shrine, and Marmaria is simply the small plateau near the road, half a mile (800 m) from the main sanctuary. Just above Marmaria and on the other side at the curve of the road is the Kastalian Spring, where pilgrims and temple priests and priestesses bathed before entering the temple grounds. Then there is the main sanctuary, including the theatre and stadium and, finally, the Delphi Museum, which contains many of the valuable artifacts uncovered during excavations by the French School of Archaeology.

ATHENA PRONAIA

Occupying a narrow strip of land on the southern slope of Parnassos and facing the twin mounds across the valley is the Sanctuary of Athena Pronaia (see Fig. 25). This site is very ancient, having been occupied during the Neolithic Period (5000–3000 B.C.) and later by the Mycenaeans. The site was eventually occupied by the Olympian deities, Athena in particular, but it belongs to an earlier cult associated with Earth Mother worship. The remains, of pottery, ashes, tools, and figurines, suggest an area devoted to sacrifice. Later, Athena, who was guardian of wisdom and consciousness, assumed her place on this sacred site, taking over the functions and bringing the devotion to the Earth Mother into the Classical Age.

This site is a puzzle. It seems unlikely that it was established only as a gateway to the main sanctuary or as a secondary gift to a goddess in the aftermath of Apollo's usurpation of the oracle from the earlier Earth Mother cult. The answer to why this narrow strip of land was sacred for so many years may lie in its surroundings. First, a spring, farther to the east from Kastalia, emerged above the plateau and served the ritual needs of the site. Its waters may have sprung from the earth below the cliffs and produced an area of abundant growth, thus sacred to the Earth Mother in her role as nurturer. Second, the landscape across the valley formed an image of the goddess, nurturing, enveloping, and in contrast to the threatening, more ominous twin peaks to the north.

THE ARCHAIC TEMPLE

There are two important structures on this narrow site. The Archaic Temple of Athena, the first of which was built in the middle of the seventh century B.C., was one of the earliest major temples in Greece. This earlier version was no doubt

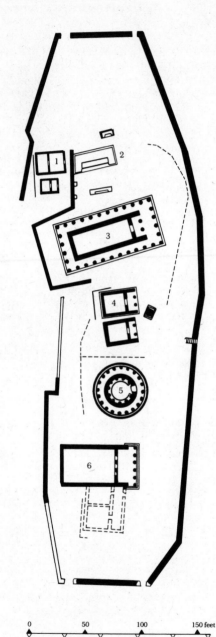

Fig. 27. *The Sanctuary of Athena Pronaia*
1. *Treasuries or Early Temples*
2. *Altar*

3. *Temple of Athena*
4. *Treasuries*
5. *Tholos*
6. *Later Temple of Athena*

destroyed by earthquake or rockfalls. Rebuilt in 500 B.C. the temple was again destroyed, this time by the Persians or by later quakes. The later temple was actually restored somewhat at the beginning of the twentieth century only to be destroyed once again by a rockfall in 1905.

Capitals from the Archaic temple may be found at the site. These early Doric designs featured a thick *echinus* (molding above the column shaft) which gives the suggestion of a great weight flattening the column supports. The design of the temple itself was also unusual. Six columns fronted the temple and twelve formed the sides, making the length of the platform or stylobate exactly twice the width, rather than the longer temples of the later pattern of six and thirteen. The reason for this unusual pattern may be the narrowness of the site itself which limited the space available.

Some might argue that a temple should have been situated in an east-west orientation, more in line with custom and with other shrines devoted to Athena. But here in Marmaria the temple had to face the double-mounded hills and cleft across the valley, no doubt to conform to the orientation of an earlier Mycenaean-Minoan shrine to the goddess located at the same spot. It is here among the ruins of at least three temples—Archaic, Classical, and Hellenistic—and in the presence of sacred landscape that one is able to sense the splendid continuity of ancient Greek religious ritual. From the Neolithic figurines found here to Roman restoration and embellishment, a long and deeply held tradition is made manifest over a period of three thousand years.

THE THOLOS

The second important structure at Marmaria is the famous *Tholos* Temple, three columns of which have been restored to support a section of entablature. Built in the early fourth century B.C., this temple, too, was constructed on a site sacred to the goddess. As is the case with other *tholoi,* these round temples may well have been closely related to Mycenaean sacrificial pits, which in turn probably reflect Neolithic rites. This *Tholos* was erected on a triple platform and was 45 feet in diameter (13.5 m). Its twenty outside columns were Doric in order, very slim and graceful. They supported an entablature which featured sculptures depicting the War of the Amazons. The inner colonnade was constructed of ten Corinthian columns, one of the earliest examples of the order. The floor, seen more clearly from the bluff above the ruins, was set in geometric patterns of Pentellic and Eleusinian marble.

The *Tholos* sits in this landscape as an ordering principle. Its round, graceful shape gathers the conflicting elements into coherence. Because it is round, there is no orientation to a particular feature, but instead, the wild gorge, deep valley, and distant sea are harmonized, given spiritual expression through the use of the circle within which smaller circles

The Tholos *Temple at Marmaria, shown in its wild landscape setting,*
Delphi.

emanate. From this circle, so carefully crafted, the circle of
the world takes shape, and from that circle the goddess who
resides here is manifest.

Remaining Structures

To the west of the *Tholos* are the remains of the later Temple
of Athena, built in 370 B.C. to replace the earthquake-
damaged main temple. This small prostyle building, fashioned of local limestone, was unadorned and had a simple
Doric facade of six columns. Next to it was a small square
building probably devoted to administration of the shrine.
The other buildings on the site, to the east of the *Tholos,*
were treasuries and were also oriented to the south in line
with the hills opposite.

A path at the western edge of the sanctuary leads down to
another plateau where the remains of the gymnasium are
found. This area is currently being excavated and may not be
accessible. There is an ancient *palaestra,* or public building,
a pool and Roman bathhouse, and, finally, the stadium. This
area may be seen to better advantage from the theatre in the
main sanctuary.

THE KASTALIAN SPRING

Along the road to the west, in its curve as one approaches the
main sanctuary of Apollo, lie the remains of the two sacred
springs of Kastalia. Here, where the great cliffs form a
chasm, both pilgrims and the priesthood gathered to purify
themselves in preparation for entering the great temple. The
spring closest to the road is the older shrine, built in the
Archaic Period, and not discovered until 1958. Stone ducts
carried the water into a rectangular basin, walled in and
fitted with stone benches. On the western wall four lion-head

The older, Archaic Kastalian Spring, Delphi.

spouts fed the basin while gates on the eastern end regulated the flow of water.

The later spring, farther into the gorge, was constructed in Hellenistic times and carved out of the cliff. It was provided with votive niches in honor of Kastalia, nymph of the sacred waters. The construction of this spring made it impossible to bathe in the spring itself. Instead, the source of water was covered and seven bronze spouts provided water needed for the purifying rites. In later years, Christian traditions added a shrine to John the Baptist, a column of which can still be seen in the large niche to the right.

The Hellenistic Kastalian Spring, with votive niches from later times, Delphi.

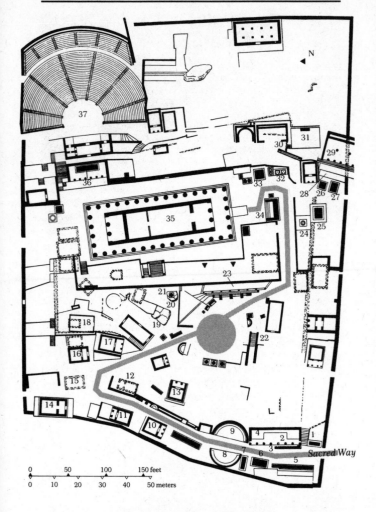

0   50   100   150 feet
0 10 20 30 40 50 meters

Fig. 28. *The Sanctuary of Apollo at Delphi*
1. *Bull of the Korcyrans*
2. *Arkadian Statues*
3. *Statue of Philopoimen*
4. *Spartan Stoa*
5. *Spartan Naval Monument*
6. *Bronze Horse*
7. *Marathon Memorial*
8. *The Seven Against Thebes*
9. *The Kings of Argos*
10. *Sikyonian Treasury*
11. *Siphnian Treasury*
12. *Megarian Treasury*
13. *Aeolian Treasury*
14. *Theban Treasury*
15. *Boeotian Treasury*

16. Poteidaian Treasury
17. Athenian Treasury
18. The Asklepeion
19. Rock of the Sibyl
20. Rock of Leto
21. Sphinx of the Naxians
22. Stairs of the Halos
23. Stoa of the Athenians
24. Serpent Column of Plataea
25. Rhodian Chariot
26. Attalus I

27. Eumenes II
28. Statue of Attalus I
29. Stoa of Attalus I
30. Acanthus Column
31. Sanctuary of Neoptolemos
32. The Golden Tripods
33. Statue of Apollo
34. Great Altar of Chios
35. Temple of Apollo
36. Offering of Krateros
37. Theatre

THE SANCTUARY OF APOLLO

It is to the visit of Pausanius to Delphi in the second century A.D. that archaeologists owe much of their knowledge of the exact placement of the hundreds of statues and buildings contained within the main sanctuary (see Fig. 26). Pausanius began his tour just as any modern visitor would, at the eastern corner where now the modern gate house is located, most fittingly at the site of the Roman *Agora,* where pilgrims purchased offerings to the god and other trinkets.

The general shape of the sanctuary, a rectangle bounded by retaining walls at top and bottom and on the sides stepping down the natural slope, was established in the sixth century B.C. and maintained throughout its active history. The fixed size made it difficult to include all the offerings desired by various cities and individuals, the result being a crowded collection of monuments along the Sacred Way, but only up to a point. Where there existed sacred ground, such as near the Rock of the Sibyl and the circular terrace of *halos,* no new monuments were added. Thus, there is a sense, even now, of the integrity of the Sacred Way leading to the entrance of the temple.

THE SACRED WAY

The Sacred Way begins at the four steps up from the courtyard of the Roman Agora. The paving which visitors tread today was laid down during late Roman times when the sanctuary was in decline. The original lies several inches lower. The route of the Sacred Way leads first to the west and passes by a succession of monuments and important treasuries before it turns due north and angles up the slope. This portion of the sacred route brings the massive cliffs of the Phaedriades into view, a sight which was unrestricted by the presence of any monument. The northern route passes the most sacred ground of the sanctuary and then turns northwest for the final approach to the temple entrance. These final steps bring the focus of attention back to the immediate surroundings and prepare the suppliant for the encounter with the oracle.

*The Sacred Way within
the sanctuary, Delphi.*

The Lower Monuments of the Sacred Way

The first section of the Sacred Way was devoted throughout most of its active history after 490 B.C. to various monuments honoring military victories or special offerings to Apollo. The first monument (no. 1), on the right at the top of the stairs, was the Bull of the Korcyrans, a huge bronze erected in the decade of 490 B.C. Pausanius tells us the story of this extraordinary gift to Apollo. It seems that on the island of Corfu a bull left its grazing and daily went down to the sea where it bellowed until one day the people saw that a huge school of tuna had appeared. After trying unsuccessfully to catch the fish, help was sought from the oracle. The people were told to sacrifice the bull to Poseidon. This done, the tuna were easily caught. In gratitude a portion of the profit from the great catch was used to erect this bronze in honor of the god.

Next (no. 2), also to the right on the long, narrow slab (nearly 31 feet or 9.4 m), stood nine bronze statues erected by the Arkadians for their victory over the Lakonians in 369 B.C. The statues reflected the ancestral line of the Arkadians, beginning with Apollo, then Nike, and followed by the founders of the state to the then living generation. Next to this grouping (no. 3) is a statue base on which stood the figure of Philopoimen of Megalopolis, a leader and general who defeated Sparta in battle (207 B.C.). The large cleared area behind (no. 4) contained a stoa with twelve columns. It is of uncertain origin, but may have been erected by the Spartans.

On the left side of the Sacred Way, just at the top of the stairs (no. 5), is an area which most likely contained a large grouping of statues, thirty-seven in number, which marked the decisive naval victory of Sparta over Athens in 404 B.C. The statues include both gods and generals and reflected Spartan arrogance at the defeat of Athens in the Peloponnesian War. Next to the Spartan display is a base (no. 6) for a monumental bronze horse, perhaps meant to be the famous Trojan Horse, erected by the Argives after a victory in 414 B.C.

In front of the horse and occupying a narrow base (no. 7) was the Athenian memorial to the Battle of Marathon, which in 490 B.C. successfully delayed Persian adventurism in Greece for a decade. The memorial was designed to include thirteen bronze statues, including Athena, Apollo, Miltiades, whose military victory at Marathon was one of history's greatest, and ten heroes of Athenian legend. The group was executed by Phidias, sculptor of the Parthenon, and was set in place around 450 B.C. Today, little remains of the base, and its location is only suggested beside the pavement of the Sacred War.

We now come to two semicircular niches, facing one another and both carved out of the rock of the hillside. Both were Argive offerings. On the left (no. 8) stood seven bronze statues representing the sons of the famous Seven Against Thebes. The legend begins with Oedipus, the most miserable of men, whose crimes banished him from Thebes and whose sons, Eteocles and Polynices fought one another for the right to rule in Thebes. The original Seven (celebrated in a play by Aeschylus) failed in their attempt to conquer Thebes, but their sons were victorious, and these two offerings celebrate that final victory.

The second niche (no. 9) was erected by the Argives after 369 B.C. and the founding of the colony at Messene. The grouping was of at least ten bronze statues, including the legendary Kings of Argos, including Herakles. These two groupings must have made an impressive showing for the Argives here at the beginning of the Sacred Way, an indication of their long history and power in Greece. The next three niches on the right are of unknown origin.

THE IMPORTANT TREASURIES

A treasury was a small temple erected by a city-state in honor of the god and used to contain and display wealth. The sanctuary depended upon the generous contributions of the rich states, who in turn depended for their welfare upon the kind oracles of the god. Several of the treasuries here at Delphi were of exquisite design and featured fine sculptures, many of which have been preserved in the Delphi Museum. As Pausanius tells us, by the time he made his trip to Delphi, the treasuries were monuments only and did not hold any gold or silver.

The first of the fine treasuries (no. 10) is the Sikyonian Treasury (early fifth century B.C.), the foundation of which remains on the left of the path. As its foundation indicates, the last of several small buildings built on this site was a simple temple *in antis* with two Doric columns before the entrance. Close examination of the foundation stones indicates that at least two other buildings were built on or near this site. One of these structures was a *tholos,* indicating the presence of an ancient sacrificial pit, perhaps an altar to Gaea, Mother Earth.

The next treasury (no. 11) belonged to the Siphnians, whose gold and silver mines produced such wealth that the island kingdom gave a tenth of the yield (or a tithe) for the construction of a magnificent Ionic treasury. Completed around 525 B.C., the treasury was without equal in the sanctuary, and fortunately for us, many of the fine marble sculptures were found and are preserved in the museum. As the plan reveals, the building faced west, and the porch was framed by two Karyatides, one of which was found nearby.

At least five other treasuries crowded the curve of the Sacred Way at this point. Across the way (no. 12) was located the Megarian Treasury, and just above it (no. 13) the Aeolian Treasury. To the west, along the huge retaining wall, was the Theban Treasury (no. 14), and just above it the Boeotian Treasury (no. 15) and above that the Poteidaian Treasury (no. 16).

As the Sacred Way turns north the famous Athenian Treasury (no. 17) comes into full view. It is a reflection of the modern importance of Athens that this treasury has been reconstructed, using most of the original blocks. The restoration was undertaken in 1906 by Replat, a French architect. The building is Doric, *in antis,* with two fluted columns supporting the porch. Thirty metopes pictured typical Athenian legends: the labors of Herakles, the battle with the

The Athenian Treasury, restored, Delphi.

Amazons, and the adventures of Theseus. The metopes currently on the building are plaster casts of originals which are displayed in the museum.

The history of the building is in doubt. Pausanius suggests that the treasury was erected after the Battle of Marathon in 490 B.C. But most observers agree that the building is older than that and place it instead around 500 B.C. Pausanius may have been mislead by an inscription below the building, on the narrow terrace upon which the Athenians erected a tripod in honor of the Marathon victory. The many inscriptions covering the walls of the treasury honor various Athenians. Late additions (138–128 B.C.) on the south wall are ancient musical notations which represent Delphic Hymns to Apollo. The museum now holds most of these valuable inscriptions.

THE ASKLEPIEION

Just behind the Athenian Treasury are the remains of a small Asklepieion (no. 18), the precinct at Delphi dedicated to the man-god Asklepios and the healing arts. It was quite natural for Delphi to have an Asklepieion since Apollo was the father of Asklepios and taught his son the art of healing. Certain elements always formed a part of such a healing center: a source of pure water, an *abaton,* where patients slept under the care of priests and met the god in dreams, and a temple dedicated to Asklepios.

In Delphi, the evidence suggests a minimal facility. There was a fountain house, which provided a source of water from a spring located at the western end of the Temple of Apollo. Stone ducts have been uncovered which brought the water down the hill. The one building which occupies the space seems more like a temple than an *abaton,* which leads to the conclusion that this sanctuary may have been less a curative site than a devotional one.

THE PRECINCT OF THE GODDESS

Ahead on the left, now roped off to prevent damage to growth and erosion of the hillside, is the sacred precinct of the early goddesses of the shrine. Here, well before the first temple was erected, stood the Rock of the Sibyl (no. 19). Upon this rock legend has it that Herophile sang her oracles. Herophile, whose father was Zeus and whose mother was Lamia, the first sibyl, sang of the Trojan War and foretold the fate of Helen. Greek history, philosophy, and religion give numerous accounts of various gifted prophetesses who sang "the will of god," which is the derivation of the word sibyl (the Doric *sio-bolla* or *theou-boule*). Herophile was the most famous of these gifted women. She is usually associated with the Temple of Apollo at Cumae (Italy), where she lived for many years in the crypts and gave oracle.

It is here, at this rock, that the Greek relationship with

The Rock of the Sibyl, first place of prophecy at Delphi.

deity has its foundation. Although the oracle at Dodona is thought to be older, and is probably more primitive in its form, here at Delphi there exists within this one sanctuary the major history of the Greek search for divine revelation. Ge, or Gaea, the Earth, spoke here, uttering her wisdom to those who came trembling to her rock, seeking to know. The rock itself may be part of the cliff, fallen in prehistoric times to its place, or it may jut from the hill itself, marking a small crevice in the hillside. It rests close to a natural spring called the Sacred Fountain which emerges from under the temple and appears to return to the earth behind the prophetic rock. A young olive tree drinks today at this fountain.

Next to the Rock of the Sibyl is the Rock of Leto (no. 20) where in myth Leto, mother of Apollo, came with her baby boy and sat with him, instructing him in the art of dragon slaying. From this rock Apollo took up his bow and arrows and slew Python to become Lord of the Word of Zeus. Behind the Rock of Leto is the foundation stone of the Sphinx of the Naxians (no. 21). This masterpiece of mythical vision stood on an Ionic column well above the height of the temple retaining wall. The sphinx, now in the museum, was erected in the mid-sixth century B.C., and had the head of a woman, the breast and wings of a bird of prey, and the lower body of a lion. Her eyes are closed as she sleeps, guarding the entrance to the temple and the precinct of Gaea.

The vision of Python and the image of the dragon represents the lower self, the unconscious, the powers of the underworld which must be conquered. The sphinx asked Oedipus the famous riddle "What is it that goes on four legs in the morning, two at noon, and three at evening?" The answer Oedipus gave was "Man." It was a vision of himself, revealed by an introspective question but only partly understood by the sighted but wisdom-blind Oedipus. The Naxian Sphinx was Archaic: still, majestic, haunting, and powerful.

It was also very Egyptian and suggests that close connection of the Naxian island culture to the more ancient religious imagery of its southern neighbor.

THE HALOS, OR THRESHING FLOOR

Just beyond the sacred precinct of the goddess and on the other side of the Sacred Way was located a circular dancing floor or threshing floor called a *halos*. The area is now cluttered with stone fragments, but was once an important place in the sanctuary. On this spot, every eight years, a drama called the Stepteria was performed in honor of Apollo. A hut, or *skene*, was constructed, within which was a table laden with religious objects. A young boy, chosen from among those whose parents were still living, was joined by other youths and raced up the stairs (no. 22) into the hut, upset the table, and then set fire to the hut. Without looking back, the boys then fled on foot, leaving the sanctuary, and went on a pilgrimage to the Vale of Tempe, to the north near Mount Olympus, where in one myth Apollo had gone to be purified of the killing of the Python. Some time later they returned to Delphi, bearing laurel leaves as a symbol of purification.

Most scholars agree that this ceremony is but a dim reflection of the myth of Apollo and the killing of the Python and more clearly involves the purification of the shrine every eight years, making pure what in the intervening years had become polluted by the temptations of office or the violence

Stairs leading to the halos, *used for the ceremony of Stepteria, Delphi.*

Temple of Apollo from the Sacred Way, with cyclopean walls. Columns of the Athenian stoa in foreground, Delphi.

of greed and hatred among the competing states and individuals. There was always the danger that the oracle would be polluted by bribery or temptation. Thus, purification was mandatory if the sanctuary was to achieve its sacred purpose, the true word of Zeus, given freely to those who desired to know it.

APPROACHING THE TEMPLE

On the left of the path as it continues north are the remains of the Stoa of the Athenians (no. 23). This simple, open colonnade was made of wood and supported by seven marble Ionic columns, three of which are standing in place. A capital of one rests on the right side of the path and shows the fine detail of this order. The stoa was erected by the Athenians around 478 B.C. to display images of naval victories.

The Sacred Way turns left, forms broad steps up the hillside, passes by three more treasuries, and enters an area once again devoted to monuments, most of which were placed on high bases overlooking the temple entrance. The first important monument (no. 24) was mounted on the existing circular base. Called the Serpent Column of Plataea, this monument celebrated the Greek victory over the Persians in 479 B.C. Three coiled serpents cast in bronze formed a high column on top of which was mounted a golden tripod, the symbol of prophecy. In the third century A.D., Constantine the Great of Byzantium stripped Delphi of many of its monuments, including the coiled snakes, one head of which now resides in a museum in Istanbul.

Farther to the right (no. 25) is the large base for a gilded chariot erected around 304 B.C. by the Rhodians. Next (nos. 26 and 27) are bases for statues of two kings of Pergamon,

Attalus I and Eumenes II. The long, narrow base to the rear (no. 28) was an image of King Attalus I, who also built a large stoa (no. 29) in 220 B.C. In the Roman era, the stoa was destroyed in order to provide a water supply to the baths off to the right beyond the retaining wall of the sanctuary.

A small base (no. 30) on the upper level of the hillside held the famous Acanthus Column of the dancing girls, an exquisite statue erected by the Athenians in the middle of the fourth century B.C. The column was 36 feet high (11 m), ending in a curl of acanthus leaves. Three girls in flowing dresses (*poloi*) dance while supporting a sacred tripod on their heads. The statue, without the tripod, has been preserved and is on display in the museum.

Next to the acanthus column was the Sanctuary of Neoptolemos—also called Pyrrhos (no. 31)—a place sacred to the Greeks. A supporting wall sheltered an altar and the grave of the hero, the son of famed Achilles. The legends of the death of this heroic figure reflect various interpretations of the rituals of Delphi. In general, the legends agree that Pyrrhos was killed by temple priests during a sacrifice at the temple hearth. Some see and understand the death to have been a just result of the hero's attempt to seize control of the sanctuary or at least an attempt to seize some degree of power from the priests. Others, of a more philosophical bent, see the killing as a ritual slaying in the mode of true sacrifice at Delphi.

Ritual slaying at Delphi, of animal or human victim, had its violent aspect, a sudden and furious wielding of the sacred knife, the death of a hero or scapegoat whose life and actions exceeded human limits and whose death was necessary to expiate the crimes of the community. Thus, Neoptolemos, the son of the greatest hero in Homeric legend, was sacrificed in order to renew life and to atone for human excess. As such, his death was sacred and his grave a place of due reverence. Interestingly, excavation has not revealed a grave on the site, but instead a Mycenaean sacrificial pit, a place revered by later Greeks wherever they were found. It was understood that the Mycenaeans knew and understood this mode of sacrifice. Such may be the function of the round temples of *tholoi* found in major sanctuaries.

THE TEMPLE TERRACE

As the pilgrim approached the temple terrace, a series of monuments caught the eye and were quite splendid in their effect. To the right were three Golden Tripods (no. 32) which were dedicated some time after 480 B.C. by the kings of Sicily. The tripods were of great value and were stolen during the Third Sacred War in the fourth century B.C. by the Phokians. Engraved *stele* or marble slabs replaced the tripods, one of which remains.

Next, on the large square base (no. 33) stood a massive

statue of Apollo in his aspect as protector of the harvest. The statue was erected by the Amphiktyonic Council sometime during the fourth century B.C. and stood over 50 feet high (16 m), dominating the entrance to the temple. The final major feature of the terrace during the Archaic through Classical periods was the Great Altar (no. 34), dedicated by the citizens of Chios, who were privileged in their relations with Delphi, being first in line when the oracle spoke. As the foundation suggests, the altar was quite large, measuring 28 feet by 17 feet (8.6 m x 5.1 m). The dark marble of the body of the altar was quarried on the island of Chios. White marble made up the base and top.

As was the case in most approaches to temples in Greece, the Sacred Way delivered the pilgrim to the gate of his sacred experience as though through a labyrinth, in this case a labyrinth which began down in the depths of the valley and wound upward through the Gate of Athena at Marmaria, through the underworld of the Kastalian Spring, and then into the sculpted and golden world of manifest divinity.

The final section of the Sacred Way, beginning at the four steps of the sanctuary, led the aspirant up through visions of order in the form of small temple buildings and human and divine forms in marble, bronze, and gold. The labyrinth passed by the awesome precinct of the Mother Goddess and directed the gaze to the cliffs rising almost directly overhead, pressing down and yet opening out to the sky. The final approach, through close walls and broad steps, shielded the temple from view until the pilgrim turned to face the massive statue of Apollo gazing out over the valley. Here was the goal of the journey, the figure of the god before his temple, within which could be gleaned a measure of understanding, should the heart be open to the experience.

THE TEMPLE OF APOLLO

The six temple columns which have been reconstructed to suggest their position in antiquity represent the last temple to occupy this sacred site. Out of the legends of the past have come the stories of six temples, only three of which can be confirmed by physical evidence, but the legends of the first three have the evidence of poetic power and a certain historical logic.

The location of the various temples depends upon two factors: the ancient belief and testimony that a cleft in the earth from which vapors arose was the source of Delphi's oracular power, and the demands of building a major temple on this particular hillside as close as possible to any specific oracular source. The myth of the cleft has to be related to the origins of oracular power in the time when the deities of the underworld spoke to mankind through natural sounds: the babbling of springs and the rustle of wind in sacred trees.

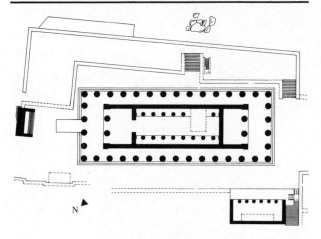

Fig. 29. *The Temple of Apollo, Delphi.*

From caves and crevices came utterings as well, and the area around Delphi was rich in such openings in the earth. The precinct of the goddess below the temple site shows physical evidence of geological fissure permitting water to rise to the surface in several places beneath the temple site. But there is no specific evidence below the foundation of the present temple of a geological fault from which volcanic vapors might arise. However, major shifting due to earthquake may have obliterated evidence of such a cleft well before the stone temples were erected and the area was prepared for their construction.

The Legends of Early Temples

Pausanius provides the legendary context for the history of temples on this site. He says that Earth gave her share of the oracular site to Themis in her aspect as protector of natural law. Themis in turn gave Apollo her share as a gift. Mankind discovered the oracle when shepherds stumbled upon the cleft and were possessed by the vapors in the name of Apollo.

Legend says that the first "temple" was a rude hut fashioned by laurel leaves from the Vale of Tempe, brought, it must be assumed, as a reenactment of the rites of purification told of in the original myth of Apollo's occupation of the site. The second temple was made of feathers and beeswax; in fact, the temple was made by bees sent by Apollo from the north. The bee in Greek myth was a sacred creature, a manifestation of pure spirit. The third temple was made of bronze, which Pausanius asserts was not an uncommon practice in early architecture. It may have been a Mycenaean structure erected during the Heroic Age when the sibyl Herophile gave oracle from the site.

The Early Archaic Temple

Temple number four was built around 650 B.C., perhaps as late as 600 B.C. It was attributed to legendary priest-architects Trophonios and Agamedes, who followed sacred inspiration in building a temple which reflected the attributes of Apollo. It is said that Apollo granted them a peaceful death at a young age as a reward for their dedication to him.

Constructed on a poros-stone base, a conglomerate commonly used in temple building, this temple was smaller than the two later temples, measuring only 140 feet (43 m) long and 52 feet (16 m) wide. Very little is known of its appearance. Slight remains indicate that it probably had a wooden roof and columns and used mud bricks for its interior walls. The temple burned in 548 B.C.

The Late Archaic Temple

By this time, Delphi was controlled by the council, which sought funds from all city-states in Greece for a new temple. The sum of 300 talents was acquired and the work begun. By 515 B.C. the Alkmaeonid family of Athens, having been exiled for their attempts to overthrow the oligarchy then in power, undertook the completion of the work. Their contribution was to complete the pediments of the temple in Parian marble, no doubt in the tradition of the fine work done on the Acropolis in Athens.

In order to prepare the site for a more massive temple, the builders first had to construct a polygonal retaining wall in

The Temple of Apollo from above, showing valley of the Pleistos River, Delphi.

order to establish a firm, flat area. This impressive wall, still standing, and the resulting terrace area above it, destroyed the evidence of several earlier buildings, including, it is thought, a temple to Ge and most of the evidence of the earlier temple to Apollo. The new temple would measure 195 feet in length (59.5 m) and 78 feet in width (23.8 m). There is some speculation that it was built in the *hypaethral* style, that is, without a roof over the *naos,* or central hall of the temple.

The Doric columns for the exterior numbered thirty-eight, six on the facades and fifteen on the sides. The interior columns were of the Ionic order. The combination of six columns on the facade and fifteen on the long side was abnormal, the usual pattern being six and thirteen. The extra length and hence the additional two columns were the result of the special requirements of the building. In the usual temple the *naos* was the only space within the temple after the *pronaos,* or outer chamber. In Apollo's temple there was the additional requirement of space for the inner sanctum or *adyton,* where the oracles were given and where the other sacred items of the temple were kept. This sanctum had to be kept separate and adequate security needed in the form of walls or screens to isolate the pilgrim from the prophetess and priests.

Earthquake and Reconstruction

In 373 B.C. this fifth temple was destroyed by an earthquake, which also damaged other buildings and monuments. Because Sparta was then the dominant power in Greece, the Spartans took the lead in raising funds for the reconstruction. A new, sixth temple was to be built on the same site, with similar dimensions. During this period the Third Sacred War deflected attention away from temple building and work was delayed.

In 350 B.C. work resumed only to be delayed again by the Fourth Sacred War. The temple was finally completed and dedicated in 330 B.C. The dimensions of this sixth temple turned out to be very nearly the same as the previous one. Also, the materials were the same: poros stone for the foundation, columns, and entablature and Parian marble for the pediments.

The Inner Life of the Temple

The contents of the *naos* and the *adyton* of this temple have been described by various writers through the ages, allowing a tentative reconstruction of the way in which oracles were given. Sayings from the Seven Wise Ones were inscribed in gold on the walls of the *naos.* Pausanius, speaking of the later temple, mentions the seven, among whom were the famous Ionian Thales and the Athenian lawgiver Solon. It was from these philosophers that the phrases "Know thyself" and "Nothing to excess" came to be associated with Delphi.

Also in the *naos* were the golden statue of Apollo and the eternal hearth.

The petitioner waiting in the outer chamber was, then, exposed to several divine principles. The sayings of the Wise Seven were designed to bring the mind to a proper appreciation of the moment. "Know thyself" the inscription said. The Greek knew that this admonition meant two things: first, be aware of the human condition, of proper place and humility before the god; and, two, from the teachings of Orpheus, Pythagoras, and Plato, know that the god resides within and through the psyche can be heard. It was Thales, one of the Wise Seven and a teacher of Pythagoras, who said, "All things are full of gods."

The other famous inscription, "Nothing to excess," was a prescription for harmony in every aspect of human life. Apollo was the god of harmony, the god whose likeness and aspect harmonized the extremes of existence. Human happiness depended upon the individual's ability to harmonize the demands of the psyche with the demands of the mind and body. Harmony was the key to success and Apollo showed the way. Harmony also meant the proper alignment of the elements of psyche, mind, and body—in that order, with the god-centered psyche in control. Here in the Temple of Apollo, after purification in the sacred waters and at the end of the labyrinth of the Sacred Way, an individual had a good chance of achieving such an alignment.

The Events in the Adyton

The inner sanctum or *adyton* was a sunken area of the temple, surrounded by Ionic columns and approached by steps leading down to the place of prophecy. The Pythia, or prophetess, dressed in the robes of a young maiden, and having bathed in the sacred Kastalian Spring, entered the *naos* and passed through the smoke and incense of the sacred hearth, or *hestia*, in which laural leaves and barley burned.

Accompanied by priests whose task it would be to record the utterings, the Pythia took her place upon the tripod, or seat of prophecy. The tripod was similar to a caldron, a large covered kettle in which were kept sacred objects. Myth held that the tripod contained the bones of the slaughtered Python, or perhaps even the bones of the slain god Dionysos. Next to the tripod was the *omphalos,* the round stone covered with a net of woven fillets, which was known to be the center of the world and also the grave of Dionysos.

Thus seated, with vapors arising from the chasm beneath the temple, and waving a branch of laurel, the Pythia entered a state of prophetic madness known by the Greeks as *enthousiasmos*. The prophetic state was probably due more to a natural ability, a tendency developed in the women selected for this task, than to any strange condition within the temple itself. Her utterings, sometimes barely grasped by the attending priests, were recorded and "translated" into Homeric hexameters. This shaping of the utterances into poetic form was one of the earliest forms of Greek writing, an art which was naturally enough associated with Apollo and connected more generally with the arts of civilization, the harmonizing of the turbulence of human existence.

THE THEATRE

The singing of hymns to Apollo was an ancient tradition at Delphi, and the area occupied by the present theatre most likely served as the place where these musical competitions were traditionally held. There is some slight evidence to suggest that an older, perhaps Classical theatre with wooden seats and scene building preceded the stone structure which followed.

Such a stone structure was built in the late fourth and early third centuries B.C., but was replaced—no doubt because of earthquake damage—several times. A major renovation was undertaken by Eumenes II, king of Pergamon, in the second century B.C., to be followed by the present construction during the Roman Imperial Period.

The present theatre, which seats 5,000 persons, has thirty-five rows of seats with a *diazoma* after row twenty-eight. The *orchestra*, in its typical Roman horseshoe shape, has a diameter of 60 feet (18.5 m). A stone scene building rose behind the *orchestra* and provided a raised stage. This late construction, then, provided for the presentation of plays as well as musical performance during various festivals, including the Pythian Games.

The Theatre at Delphi—Roman Imperial Period—Athenian Treasury below.

THE STADIUM

Nestled among the pines farther up the hillside are the remains of the Stadium. Along the way the visitor passes several votive niches and fountains where natural springs provided water. Evidence suggests that the hillside now occupied by the stadium was first flattened in Classical times, sometime around 450 B.C. Before that time the Pythian Games, as they came to be known, were primarily musical contests in honor of Apollo. Later, athletic contests were added and eventually overshadowed the artistic competitions.

The present appearance of the stadium is attributed to Herod Atticus, the wealthy Athenian whose works in Athens include the Odeion near the Acropolis. His contributions to the stadium include the monumental entrance, the remains of which are still evident, and the stone seating. At the entrance the four limestone posts, two with votive niches, were the supports for three Roman arches, through which the athletes entered the arena.

Runners took their positions at the marble slab, which was provided with indentations, the Roman equivalent of starting blocks. Holes in the slab indicate the positions for posts which marked the running lanes. Roughly twenty lanes were available. The course was 195 yards long (178.3 m), which equaled 1 Pythian *stadion*. Some races were two lengths of the stadium, and some involved horses and chariots.

The Roman Imperial stadium of Atticus was provided with stone seating for 7,000 spectators. Included in the center were backed seats for the judges. The seating was arranged

The Stadium at Delphi.

in a series of twelve sections, each with twelve rows, except at the rounded end, or *sphendone,* where there were only six rows. Recent excavation has revealed the remains of an Archaic fountain at the rounded end of the stadium, suggesting something of the ritual history associated with the Pythian Games.

THE MUSEUM

Because the museum reflects the cooperation throughout excavations between the French School of Archaeology and the Greek government, all the accompanying inscriptions for the collection are written in Greek and French only. Those wishing a comprehensive description of the collection and an English translation of the inscriptions will find at the desk several fine full-color guides with adequate descriptions. This guide will highlight only a small selection of this extraordinary collection in an effort to emphasize its high quality and sacred intent.

THE OMPHALOS

At the top of the stairs on the main level of the museum is the marble *omphalos* which was found at the entrance to the temple. This Hellenistic copy of the original which stood in the *adyton* reflects the general design of such symbols throughout ancient history. The *omphalos* was both a grave marker and an image of a matrix; it was a point of origin and a tomb. Some have speculated that its shape also reflects the mound of white ash that was built up into this shape around a core of hot coals to keep a source of fire safe when not in use. The carving on the marble imitates the covering of wool fillets woven like a net over the stone.

Of interest nearby are the Archaic tripod and an example of a bronze caldron. These two particular pieces would not have been seen or used together, but they illustrate the principle of the tripod and caldron upon which the prophetess sat when giving oracle. These examples are votive offerings.

THE KOUROI

Inthe Hall of the Kouroi stand two magnificent figures from Argos, sculpted by Polymedes, whose name appears on the base. The *kouroi* date from around 600 B.C. and represent the sacred principles of form so evident in the early Archaic Period. The symmetry of the pair reflects the ancient knowledge of the human form as an expression of the ideal. The symmetry of design is not a reflection of awkwardness or a primitive conception on the part of the artist or his culture, but an expression of perfection rather than appearance. Here is a human being, a manifestation of the creation in perfect form.

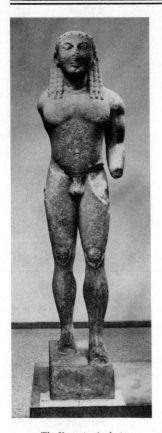

The Kouroi—*Archaic figures from Argos.*

These two figures were inspired by the myth of Cleobis and Biton, two youths from Argos whose mother was a priestess in the Temple of Hera in the Argolid. In the legend the two youths yoked themselves to a chariot in order to take their mother to the temple, a distance of 5 miles (8 km). Once there, the mother-priestess prayed to the goddess to reward her sons for their devotion and service. The goddess responded to the prayer by taking life from the youths while they slept in the temple, thus giving them the reward of a peaceful death without suffering.

THE SILVER BULL AND GOLD TREASURES

In Room #5, a relatively new addition, the museum has displayed a valuable collection of silver, gold, and ivory treasures which were all discovered in 1939 by the French archaeologist Amandry. Central to this display is the head of a bull, of Ionian design from the Archaic Period. The bull was fashioned from thin silver sheets fixed onto a wooden framework. As was the custom from earlier times, the horns, ears, hooves, and genitals of the bull were gilded, indicating its sacred function and purpose as a sacrificial animal.

Also noteworthy in the room are several gold sheets with hammered panels depicting sacred animals. From the Archaic Period, these panels were part of the garment of a large statue and reflected the interest during Archaic times in connecting the image of the gods with animal attributes, both real and imaginary. Pictured are griffins, bulls, lions, goats, an antelope, and a sphinx.

THE NAXIAN SPHINX

The contents of this room illustrate the Archaic vision of two prominent Aegean islands, Naxos and Siphnos. The sphinx has already been described (see p. 288). What becomes evident in its presence is the remarkable symmetry of the disparate elements. Here, after all, is a woman, very much like a *kore,* poised, enigmatic, who has the wings of a bird and the body of a lion. The body in particular, which is slim and graceful, seems to support the mythic wings and head so naturally that one might suppose such a creature to exist. The secret of this symmetry lies in the expression. The eyes are closed. The lips betray a smile expressive of secret knowledge, both dangerous and personal.

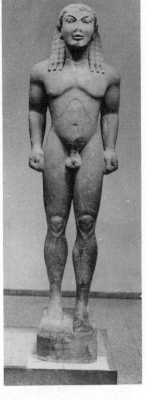

The rest of this room contains elements from the famed Treasury of the Siphnians. Of particular interest are the Archaic frieze sculptures. These are very rare because in most cases Archaic pieces from temples throughout Greece were destroyed or lost in the process of Classical and Hellenistic reconstruction. The subject matter here is the Trojan War. The gods pictured are Ares, with shield, Aphrodite, who is leaning over the back of Artemis, both of whom appear to be talking to Apollo, presumably pleading with him for the cause of the Greeks. Zeus the Father sits (headless) to the right.

To the Greeks such representations were full of mythical and sacred meaning. Here was a harmonizing scene in which Ares, god of war, sits poised and awesome in his strength. At the other end Zeus sits with his arm held in the same gesture. In between are the goddesses whose love and lawful order attempt to balance the wrath of Ares and Zeus, while Apollo turns to receive their pleas. Such balance and structure in Archaic sculpture were typical and illustrate the means by which myths were transmitted and meaning established through the plastic arts.

THE HYMNS TO APOLLO

In the room dedicated to the Athenian Treasury (#6), are the inscriptions from the Athenian Treasury which represent Greek musical notation of two hymns to Apollo. These two hymns date from 128 B.C. and were inscribed at that time in honor of the Pythias, the religious festival celebrated by the Athenians. Two German scholars deciphered the notations, which make use of letters and dots in various positions to signify notes on the scale and finger positions on the lyre.

Delphic Hymn A says in part:

> Listen, pale-skinned daughters of thundering Zeus,
> Maidens who dwell on forested Helicon,
> Come sing and dance in honor of your kinsman Phoibos,
> He who shall come to the twin-peaked cliff of Parnassos
> And the rushing waters of Kastalia with the famed
> Maidens of Delphi, to visit the oracular hill of Delphi.

THE DANCING MAIDENS AND DIONYSOS

In the large room (#11) dedicated to Classical sculpture, two important works are displayed. The first is the Acanthus Column of the dancing girls (see p. 291). Here again is the harmonizing symmetry so typical of the themes of Delphi. The three maidens emerge from the natural fecundity of the acanthus-leaf column to swirl in frozen dance, while holding the sacred tripod upon their heads. The image speaks of the human connection to oracular power and of feminine beauty as the image of harmony and grace in such power. The column combines the imagery of the Corinthian column with the beauty of the Karyatides in a single expression of the sacred attributes of the Mother Goddess.

The second statue of great interest in the room is the figure of Dionysos, one of the monumental sculptures which decorated the southwestern pediment of the last Temple of Apollo. This piece, executed by Androsthenes of Athens around 340 B.C., was accompanied on the pediment by the Maenads, the female celebrants who performed the orgiastic rites in honor of the god. This statue shows the feminine aspect of the god, his grace and beauty. Here is a dramatic contrast to the figures of Ares, Zeus, and Poseidon, those powerful, masculine gods of the pantheon.

The image of Dionysos shown in this statue has another sort of power. By this date, the image has a fleshy quality and the artist's touch reflects the style of Late Classical Period, but the image of Dionysos remains the same as earlier conceptions. He is the product of the union between the demigoddess Semele and Zeus. Semele in turn came from the union between Harmonia, the daughter of Aphrodite and Ares, and the hero Kadmos, a mortal. To the Greeks,

Dionysos was a sympathetic and accessible god, but also one who was dangerous when crossed. This statue is one of the finest extant depictions of the god.

THE BRONZE CHARIOTEER

The final room of the museum houses its greatest treasure, the bronze Charioteer, whose grace and poise represent the best of human achievement and spiritual aspiration. There is an interesting legend about the charioteer, which is often told by guides to the visitors to Delphi.

It seems that during the 1890s, before the start of excavations, when the French were in the process of clearing the town of Kastri off the site of the sanctuary, one matriarch in particular would not leave her little house to relocate to the new town then under construction. Her refusal was holding up the whole relocation project. One morning she arrived at the house where the archaeologists were gathered and announced that she was ready to leave her house. When asked why she had so suddenly changed her mind, she reported a dream from the previous night. In her dream a boy who seemed to be trapped beneath the green sea called to her, "Set me free! Set me free!" The dream frightened her and was, she thought, an omen. When the excavations began, the charioteer was discovered beneath the old woman's house.

Such are the legends which have grown around this magnificent bronze. It was produced in 470 B.C. as a monument to a victory in the Pythian Games. The group included four horses and a chariot. A separate group in front pictured a groom leading a single horse. The intent was to honor the victor and to demonstrate what Plato gave as the definition of mastery: control of four horses running in perfect synchrony drawing a chariot.

What is pictured in this figure is the control under pressure and the look of human achievement and perfection that was the Greek ideal of human life. The style is early Classical, sometimes referred to as the severe

The Charioteer, fifth century B.C., Delphi Museum.

style. Still evident is the idealized form of the Archaic Period, what we see in the *kouroi*. What is yet to come is the so-called naturalism of the later Classical style and the still later decadence of the Hellenistic. Here is the human being inspired by spiritual attributes pictured in the moment of victory in one of life's most demanding exercises. Surely it is how the Greeks envisioned Apollo arriving at his sanctuary drawn by four of Poseidon's finest horses.

4
THE LESSER PALACE AND TEMPLE SITES

Dotted throughout the mainland and islands of Greece are sites where palaces were constructed and temples were placed in honor of the gods and which celebrate the existence of ancientsanctuaries of Minoan, Mycenaean, or Neolithic origins. Such sites range in magnitude and importance from the great Olympia in the far-western Peloponnese to the oracle of Zeus at Dodona in the north to the barren remains of Delos in the Aegean.

Part 4 lists several of the more important sites not given full treatment by this book. Those travelers interested in greater detail will usually find materials at the sites; at some are full-color guides at reasonable prices. One warning, however, may avert some degree of disillusionment. Locally produced pamphlets designed to meet the demand for information and some degree of interpretation tend to be carelessly translated and edited.

BASSAE

Also spelled Bassai, Vassae, and Vasses—the Greek beta being pronounced as V in Greek—Bassae means "glens" or "ravines," and the site of the Temple of Apollo Epikourios (the Helper) at Bassae sits in dramatic isolation among mountains and gorges in Elis, the Western Peloponnese. The drive alone is worth the trip, particularly the last 9 miles (15 km) from Andritsena. The road winds through the hills, moving up to an altitude of 3,700 feet (1,127 m) where the temple rests in the slope of Mount Kotilion.

The area surrounding the temple was sacred to Artemis in her aspect as goddess of wild things and places and to Aphrodite, the remains of whose temple has been found higher on Mount Kotilion. Preserved here is Greece as it was two thousand years ago, at least in the forms of the landscape. Even the spring mentioned by Pausanius when he visited the site still runs, at least in the winter.

The archaeological evidence tells us that an Archaic temple of the seventh century B.C. stood on this site and could have been dedicated to Artemis, likely enough in the light of the landscape elements. Apollo appeared here as the result of a dedication by the people of Phigalia, who during the Peloponnesian War in the fifth century B.C. were spared the ravages of the plague and in gratitude built the present temple.

The great attraction of this temple is its design. Attributed to Iktinos, architect of the Parthenon, it was probably completed between 420 and 417 B.C., although some scholars argue for the earlier date of 450 B.C., making the use of Corinthian columns in the interior the earliest on record.

The excellent state of preservation is a testament to its isolation. Indeed most of its columns are now standing, having been restored to their proper places early in this century. Of especial interest are the ten "engaged" columns, two of which at the southern end were Corinthian. Also interesting is the eastern door, so located in relation to the cult statue of Apollo to catch the first rays of the morning sun, no doubt lined up exactly on festival days.

BRAURON

Also spelled Vravron, the sanctuary of Brauron is located 15 miles (24 km) east of Athens. Sacred to Artemis, the site rests at the foot of Agios Georgias Hill and dates well back into Mycenaean times and was continuously occupied throughout the Classical Period.

The site is neatly laid out and has been well excavated, revealing a Classical Temple of Artemis, a peristyle court around which a dozen columns are standing, numerous small rooms for the priestesses of Artemis, and a sacred spring. This sanctuary was important to the life of young girls, who served the goddess and experienced the initiations of maidenhood in her precinct.

CORINTH

Also Korinthos, Corinth sits at the entrance to the Peloponnese, a location which gave the city much power in ancient times but also made it the target of frequent invasion and destruction. The present ruins are nearly all Roman, with evidence of Archaic and Classical stonework used in later buildings and monuments.

Central to the present ruins is the ancient spring, a source of water held sacred from the Bronze Age. For most of its

Temple of Apollo at Corinth, with Acrocorinth in background.

history Corinth was regarded as a place of pure waters and healing baths. The sanctuary of Apollo remains, with an Archaic temple to the god having been partly restored. Nearby was also an Asklepieion, second only in fame to the sanctuary at Epidauros.

The imposing acropolis of Acrocorinth rises above the site and contains ruins of fortresses from Byzantine through Venetian times. Hearty souls may wish to scale these heights and explore the ruins, but little of ancient times remains.

DELOS

The island of Delos, also Dilos, is the smallest of the Cyclades but is central in the group. Occupied from Neolithic times, the island was of strategic importance during the period of Athenian domination in the fifth century B.C. Now abandoned, except by archaeologists, staff, and visitors, the island is accessible from Mykonos by small boats, which make daily visits during most of the year.

Delos is the most sacred island in the Aegean. Its history suggests that it was sacred to the Earth Mother Goddess from earliest times, and in the Olympian tradition, that devotion was carried on by Artemis, whose temples and sanctuaries on the island were really more important than Apollo's. The stark isolation of the island made it ideal as sacred to the virgin Artemis, goddess of wild places and windswept bluffs.

Here on this centrally located island were celebrated the cycles of the sun (Apollo) and the moon (Artemis) in yearly festivals and sacrifices. Near the ancient sacred harbor lie the remains of the major sanctuaries. Mycenaean remains have been found amidst the Archaic and Classical temples erected to both gods.

To the north of the harbor lies the Sacred Lake, the entranceway to which is guarded by the famous Archaic Naxian lions. Highly stylized and roaring, these beasts guarded the sacred precinct of the lake and reminded pilgrims of the nature of their son-god Apollo.

DODONA

Far to the north, near the Albanian border and some 12 miles (19 km) from Ioannina, lies the famed sanctuary of Dodona, the first oracular site in Greece and sacred to Zeus the Father. Dodona was home to the *selloi,* priests of Zeus famous for sleeping on the snow-covered earth and for their special gifts of prophecy.

The priests of Dodona were devoted to nature's revelations, the prophetic utterances provided by the voices of streams and the language of leaves stirred by the wind in the sacred oak trees. The legends of the sanctuary held that a pigeon had flown from Thebes in Egypt and landed in an oak tree from which it declared that an oracle of Zeus himself should be established at the site.

The main sights at Dodona are the impressive Hellenistic theatre, which holds 18,000 spectators for modern productions of the Classical plays, and the Zeus sanctuary, within which was preserved for many years the sacred oak tree.

OLYMPIA

Most people know the history of Olympia from its famed stadium, where the first Olympic Games were held beginning in 776 B.C., the date from which much of ancient history has its point of reference. Its sacred history is no less important and dates from much earlier, around 2000 B.C., when settlement near Mount Kronion began.

The fertile land in Elis which was set aside for the Panhellenic sanctuary to Zeus and Hera was first occupied by Kronos, father of Zeus, and Gaea, the Earth Mother. Sacred here was the marriage of spiritual elements, a union of forces where two rivers converged in fertile plain and where Greeks from every city came to prove their athletic ability. The games were expressions of the ideal of human accomplishment. To win the crown of laurel was to celebrate the godlike qualities inherent in every man.

The main sanctuary of Olympia, the Altis, houses the major monuments in the sacred tradition of Olympia. Central

Engraving of the Temple of Zeus at Olympia.

was the Pelopion, a raised section surrounded by a pentagonal wall and sacred to the memory of Pelops, the mythical hero of the games. Also in the Altis were the two temples of Hera and of Zeus, both in the Doric style and very distinctive in construction.

The Archaic Temple of Hera, now cleared to its foundations, was unusually long, with sixteen columns on the long sides and six across the front. As the existing columns show, Hera's temple was also quite low, lesser in stature than its neighbor the huge Temple of Zeus.

Built in 472 B.C. in the Doric style, the Temple of Zeus rose above the plain on a high platform (nearly 9 feet) and was 210 feet long (64 m) and 88 feet wide (27 m). The museum contains important Archaic sculptures from the friezes of both temples, including scenes of the labors of Herakles.

PYLOS

Beyond the Argolid, far to the west in Messenia, on the other side of the Peloponnese, lie the ruins of the Palace of Nestor at Pylos. This storied palace, so brilliantly pictured in the *Odyssey*, was uncovered in 1939 and contains the remains of a Bronze Age megaron second to none in Greece. Those with the time to explore the Western Peloponnese will want to include Pylos in their itinerary.

It was not until 1939 that archaeologists discovered the site of King Nestor's Palace near Pylos. The location, just over 9 miles (15 km) from Pylos on the hill called Ano

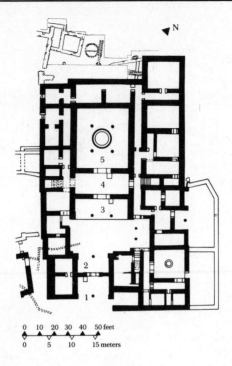

Fig. 30. *Pylos*
1. *Propylon*
2. *Outer Court*
3. *Porch*
4. *Lobby*
5. *Megaron*

Englianos, is a truly beautiful site. One is reminded more of Knossos than of Mycenae in that Pylos appears not to have been fortified. Like Knossos, it depended more on seapower to protect the citadel than upon monumental walls to withstand siege.

The palace is well preserved and offers a clear understanding of Mycenaean construction. The main, or central, complex of the palace is of major interest. The propylon reminds us of similar main entrances at Mycenae and Knossos. A single column, the base of which remains, supports the porch and yields to a second single column in the vestibule. Before the main portico of the palace is an open court where visitors awaited entrance before the king.

The visitor has a clear sense of the majesty of this palace in the good state of preservation of the vestibule and central megaron. The hearth, which is the heart of the palace, shows the history of the circular offering pits and their importance to Mycenaean culture. We are able to trace circular pits and hearths of this type and size from Neolithic times, through the Mycenaean into the Classical in the form of the *tholos* temples. Also, like Knossos and Mycenae, the wood-and-ivory throne was placed on the right-hand wall and was framed by griffin frescoes, symbols of wisdom and power.

SUNIUM

One of the most beautiful places in Greece was chosen as a sanctuary of Zeus and Poseidon. On a bluff 200 feet (60 m) above the Aegean on the southernmost tip of Attica sits the famed Temple of Poseidon. Built in 440 B.C., its very thin Doric columns of pure white marble made the entablature float above the sea and told returning sailors that home was in sight.

One of the legends of Sunium (or Sounion) is that it was here that King Aegeus waited for his son Theseus to return from Crete and saw the black sail in the distance. Thinking his son dead, Aegeus threw himself from the cliff into the sea which bears his name.

TIRYNS

Excavations beginning in 1887 and continuing to the present have uncovered numerous ancient sites in the Argive Plain, although none are so impressive or important as Mycenae. The Bronze Age citadel of Tiryns offers another glimpse of a fortress along the lines of Mycenae and contains examples of monumental stonework of the highest order.

Those who find accommodation in Nauplia or who merely wish to visit this beautiful seaside town and sample some of the best seafood in Greece, will want to stop briefly at the citadel of Tiryns, which is no more than 50 yards (46 m) off the main road. Because Tiryns is not a major site, its open hours are confined to the middle of the day. Visitors need to plan accordingly.

The first and major impression of Tiryns is that it sits very low in the landscape, only 60 feet (18 m) higher than the alluvial plain. Indeed, many scholars who have worked extensively in this plain have expressed the opinion that when Tiryns was occupied and was an important extension of the power of Mycenae, the citadel was very close to the water and functioned as a port. In other words, the Gulf of Argolis reached higher into the Argive Plain than it now does.

Most of the remains at Tiryns date from 1250 B.C., the last period of construction for this fortress. The outstanding features include the long ramp leading to the entrance, the main gate which lies within the major fortress walls, the double walls with corridors leading throughout the citadel, the corbel gateway in the west wall, and the corbel-shaped passages built within the thickness of the main walls.

After the Dark Age, in the early Geometric Period, a temple dedicated to Hera was imposed over the ruins of the old megaron. As well, inscriptions indicate that during later periods, both Zeus and Athena worshipped here. This evidence of cult activity suggests that a continuity of worship at the site establishes Tiryns as a sacred place, one particularly devoted to the goddesses of the pantheon.

GLOSSARY

abaton	sleeping quarters for patients
adyton	inner sanctum
aegis	shield
agon	conflict
agora	marketplace
agyrmos	the gathering
anaktoron	small building within telesterion
ananke	necessity
antae	extended walls
arche	head, leader
archons	officials
arete	excellence
aristoi	the few, aristocracy
arrheton	ineffable
basileus	king
cella	inner room (Greek, *naos*)
daemon	spirit, genius
deme	district, town
diazoma	inner circle
Dike	justice
dromos	entry to tomb
echinis	molding above column
ekkyklema	rolling platform
en theos	with God
enkoimisis	sleep cure
entasis	bulge in column
enthousiasmos	prophetic madness
epoptai	those gone before
eschara	underground altar
eurharmostia	harmony
gephyrismoi	"bridge jests" or hazing of initiates
guttae	decorative temple elements (drops)
halos	circular terrace
hecatomb	100 or large number
heiron	sanctuary
hestia	sacred hearth
hexastyle	6-column front of temple
hoi polloi	the many, people
hubris	arrogance
hypaethral	without a roof for central hall
in antis	projection of temple walls beyond enclosing walls
karyatid	column in the form of a maiden
kernos	offering table
kiste	basket
Kore	name of Persephone
kore	figure of a young woman
kouros, kouroi	idealized male youths—statues

labrys	double ax
mechane	crane
metope	sculpted panel
moira	fate
myesis	beginning of initiation
mystai	worshippers
naos	inner room of temple (Latin, *cella*)
nomoi	customs and laws
nomos	law
nous	universal mind
omphalos	world navel
orchestra	circle in theatre
ostrakon	shard used in voting for banishment
palaestra	public building
paradoi	entranceways to theatre orchestra
parthenos	maiden
peplos	robe
peripatos	encircling road
physis	nature
pithoi	storage jars
polis	city-state
poloi	flowing dresses
pronaos	porch, entranceway to *naos*
propylaia	buildings forming entranceway
propylon	formal entrance to sanctuaries
proskenion	Roman theatre facade
psyche	soul
sekos	inner temple chamber
skene	scene building
stele	relief sculpture, grave marker
stoa	narrow building with colonnade
techne	skilled artisans
tholos	round temple or tomb
wanax, wa-na-ka	Mycenaean priest-king
xenon	guest room
xoanon	ancient cult statue

FURTHER READING

The authors represented below are those whose views and insights into the vitality of the Greek experience informed this book. Added to this list would also be the original documents of the time, the plays of the great dramatic poets, the dialogues of Plato, the histories of Herodotos and Thucydides, the poetry of Pindar and Hesiod, the philosophies of Heraclitus and Parmenides, and, of course, the great epics of Homer, the *Iliad* and the *Odyssey*.

Burkert, Walter. *Greek Religion.* Cambridge, Mass.: Harvard University Press, 1985.

Brunés, Tons. *The Secrets of Ancient Geometry.* Copenhagen: Rhodos, 1967.

Diel, Paul. *Symbolism in Greek Mythology.* Boulder and London: Shambhala, 1980.

Döczi, G. *The Power of Limits.* Boulder and London: Shambhala, 1981.

Dodds, E. R. *The Greeks and the Irrational.* Berkeley: University of California Press, 1951.

Graves, Robert. *The White Goddess.* New York: Farrar, Straus, and Giroux, 1948.

———*The Greek Myths, vols. 1, 2.* Middlesex: Penguin, 1960.

Harrison, J. *Epilegomena and Themis.* New York: University Books, 1962.

James, E. O. *The Ancient Gods.* New York: G. P. Putnam's Sons, 1960.

Lawlor, R. *Sacred Geometry.* New York: Crossroad Publishing Co., 1982.

Miller, H. *The Colossus of Maroussi.* New York: New Directions, 1941.

Neumann, E. *The Great Mother.* Princeton, N.J.: Bollingen Foundation, 1963.

Scully, V. *The Earth, the Temple, and the Gods.* New Haven, Conn.: Yale University Press, 1962.

Vernant, J. *The Origins of Greek Thought.* Ithaca, N.Y.: Cornell University Press, 1982.

INDEX

abacus, 87
abaton, 256, 263–4, *illus.* 263
Academy, Plato's, 31
Acanthus column, 291, 302
Achaeans, 146
Acrocorinth, 309
Acropolis, Athens, 178, 184–204,
    plan 186
    Erechtheion, 199–201
    history, 12
    museum, 178, 196, 201–4
    Propylaia, 178, 187
    Temple of Athena Nike, 184,
    204
    Parthenon, 178, 180, 184–5,
    189–99, *illus.* 19, 190, 197
adyton, 295–7
Aegeus, 103, 181
Aegisthus, 53, 154, 168
Aeschylus, 24, 205, 208
    Oresteia, 25, 154
Agamemnon, 151, 154
    mask of, 226, *illus.* 227
Agora, Athens, 216–26
    Altar of Twelve Gods, 216, 222
    Eleusinion, 218, 238
    entrances, 216
    Fountain House, 219
    history, 216
    museum, 219, 225–6
    State Prison, 224–5
    Temple of Hephaistos, 217,
    222–4, *illus.* 223
    Tholos, 217, 224
agora, 15, 31, 216–26
Agra, 237
agyrmos, 239
Akrotiri (Santorini), 8
Alaric the Goth, 233
Alexander the Great, 19, 31
Almond-Eyed *Kore,* 202, *illus.* 16,
    202
American School of Classical
    Studies, 216, 225
Amphiktyonia, 272
Amphiprostyle, 87
anaktoron, 241–2

Anaxagoras, 191
Aphrodite, 43, 49–50, 276
Apollo, 43, 46–8, 52, 101, 227,
    253, 269–76
Apollo, Temple of (Delphi), 277,
    290–7, *illus.* 270, 290, 294
Apollo Patroos, 225
Arch of Hadrian, 215
Archaeological Museum of Irak-
    lion, 137–45
Archaic Period, 14–19, 202–3
Architect (defined), 83–4
architrave, 87–8
archons, 179
Arditos Hill, 237
Areopagus, 213
Ares, 43, 48–9
Ariadne, 102–3, 181
aristoi, 179
Aristophanes, 26–7, 205
Aristotle, 32, 68
arrheton, 230
Artemis, 48
Asklepieion, Athens, 211–2, *illus.*
    211, 212
Asklepieion, Delphi, 287
Asklepieion, Epidauros, 256, 259
Asklepios, 211–12, 224, 238, 250,
    252–5
Athena, 43, 51–3
    statue of, 198–9, 229, *illus.* 52
Athena Nike, 188
Athena Pronaia, 277–80
Athenian Treasury, 286–7, *illus.*
    286
Athens, 16, 177
    see also Acropolis, Agora, Ask-
    lepieion, Kerameikos, Odeion
    of Herod Atticus, Odeion of
    Pericles, Olympic Stadium,
    Olympieion, Omonia Square,
    Parthenon, Plaka, Pnyx,
    Street of the Panathenaia,
    Temple of Athena Nike,
    Temple of Zeus, Theatre of
    Dionysos, Theseion, Walls of
    Themistocles

Atreus, 152–4
Attalos II, 225

Bassae, 307–8
Bhagavad-Gita, 244
Bouleuterion, 250
Brauron, 308
Brazen Age, 40
British Museum, 196
Bronze Age, 3, 5, 6–12, 38, 98, 176, 230
Buddha, 71
bull-leaping, 113, 143, *illus.* 10, 138
bull's head rhyton, 139, *illus.* 142

Calendar, Attic, 58–9
Calf-Bearer, 202, *illus.* 21
Campbell, Joseph, 84
Celeus, King, 234
Central Court
    Knossos, 113
    Phaestos, 127
    Mallia, 133
Charioteer, bronze statue, 303, *illus.* 303
Chavos chasm, 148
Chiron, 255
chthonic (defined), 236
circle (symbolism), 70
Cleisthenes, 21, 51
Clement of Alexandria, 242
Clytemnestra, 151, 154
Code of Law, 122
Colonus, 31
Confucius, 71
Corfu, 284
Corinth, 34, 308–9
Corinthian Order, 88, *illus.* 88
cornice, 87
Coronis, 255
Corridor of the Procession, 109
Croesus, 228
cult center, 162
Cycladic, 226–7
Cyclops, 152

Daedalus, 101
daemon, 28
Daktyls, 102
Danaans, 146
Dark Age, 11, 12–14, 175
Delos, 28, 47, 309–10
Delphi, 30, 33, 56, 181
    oracles of, 270–1
Delphi, The Site, 269–304
    Marmaria, 277–9, *plan* 278
    museum, 277, 299–304

sanctuary, 277, 283–97, *plan* 282
    stadium, 277, 298 and *illus.*
    Temple of Apollo, 290–7, *illus.* 270, 290, 294
    Theatre, 277, 297 and *illus.*
Demeter, 66, 152, 229, 230–6, 240, 242–3, 247, 251
Demophon, 234
Diel, Paul, ix, 45
dike, 213
Dikte, Mt., 129
    caves of, 61
Diodorus, 117
Dionysos, 43, 54–6, 66, 237, 276, 302
    cults of, 24
    festivals of, 205–8
    tomb of, 296
dipteros, 87
Dipylon Gate, 187, 215
Dithyramb, 205–6
Dodds, E. R., 54
Dodona, 288, 310
Dorians, 11, 13, 150
Doric order, 87 and *illus.*
double ax, 105, 119, 154
drama, Classical, 23–6
dromos, 168–71, *illus.* 169, 170

Earth Mother Goddess, 4, 5, 8, 13, 37–8, 41, 64, 66, 74, 82–3, 97, 122, 137, 152, 159, 227, 233, 243, 254, 269–70, 277
Earth Spirit, 36
echinus, 87, 279
Egypt, 9, 18, 33, 71, 289
ekkyklema, 207
Electra, 151, 153
Eleusinian Mysteries, 20, 66, 117, 218–9, 228, 231, 245
    rites, 238–40
    secret, 243–5
Eleusinion, 218, 238
Eleusis, 20, 215, 230–51
Eleusis, The Site, 245–51
    museum, 250–1
    Precinct of Plauton, 246, 248, *illus.* 241
    propylon, 247
    Sacred Way, 245, 247
    Telesterion, 240–2, *illus.* 249
    Well of dances, 240, *illus.* 234
Elgin, Lord, 196
Elis, 310
Emerson, Ralph Waldo, 200
enkoimisis, 263

enneagram, 75, *illus.* 74
entasis, 89
Epidauros, 16, 89
Epidauros, The Site, 252–68
    abaton, 256, 263–4, *illus.* 263
    cures, 264–5
    museum, 256
    propylon, 258
    sanctuary, 256, 259, *plan* 256
    Temple of Asklepios, 256,
        260–1
    Theatre, 265–8, *illus.* 26, 253,
        265, 266
    Tholos, 256, 261–2, *illus.* 261,
        262
Erechtheion, 178, 184, 199–201,
    illus. 199, 201
Erechtheus, 179, 197
eschara, 247
eurharmostia, 236
eurhythmia, 236
Euripides, 25, 205, 208
    Bacchae, 26, 54
    Electra, 26
    Helen, 239
    Medea, 26
Europa, 100
Evans, Sir Arthur, 105–6, 116

festivals, 57–61
frieze, 87

Gaea (Ge), 41, 270, 288
Garden of Eden, 244
Geometric Period, 216
Golden Age, 39
Golden Proportion, 76–9, 192,
    194, 267, *illus.* 77–8
Golden Verses, 65
Gortyn, 15
Gournia, 123, 135
Grand Staircase
    Knossos, 118
    Phaestos, 126
Grave Circle A, 155, 160
Grave Circle B, 160
Graves, Robert, 237
Great South Propylon, Knossos,
    109–10
Greater Dionysia, 206, 208
Greek foot, 193
guttae, 198

Hades, 51, 236
Hagia Triada, 129–32, 142
    sarcophagus, 104, 134, 144
Hall of Colonnades, Knossos,
    118

halos, 289
Harrison, Jane, 190
heira, 238
heiron, 259
Helen, 151, 153, 182, 287
Helios, 197, 275
Hellenistic Age, 33
Hephaistos, 43, 53
    Temple of, 222–4
Hera, 43, 45
Heraclitus, 18
Herakles, 95, 181, 224, 283, 311
Hermes, 43, 50–1
Herodotos, 13, 232, 273
Heroic Age, 40
Heroic Tradition, 149
Herophile, 287
Hesiod, 17, 39–42
    The Five Ages, 39–42
    Theogony, 17, 18, 39–42
Hestia, 43, 53–4
hestia, 296
Hezekiah, 153
Hierophant, 28
Hippokrates, 253–4
Hippolytos, 241
Homer, 17
    Hymn to Demeter, 230, 233
    Iliad, 17
    Odyssey, 17, 164, 311
Hopi symbol, 83
Horns of Consecration, 112, *illus.*
    94
hubris, 46
Huxley, Aldous, 35
Hygieia, 212
Hymettos, Mt., 191
Hymns to Apollo, 287, 302

Idha, Mt., 102, 125, 127, 129
    caves of, 61
Iktinos, 191, 308
Ionic Order, 87, *illus.* 70, 88
Iraklion, 95
    museum, 106, 137–45
Iron Age, 40
Isopata Ring, 140

Jouctas, Mt., 97, 102, *illus.* 96
Julian the Apostate, 273

Kairtos River, 96
Kallikrates, 188, 191
Kamares, pottery, 139
Kanakis, Z., 143
Karyatides, 200, 204 and *illus.*
    at Delphi, 286
    at Eleusis, 251

Kastalian Spring, 276, 280–1,
   illus. 281
Kephisos River, 239–40
Kerameikos, 213–5
kernoi, 134, 251
Kitto, H. D. F., 266
Klepsydra Spring, 187
Knossos, 8, 10, 83, 93, 181, 228,
   illus. 81–2, *plan* 110–11
Knossos, the Site, 95–121
   Central Court, 113
   Grand Staircase, 118
   King's Megaron, 118
   Labyrinth, 117
   North Lustral Basin, 108
   plan 110–11
   Queen's Megaron, 119
   Royal Road, *illus.* x, 107
   South Propylon, 109–10
   Theatral Area, 107
   Throne Room, 115–16
   West Court, 106
"Know Thyself," 295
Kodros, 179
Korykeion Cave, 270
kouros, 228, 304
   of Croesus, 228, *illus.* 229
   of Delphi, 299–300, *illus.*
     300–1
Kritos Boy, 203
Kronos, 44
Kynortion, Mt., 257

labyrinth, 83, 105, 117, 262–3
Lao-tzu, 71
Leto, 273
Linear B Script, 9, 140, 251
Lion Gate, 82, 116, 150, 155,
   159–61, *illus.* 6, 158, 159
Logos, 269
Lyceum, 68
Lycurgas, 207

Mallia, 123, 133, 138, *plan* 134
Marathon, 19–20, 284, 287
Marmaria, 277–9, *plan* 278
Marta, Mt., 150
Medea, 181
Medusa, 151–2, 260–1
megaron, natural, 80–1
Melville, Herman, 184
Menelaus, 153, 164
Mesara Plain, 122
Metaneira, Queen, 234
Meter, 216
metope, 196
Milesian thinkers, 18, 66
Miller, Henry, 121, 124, 166

Minos, King, 7, 101–2
Minotaur, 101–2, 181
Mnesikles, 200
museums
   Acropolis, 178, 196, 201–4
   Agora, 219, 225–6
   Delphi, 277, 299–304
   Epidauros, 256
   Iraklion, 106, 137–45
   Kerameikos, 215
   Mycenae, 171
   National Archaeological, 177,
     196, 226–29
Mycenae, 93, 147
Mycenae, The Site, 148–71
   Cult Center, 162
   Grave Circle A, 155, 159, 160
   Grave Circle B, 160
   Great Ramp, 161
   Lion Gate, 82, 116, 150, 155,
     159–61, *illus.* 6, 158, 159
   Megaron, 164
   North Gate, 165
   Secret Cistern, 166
Mycenaean Age, 7, 226
Mykonos, 309
Mylonas, G., 155, 162
mystai, 230, 240, 247
Mystery Religions, 61–6
myth (defined), ix, 100

naos, 295
National Archaeological Museum,
   177, 196, 226–9
Nauplia, 154, 155
Neolithic Period, 5, 37, 226–7
Neoplatonism, 68
Neoptolemos, Sanctuary of, 291
Nereid, 225
Nine Springs, 220
nomadic culture, 3–4
nomos, 262
"Nothing to Excess," 295
nous, 191, 203

octave, 65
Odeion of Herod Atticus, 208,
   212
Odeion of Pericles, 21, 207
Odysseus, 61, 151
Oedipus, 151, 182, 285, 288
Olympia, 310–11
Olympic Airways, 95
Olympic Stadium, Athens, 237
Olympieion, 215 and *illus.*
Olympus, Mt., 255, 289
Omonia Square, 177
omphalos, 248, 271, 296, 299

Oresteia, 25, 154
Orestes, 151, 154
Orpheus, 61, 62, 117, 296
    Orphism, 62
    Petelia tablet, 63
ostrakon, 22
Ouranos, 41

Palace of Nestor, 311
Pallas Athena, 51–2
Pan, 274–6
Panathenaia, 59, 60, 185
Pantheon of Gods, 42–56
Paris, 50
Parmenides, 18
Parnassos, Mt., 276
Parthenon, 178, 180, 184–5,
        189–99, *illus.* 19, 176, 190,
        197
    destruction of, 180
Pasiphae, 101–2
Pausanius, 187, 219–20, 287, 295
Peirithous, 182
Peloponnesian War, 28–30
Pelops, 151–2
Penrose, F. C., 190, 195
Pentelicus Mt., 195
peplos, 187, 196, 229
Pericles, 21–3, 191, 207
    funeral oration, 23
peripitos, 187, 211
peripteros, 87
Persephone (Kore), 66, 181, 229,
        232–7, 240–2, 251
Perseus, 151–2
Persian Wars, 19–20, 29, 232,
        276
Phaedriades, 276
Phaestos, Disk, 128, 139, *illus.*
        128
Phaestos, 106, 138, Site, 122–32
    Central Court, 127
    Grand Staircase, 126
    Northeast Complex, 128
    Royal Apartments, 127
    Temple of Rhea, 129
Phidias, 52, 191, 199, 229
Philip II, 30
physis, 262
Piano Nobile, Knossos, 112–13,
        plan 114
pig sacrifice, 238
Pinakotheke, 189
Pindar, 64, 255
Plaka, Athens, 177
Plato, ix, 31–2, 266, 296
    Academy, 178
    Critias, 5

Gorgias, 69
    Meno, 67
    Phaedo, 224
    philosophy, 28, 32
Pleiades, 165, 190
Pleistos River, 276
Plotinus, 68, 101
Plutarch, 149, 191
Pnyx, 23, 213
Poe, E. A., 191
polis, 14, 15, 175
Polykleitos, 265
Poppy Goddess, 142
Porphyry, 68, 101
Poseidon, 43, 45–6, 101
prepalatial, 107
priest-king, 93, 100, 115
Prometheus, 244
pronaos, 85
Propylaia, Athens, 178, 187
propylon
    Eleusis, 247
    Epidauros, 258
    Mycenae, 163
    Phaestos, 126
Prostyle, 87
Protagoras, 77
protopalatial, 98, 126
psyche, 203, 235
Pylos, 147, 311–12, *plan* 312
Pyrrhos, 291
Pythagoras, 18, 64, 274, 296
    Golden Verses, 65
    number system, 65, 71–5
    Sacred Tetractys, 75
Pythia, 296
Pythian Games, 303
Python, 274–5, 288

religion, 56–68
    Minoan, 104–5
repression (defined), 236–7
Rhadamanthys, 124
Rhea, 44, 129
Rock of Leto, 288
Rock of the Sibyl, 288 and
        illus.
Royal Villa, Knossos, 120

Sacred Gate, 239
Sacred Landscape, 122–3
Sacred Number, 69, 71–5
Sacred Tetractys, 124, *illus.* 75
Sacred Way
    Athens, 218, 239
    Eleusis, 246–7
Salamis, 20, 179
sally port, 166

Schliemann, H., 105, 155, 160, 226
Scully, Vincent, 80–2, 85, 122, 158, 191
Secret Cistern, 166
Serpent Column, 290
shaft, column, 87
sibyls, 270–1
Sikyonian Treasury, 285
Silver Age, 39
Siphnian Treasury, 286, 301
skene, 207
Socrates, 27, 28, 67, 224–5
Solon, 231, 295
Sophocles, 25, 205, 208, 211
  Antigone, 25
  Oedipus at Colonus, 25
  Oedipus Tyrannus, 25
Sparta, 16, 30
Sphinx of the Naxians, 288, 301
stadium, Delphi, 277, 298, *illus.* 298
State Prison, Agora, 224–5, *see also* Socrates
State Religion, 56–61
stele, 214, 226, 264, 291
Stonehenge, 71
Street of the Panathenaia, 218
stylobate, 87
sublimation (defined), 236–7
Sulla, 254
Sunium, 313

Tantalus, 151–2
Taylour, Lord, 162, 170
Telemakhos, 164
Telesterion, 240–2, *illus.* 249
temple design and placement, 84–7
Temple of Apollo, Corinth, 308–9
Temple of Apollo, Delphi, 290–7, *illus.* 270, 290, 294
Temple of Artemis, (Brauron), 308
Temple of Artemis, (Epidauros), 256
Temple of Asklepios, 256, 260–1
Temple of Athena, Delphi, 280
Temple of Athena Nike, 184, 204
Temple of Athena Parthenos, *see* Parthenon
Temple of Hephaistos, 217, 222–4, *illus.* 78, 223
Temple of Hera, 311
Temple of Hera (Argos), 300
Temple of Zeus (Athens), 215 and *illus.*
Temple of Zeus (Olympia), 310–11, *illus.* 311

Thales, 296
Theatral Area, 107–8, 125
Theatre of Delphi, 297
Theatre of Dionysos, 205–11, *illus.* 24, *plan* 210
Theatre of Epidauros, 265–8, *plan* 267
Thebes, 285–6
Thera eruption, 7, 99
Thermopylae, 150
Theseion, 222, 224
Theseus, 102–3, 181–2, 224
Thespis, 24, 205
tholos temples, 140
  Agora, 224
  Delphi, 286
  Epidauros, 261–3
  Marmaria, 278–9
tholos tombs, 161, 167–71, *illus.* 146, 167
Thrasyllos, 209
Throne Room, Knossos, 115
Thucydides, 29
Thyestes, 152
Tiryns, 147, 313–14, *illus.* 13
Town Mosaics, 138
transmigration, 63–4
Treasury of Atreus, 168–9
Tricolumnar Shrine, 138
triglyph, 87
tripod, 291, 296, 299
Triptolemos, 219, 235
Troy, 40, 147, 151, 153, 208
Tsountas, B., 155

Universal Being, 72

Valentinian, 231, 244
Vale of Tempe, 274, 293
Venetians, 95

Walls of Themistocles, 180
wa-na-ka (wanax), 12, 14, 149–50
Well of dances, 240, *illus.* 234
Winged Victory, 204, 229

Xenophanes, 18
Xerxes, 20–1
xoanon, 199

Yahweh, 153

Zakros, 123, 135–6, 142
Zara, Mt., 158, 167
Zeno, 18
Zeus, 13, 35, 41–7, 100–2, 150–2
Zoroaster, 250

A Note About the Author

Richard Geldard studied classical Greek theatre with William Arrowsmith at the Bread Loaf School of English and with the late T. B. L. Webster at Stanford University, where he earned his doctorate in 1972. This book grew out of a student tour to Greece in 1981 and subsequent summer study at Oxford University. A more recent Greek visit infused the earlier experience with a deeper appreciation of the sacred life of the ancient Greeks. Dr. Geldard now teaches and is Coordinator of General Studies for Secondary Education at Yeshiva University, where, he says, "the sacred and the profane live together in uneasy but creative harmony." He also lectures in New York on classical and Emersonian philosophy. He and his wife, the artist Astrid Fitzgerald, live in Manhattan and upstate New York, where they are renovating a neolithic farmhouse.

A Note on the Type

This book was set on the Linotype in a face called Primer, designed by Rudolph Ruzicka (1883–1978). Mr. Ruzicka was earlier responsible for the design of Fairfield and Fairfield Medium, Linotype faces whose virtues have for some time been accorded wide recognition.

The complete range of sizes of Primer was first made available in 1954, although the pilot size of 12-point was ready as early as 1951. The design of the face makes general reference to Linotype Century—long a serviceable type, totally lacking in manner or frills of any kind—but brilliantly corrects its characterless quality.

Composed by Americomp, Inc., Brattleboro, Vermont. Printed and bound by R. R. Donnelley & Sons, Crawfordsville, Indiana.
Book design by Claire M. Naylon, adapted from a
design by Christine Aulicino.